HOW TO SURVIVE

MIDDLE SCHOOL

SCIENCE

Visit us on the Web! rhcbooks.com

Educators and librarians, for a variety of teaching tools, visit us at RHTeachersLibrarians.com

Library of Congress Cataloging-in-Publication Data is available upon request.

ISBN 978-0-525-57143-8 (trade)

ISBN: 978-0-525-57148-3 (ebook)

Printed in the United States of America

10 9 8 7 6 5 4 3 2 1

First Edition

Writers: Rachel Ross, Maria Ter-Mikaelian, Ilse Ortabasi

Curriculum Consultant: Kimberly Coniglio

Sideshow Media Editorial and Production Team: Dan Tucker, Liz Dacey, Julia DeVarti

Penguin Random House Publishing Team: Tom Russell, Alison Stoltzfus, Brett Wright, Emily Harburg, Eugenia Lo, Katy Miller

Produced by Sideshow Media LLC

Illustration and Design by Carpenter Collective

HOW TO SURVIVE
MIDDLE ✦ SCHOOL

A DO-IT-YOURSELF STUDY GUIDE

SCIENCE

RACHEL ROSS, MARIA TER-MIKAELIAN

BRIGHT
MATTER
BOOKS
NEW YORK

TABLE OF CONTENTS

CHAPTER 3

79

THE FORCES THAT SHAPE THE EARTH

CHAPTER 4

109

WATER, WEATHER, AND CLIMATE

CHAPTER 5

149

EARTH AND HUMAN ACTIVITY

CHAPTER 6   197

FROM CELLS TO ORGANISMS: STRUCTURES AND PROCESSES

CHAPTER 7   245

ECOSYSTEMS: INTERACTIONS, ENERGY, AND DYNAMICS

CHAPTER 8   277

HEREDITY: INHERITANCE AND VARIATION OF TRAITS

CHAPTER 9   315

BIOLOGICAL EVOLUTION: UNITY AND DIVERSITY

CHAPTER 10   347

MATTER AND ITS INTERACTIONS

CHAPTER 14   489

HOW TO THINK LIKE A SCIENTIST

TEXT CREDITS   515

A JOURNEY INTO SCIENCE

Welcome to a wild adventure full of perils, daring feats, and amazing discoveries, also known as Middle School Science! On this journey, you will camp under the stars, hike up mountains, head to the beach, bike along scenic trails, visit different ecosystems, and even zipline through the forest!

CHAPTER CONTENTS

THINKING LIKE A SCIENTIST
· The Scientific Method

WHAT'S IN THIS BOOK

EQUIPMENT FOR LEARNING

THINKING LIKE A SCIENTIST

To make the most of this journey, you will need to adopt the mindset of a scientist. This means being curious and keeping an open mind. For example, if a topic seems familiar, don't assume you already know everything about it. And if you observe something new, don't jump to conclusions about what it means.

Observations are key to learning about the world around you. Scientists love jokes, so let's begin with one that illustrates how scientists make observations:

> Three scientists were driving through an unfamiliar area. They noticed some sheep grazing in a pasture near the road. "Oh, look," said the biologist, "This region has black sheep!" "No, wait," said the physicist, "We only know that this region has at least one black sheep." "Now hold on," said the geologist, "All we know for sure is that this region has at least one sheep that's black on at least one side."

What does this joke remind you to do? Or rather not do—it's important not to make assumptions about phenomena you notice in nature or in your experiments. Rather, you need to observe things carefully, using all of your senses and any measuring tools you might have. Be sure to note down just what you see without embellishing.

THE SCIENTIFIC METHOD

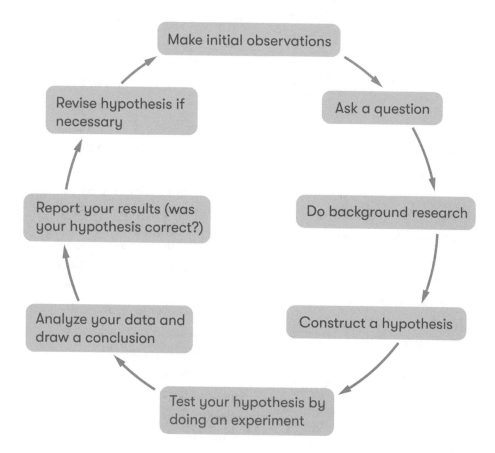

Anybody who asks "why" questions and wants to know how the world works can use the scientific method—no Einstein hairdo or lab coat required. For example, your initial observation ("Hey, one of the sheep here looks black!") might lead you to wonder whether coat color makes any difference for sheep. Ta-da! Now you've got a scientific question.

What comes next? You guessed it: you formulate a hypothesis. This is like penciling in an answer to the question. Why pencil? Because your answer may or may not be correct, or it may be partially correct. With a pencil, you can erase bits and refine them as you test your answer. This is an important part of the scientific method, so don't just make something up. Instead, take an educated guess based on what you already know about the topic.

For example, you may already know that an animal's coat color can help it blend in with its surroundings and hide from predators. Therefore, you might suspect that a black sheep among so many white ones would stand out and become an easy target. So, your hypothesis might be that black sheep get eaten by wolves more often than white sheep, making their coat color a disadvantage.

LOTS OF HYPOTHESES

Keep in mind that there is no single correct hypothesis: different scientists may come up with many different hypotheses from the same observation. For example, someone else might hypothesize that the black sheep's color absorbs sunlight and helps keep it warm, so that they actually survive the winter better than white sheep. As long as there is some logic behind a hypothesis, it's never incorrect. To be scientists, you have to let go of trying to be right the first time and embrace trial and error. That's a relief, isn't it?

Now that you've got a hypothesis, you are ready to conduct an experiment. A well-designed experiment should produce results that help you determine whether your hypothesis is correct or incorrect. Take your first hypothesis that black sheep get caught by wolves more easily than white sheep. How can you test that?

Pretend that you have a few flocks of sheep. One experiment could be to observe a flock from a distance over several months and count how many sheep of each color got caught by wolves. In another experiment, you could split the flocks up and put them into different environments. You could observe if the different environments change how many sheep of each color get caught by wolves. There are many other creative experiments you can probably think up.

Your experiment should produce some results or data. These results might be *qualitative*, which means descriptions without numbers. For example, noting which environment may allow fewer sheep to be caught by wolves would be a qualitative result. Results can also be *quantitative*, in other words, involving numbers or measurements. Counting how many sheep of each color were caught by wolves over three months would be a quantitative result. Some experiments can produce both qualitative and quantitative results, while others yield only one of these types of data.

Analyzing your results should allow you to conclude whether your hypothesis was correct or not. If it turns out to be incorrect, do you hang up your imaginary lab coats and go home? Not a chance! This is where trial and error comes in. Remember, you wrote your hypothesis in pencil. You can tweak it as many times as you need, or even erase it completely and write a new one. When your experiment gives you *new* information, or when you observe something new in nature, you can revise your hypothesis and design another experiment. The best part is that you learn a bit more with each new experiment.

It might be helpful to think of this as an *engineering approach* or "tinkering." You know those people who are always fiddling with their motorcycle, seeing if they can get it to go a little faster or sound a little cooler? They're always working on it, and even though it runs okay, it's never quite finished. That's how it is with science. We will never be done acquiring knowledge about the universe, but our understanding of the world keeps getting a little deeper with every new experiment.

WHAT'S IN THIS BOOK

On this journey, we will explore three major branches of science:

1. **Earth and space sciences (Chapters 1, 2, 3, 4, and 5):** In these chapters, we will travel across the solar system, learn about the Earth's history, study the forces that shape Earth's surface, explore what causes weather, and find out how human activity is changing the natural world.

2. **Life sciences (Chapters 6, 7, 8, and 9):** In these chapters, we will zoom in to explore the tiniest building blocks of life and then zoom out to understand how whole ecosystems work together. We will also look at the ways genetics and evolution determine how organisms develop and change.

3. **Physical sciences (Chapters 10, 11, 12, and 13):** In the final chapters, we will find out what everything is made of, explore the laws that govern how substances transform, and learn how objects move and interact.

Throughout the chapters, there are questions and prompts to help you understand what you've read. You can find answers to these questions in the answer keys at the end of each chapter.

EQUIPMENT FOR LEARNING

When you go on an adventure, including learning about science, you need tools that will help you survive and thrive. That's where we come in. We are not only giving you the tools below, we will remind you to use them. In the pages ahead, you'll see the tools pop up, along with some questions and ways to think about what you're reading.

SYMBOL/ TOOL	WHAT IT IS	HOW TO USE IT WHILE YOU READ
	In science, a phenomenon is an event or fact that is observable using the five senses.	The phenomenon icon, based on St. Elmo's Fire (look it up), tells you to sharpen your senses and open your mind to investigate an observable fact that raises a scientific question.
	People use a GPS so they don't get lost. It helps them figure out where they are, get directions, or explore a new area.	When you see the GPS, stop and pay attention to the big picture. You might… • Ask yourself some big picture questions before you read. • Get oriented with the basic facts. • Preview the text by skimming the headings, timelines, charts, and illustrations.
	Boots give hikers sure footing, even on rocky paths. All serious hikers pull on their boots before setting out.	Activate prior knowledge. When you see the boots, it's time to: • Think back on what you already know about the topic. • Build on what you already know with new information.

	A pickaxe is a digging tool. Notice how it has a sharp point to get into small places!	Your pickaxe will help you dig deeply for meaning. • Use it to pick an idea apart and examine it critically. • Use it to look for evidence and important details.
	People use a magnifying glass to examine something up close.	The magnifying glass will remind you to stop and zoom in. Use your magnifier to: • Reflect on what you just learned. • Make conclusions based on your new information.
	A measuring tape is an essential measuring tool.	Scientists often have to measure things, whether they're objects like fossils, liquids, microscopic particles, or the vast dimensions of space. When you see the measuring tape: • Think about what you are measuring, and the best way of measuring it. • Be sure you are accurate!
	Stop and pay attention.	• Beware of a common misconception or a common error.

Familiarize yourself with these tools, and when you're ready, buckle your seatbelt, and off we go!

CHAPTER VOCABULARY

conclusion: the analysis of the data after the experiment ends to determine whether the hypothesis was correct or not.

experiment: the process of testing a hypothesis.

hypothesis: a proposed explanation for the scientific question to use as a starting point for an experiment.

observation: the first step in the scientific method—taking note of something interesting and beginning to make connections.

results/data: evidence and facts from the experiment that can be used to help answer the scientific question.

scientific question: the second step in the scientific method—turning your initial observations into a question that can be answered by performing an experiment.

You'll notice that vocabulary terms appear throughout the book highlighted in bold yellow type. Definitions for these terms are collected for you at the end of each chapter in a list like the one on this page.

1 EARTH'S PLACE IN THE UNIVERSE

Tonight, you'll be camping out in the woods. While roasting marshmallows on sticks, take a look up at the starry sky. Tonight the Moon is just a tiny sliver—what some people call a young moon. You may think about the full moon you saw last time you checked out the night sky and wonder. . . what causes the Moon's appearance to change over time? In this chapter, you will learn about that and more, using astronomy as your guide.

CHAPTER CONTENTS

THE SOLAR SYSTEM

The Sun, Moon, Earth, and all the other planets are part of the solar system. Scientists have made observations of the solar system—and of the vast expanse of space surrounding it—to develop theories of how our solar system formed. The primary theory is that about 4.6 billion years ago, our solar system was just an enormous cloud of dust and gas called a nebula. Over millions of years, those gases and bits of dust slowly formed into objects. Eventually those objects took shape into the Sun, planets, moons, and all the other objects in the solar system.

Scientists believe that over millions of years, a nebula of gases and bits of dust formed the solar system.

The Sun is in the middle of the solar system. Orbiting around it are eight planets, including Earth, as well as many moons, asteroids, comets, and much more.

OUR NEIGHBORHOOD: THE MILKY WAY

The solar system is part of the Milky Way galaxy. If you think of the Earth as your house, then the solar system is your street, and the Milky Way is your local neighborhood. But on a much, much bigger scale.

In fact, you might be able to see the Milky Way tonight if you look carefully! It looks like a hazy trail of light passing among the stars, almost in a straight line.

Early astronomers thought the Milky Way looked like milk after someone pours it into a dark liquid, when it's just starting to mix together—kind of like one of those fancy drinks some people order at coffee shops. In fact, the word "galaxy" actually comes from the Greek word for "gala," which means milk.

Scientists have learned that the Milky Way is just one of many galaxies in the universe. Scientists estimate that the observable universe—the part of the universe that humans can see with current technology—contains at least **two trillion** galaxies! That's a million million, or a number with 12 zeroes! That's a number so big that scientists prefer to write it in scientific notation.

WRITING VERY, VERY BIG NUMBERS: SCIENTIFIC NOTATION

For scientific notation, you need to count how many digits the number in standard form contains. For example, the value of two trillion in standard form is 2,000,000,000,000, which contains one 2 plus twelve zeroes. Start with the leftmost digit, in this case the 2, which is often called the leading digit. Then, put a decimal point to the right of that number. Write any numbers that are not trailing zeroes to the right of the decimal point. Then, multiply that number by 10 raised to the power of the number of placeholder digits. So, 2 trillion would be a 2 times 10 raised to the 12th power: 2×10^{12}. Therefore, 207,000,000,000,000 (207 trillion) would be written in scientific notation as:

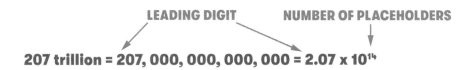

LEADING DIGIT **NUMBER OF PLACEHOLDERS**

207 trillion = 207, 000, 000, 000, 000 = 2.07 x 10^{14}

You can also do the reverse. If you start out with a number in scientific notation, for example 1.01×10^{11}, you can write out the full number. Start with the leading digit, which is 1. Write the digits that are on the right of the leading digit, followed by as many zeroes that are needed to get to that 11 in the exponent. So, you would have 101 followed by nine zeroes:

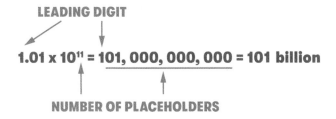

LEADING DIGIT

1.01 x 10^{11} = 101, 000, 000, 000 = 101 billion

NUMBER OF PLACEHOLDERS

And what is significant about the approximate number of 101 billion? It is the estimated number of stars in the Milky Way! Wow, that's a lot of stars! Now, let's do some practice converting between scientific and standard notation with some other very large numbers. Fill in the blank boxes in the table.

THE MILKY WAY IN NUMBERS

MILKY WAY GALAXY OBJECT	DISTANCE TO EARTH IN KILOMETERS	
	STANDARD NOTATION	SCIENTIFIC NOTATION
Moon	384,400	3.844×10^5
Sun		1.48×10^8
Proxima Centauri (the closest star other than the Sun)		3.974×10^{13}
Sirius (the brightest star in the night sky)	81,500,000,000,000	
The center of the Milky Way	247,000,000,000,000,000	

GETTING STREETWISE: EXPLORING THE SOLAR SYSTEM

 Remember the analogy that the solar system is your street and the Milky Way is your neighborhood? Let's see how well you know your street. We bet there are some nooks you haven't explored.

The solar system is home to many objects, in addition to the eight planets orbiting the Sun.

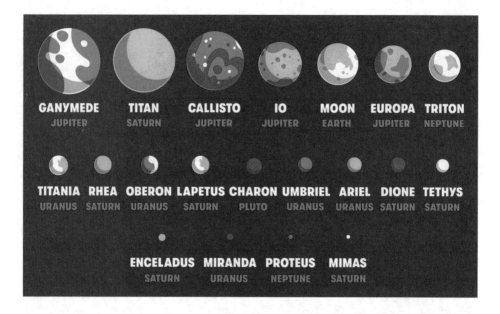

GANYMEDE JUPITER   **TITAN** SATURN   **CALLISTO** JUPITER   **IO** JUPITER   **MOON** EARTH   **EUROPA** JUPITER   **TRITON** NEPTUNE

TITANIA URANUS   **RHEA** SATURN   **OBERON** URANUS   **LAPETUS** SATURN   **CHARON** PLUTO   **UMBRIEL** URANUS   **ARIEL** URANUS   **DIONE** SATURN   **TETHYS** SATURN

ENCELADUS SATURN   **MIRANDA** URANUS   **PROTEUS** NEPTUNE   **MIMAS** SATURN

For example, the Earth has one moon orbiting it. Most of the other planets in the solar system also have their own moons and, in fact, many have more than one. Saturn holds the current record for the number of known moons at 82. Can you imagine looking up and watching 82 moons move across the sky?

In fact, there are more than 200 moons in the solar system, including an estimated 79 for Jupiter, but zero for Mercury and Venus!

Another neighbor on your solar system street is the asteroid belt. This region between the orbits of Mars and Jupiter is occupied by many asteroids, which are solid, rocky objects. Ceres, a dwarf planet, also lives amongst the asteroids in the asteroid belt. Despite what you may have seen in movies, the asteroid belt is mostly empty space, not lots of large rocks hurtling toward each other. So if you plan a trip that takes you through the asteroid belt, your chances are very high that you will come through the other side catching a glimpse of only a handful of distant asteroids.

Very similar to the asteroid belt is the Kuiper belt. The primary difference between the asteroid belt and the Kuiper belt is that the Kuiper belt is beyond Neptune's orbit. Dwarf planets Pluto, Haumea, Makemake, and Eris all live among the rocky bodies within the Kuiper belt.

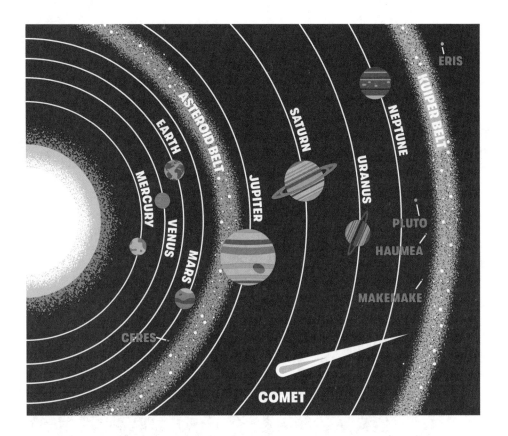

There are also numerous icy, rocky comets in the solar system. If the planets are houses on your street, comets are sort of like stray cats, passing across the road in different directions and trailing a "tail" of gases and dust. So far scientists have discovered more than 6,600 comets, and they estimate that there are many thousands more lurking in the furthest reaches of the solar system.

CHECK YOUR UNDERSTANDING

Order the following objects from smallest to largest:
Sun, asteroid, Earth, galaxy, Moon, solar system

SMALLEST   LARGEST

BUILDING A MODEL OF THE SOLAR SYSTEM

 If someone asked you to draw a map of the solar system, you'd have to know how big things are in relation to one another, just like on a globe of the Earth. You'd also have to know how far apart things are in order to get an accurate picture.

SIZES IN THE SOLAR SYSTEM

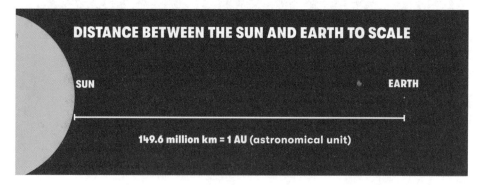

DISTANCE BETWEEN THE SUN AND EARTH TO SCALE

SUN

EARTH

149.6 million km = 1 AU (astronomical unit)

Of course, when you look at a picture of the solar system like the one in this chapter, remember that it's not to scale. But wait, what's scale? Scale is the representation of really big objects in a size that you can understand, like taking the entire solar system and squishing it to fit into these pages. The other part of scale is proportion, which involves comparing the sizes of objects and distances between them to others. For example, the Earth has a diameter of 12,756 kilometers, while the diameter of the Sun is 1,391,016 kilometers—more than 100 times as big! So in order to show the Earth and the Sun—and the other planets, for that matter—in the same drawing or model, scientists take liberties with the distances and sizes of the planets.

FITTING PLANETS IN PLANETS!

In the pictures of the solar system in this book, it looks like all the planets are kind of similar in size and are packed together so close that they might bump into each other. But in reality, the planets vary greatly in size and are much farther apart than they seem. Did you know that 1,300 Earths can fit inside Jupiter? And 1,000,000—yes one million—Earths can fit inside the Sun!

DISTANCES IN THE SOLAR SYSTEM

Here's how you can picture how far apart things really are in the solar system.

Pretend the Sun is roughly the size of a regular basketball. Place it on one end of a basketball court. On that scale, the Earth will be the size of a flea—those tiny insects that like to live in the fur of cats and dogs. To keep the distance scaled properly, that flea will be all the way on the other side of the basketball court.

On that same scale, Mercury would be so tiny you wouldn't even be able to see it! And it is far enough away from the Sun that it would be just outside the 3-point line on the basketball court.

THE FARTHEST OUT

Neptune, the most distant planet in the solar system, would be about 26 basketball courts away from the basketball/Sun. It's a piece of gum stuck to the ground in the most distant corner of the parking lot outside the stadium. Clearly, there is no chance the flea is bumping into that piece of gum! Similarly, there is no way the planets of the solar system will collide as they travel along their orbits around the Sun.

THE FORCE: GRAVITY AT WORK

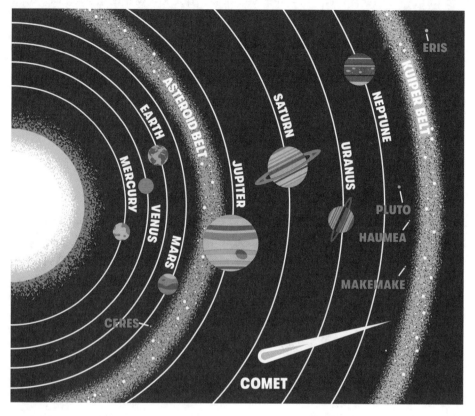

Now you have some idea of the enormous distances between objects in the solar system. But how do all the planets in the solar system stay in their proper places, anyway? Why do all the planets orbit around the Sun, and why don't we wake up one day to find that we all floated away from Earth?

SIR ISAAC NEWTON AND THE APPLE

The answer is that objects in the Solar System "use the force." Not the one from *Star Wars*, though—rather, it's the force of gravity. The first scientist to name gravity and some of its properties was Sir Isaac Newton (1643–1727), who shared his discovery in the 1680s. According to legend, Newton was sitting under an apple tree when an apple fell and hit him on the head. That's when Newton realized that the apple was pulled down toward the ground by an invisible force that he called gravity.

All objects in the solar system are able to wield this force. But some objects have a more powerful pull than others. The Sun exerts the strongest gravitational force in the solar system, and that's because it is the largest object in the solar system. The amount of gravitational force an object is able to exert on other objects is directly related to its mass—the amount of matter that makes up an object. You'll learn more about mass in a later chapter.

THE EARTH-MOON-SUN SYSTEM

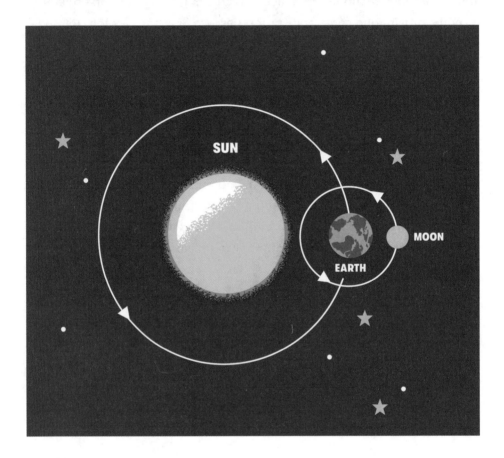

Gravity is the reason that Earth keeps orbiting around the Sun, sort of like a hungry kid who keeps circling the snack table at a party. Gravity also makes sure the Moon keeps orbiting the Earth. In the analogy, the Moon is a dog that keeps circling around the hungry kid who keeps snacking. They're like a package deal: the snack table attracts the kid, and the kid attracts the dog. You could say it's a "kid–dog–snack table system." Similarly, scientists talk about the "Earth–Moon–Sun system."

ROTATION VS. ORBIT

What's the difference between a rotation and an orbit? A rotation is one complete spin of an object. In 24 hours, or one day, the Earth makes one full rotation. An orbit is the time it takes to go around another object. It takes 365 days, or one year, for the Earth to orbit the Sun.

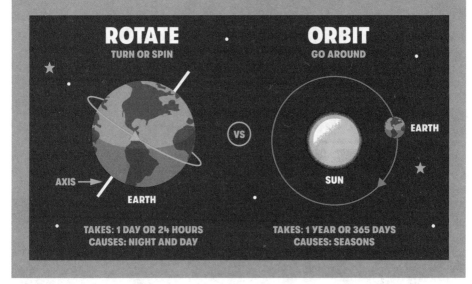

ROTATE
TURN OR SPIN

ORBIT
GO AROUND

VS

AXIS

EARTH

EARTH

SUN

TAKES: 1 DAY OR 24 HOURS
CAUSES: NIGHT AND DAY

TAKES: 1 YEAR OR 365 DAYS
CAUSES: SEASONS

SOLVING THE MYSTERY OF THE SEASONS

The Earth–Moon–Sun system can help explain many mysterious phenomena. Why is it cold during part of the year and warm during another part of the year? The Earth–Moon–Sun system can explain the phenomenon of the changing seasons.

THE CYCLE OF SEASONS

Picture a globe, like one you might have seen at the library or in science class. A globe is a 3-dimensional model of the Earth, and it shows that the Earth spins around its own axis.

THE AXIS OF ROTATION

Now let's look more closely at this globe. Notice how it's mounted on an angle? Rather than the North pole being right at the top and the South pole being just above the stand, the globe's spin axis, also called the axis of rotation, is tilted. Why did globe makers go to the trouble of mounting the globe on an angle like this? Take a look at this picture of the Earth as it travels around the Sun:

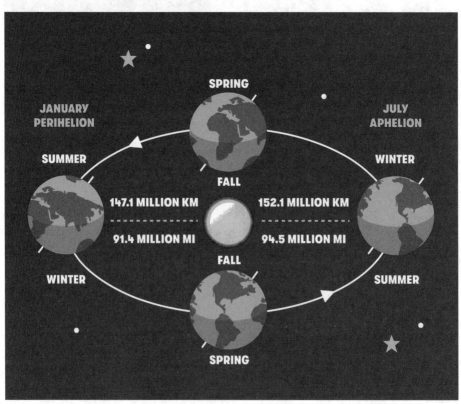

What do you notice about Earth as it travels around the Sun?

_____

_____

_____

_____

If the Earth didn't have this orientation, there would be no seasons at all! Let's take a closer look.

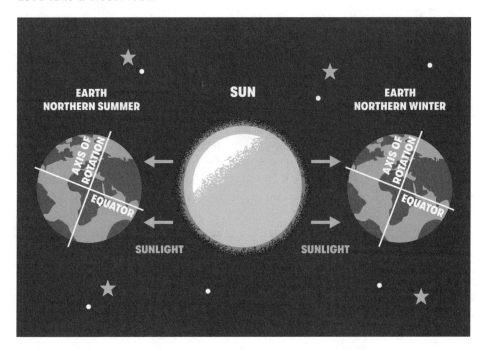

The Earth spins around the axis of rotation, like the stem of a top that you twirl to make it spin around. That axis of rotation is tilted. And that tilt stays exactly the same as Earth travels along its orbit. Take a look at Earth during the northern summer and the Earth during the northern winter. How do you think this tilt causes the summer and winter seasons in the Northern Hemisphere? Write your thoughts down in the space provided on the next page.

IN YOUR OWN WORDS: EARTH DURING NORTHERN SUMMER	IN YOUR OWN WORDS: EARTH DURING NORTHERN WINTER

Okay, so when people in the Northern Hemisphere are on summer vacation from school, what are people in the Southern Hemisphere experiencing? The Southern Hemisphere experiences the opposite seasons than the Northern Hemisphere does! Why do you think that is?

_____

_____

_____

_____

_____

_____

_____

_____

_____

The next time someone tells you that it is summer because Earth is closest to the Sun, ask them why it is winter in the other hemisphere. What do you think they might say? Hmm. . . you will probably get a lot of answers.

Earth does in fact travel slightly closer and farther away from the Sun during its orbit. Earth is about 5 million kilometers closer to the Sun in January than it is in July! But in January, the Northern Hemisphere experiences winter. This is because the tilt of Earth's axis of rotation causes the seasons, not how close it is to the Sun.

SOLVING THE MYSTERY OF THE MOON'S PHASES

The seasons are just one of the phenomena that the Earth–Moon–Sun system explains. So, what about the movement of the objects in the Earth–Moon–Sun system? How can the movements of Earth and the Moon explain other phenomena? Like why the Moon's appearance keeps changing?

THE GROWING AND SHRINKING MOON

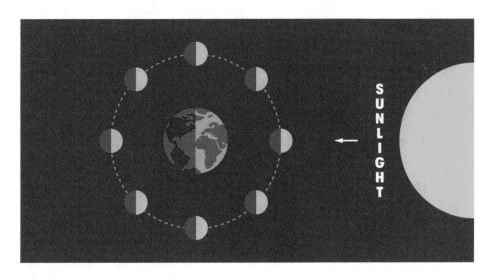

Before you continue along on your adventure, it is important to note that all of the light we see coming from the Moon is actually from the Sun. The Moon is basically a big rock, and rocks can't make their own light. Sunlight hits the Moon and lights it up, just like how sunlight lights up the daytime side of Earth. This allows us to see the Moon at night!

The Moon travels around Earth. Let's tag along as it completes one orbit and organize our travel log in the table below. Our starting point is when the Moon is in between Earth and the Sun. This is what we call a new moon.

 Draw what you think a new moon looks like in the right column of the table.

OUR LUNAR ORBIT TRAVEL LOG

LUNAR LOCATION	LUNAR PHASE NAME	LUNAR OBSERVATIONS	YOUR NEW MOON DRAWING
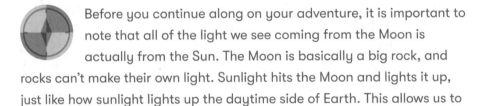	New moon	All of the sunlight falls on the side of the Moon that is facing away from Earth.	

Did you draw a black circle where the Moon should be? Because all the sunlight lands on the side of the Moon that isn't facing Earth, you won't be able to see any part of the Moon. Continue your journey.

In the right hand column of the chart on the following page, draw what you think the Moon will look like from Earth. Think about the shapes of the Moon that you have seen when you look up at the sky.

LUNAR LOCATION	LUNAR PHASE NAME	LUNAR OBSERVATIONS	YOUR LUNAR PHASE DRAWING
	Waxing crescent	You can see a sliver of the lit side of the Moon from Earth. The Sun is barely hitting the right side of the Moon.	
	First quarter	You can see the right half of the lit side of the Moon from Earth.	
	Waxing gibbous	The lit side of the Moon keeps moving left, and you can now see more than half of the Moon's face.	
	Full moon	The entire lit side of the Moon faces Earth. You can see the whole face lit up.	

Hey, you made it halfway around the Moon's orbit! You went from being able to see none of the Moon during a new moon to the whole face of the Moon during a full moon! What do you think will happen during the rest of your journey? Here's a hint: the process will start to go backwards.

Try to fill in the lunar observations and draw a picture of the shape of the Moon.

OUR LUNAR ORBIT TRAVEL LOG, CONTINUED AGAIN

LUNAR LOCATION	LUNAR PHASE NAME	LUNAR OBSERVATIONS	YOUR LUNAR PHASE DRAWING
	Waning gibbous		
	Third quarter		
	Waning crescent		
	New moon		

People in the Northern and Southern Hemispheres experience opposite seasons. Not only that, but the phases of the Moon also appear differently to people in the Northern and Southern Hemispheres.

Now take a moment to think back to the question from the beginning of this chapter. Why does the Moon's appearance keep changing?

_____

_____

_____

_____

_____

_____

_____

The shape of the Moon is not the only thing that changes. Sometimes, the Moon turns a bright red color. What? Let's figure out why!

SOLVING THE MYSTERY OF BLOOD MOONS AND RINGS OF FIRE

Whoa, did someone spill some red paint or blood on the Moon? What's going on? Sometimes when the Moon is full, it passes directly into Earth's shadow. Wait, Earth has a shadow? Yes! Just like the Sun causes you to have a shadow, the Sun causes Earth to have a shadow. You just can't see it.

 You are observing your shadow on the grass. Where is the Sun located?

A. To your right

B. To your left

C. In front of you

D. Behind you

The Sun causes Earth's shadow to point directly behind it. Remember, images like this are not to scale. What does that mean again? Oh yes, that means that the distances and sizes of the objects in the picture are not actually accurate, but they do illustrate how the Earth can cast a shadow on the Moon. In this case, the actual width of the Earth's shadow that the Moon can travel through is pretty narrow, which is part of the reason you don't see the Moon turn bright red every month.

This phenomenon is called a lunar eclipse. Lunar eclipses always occur during a full moon, and only when the Sun, Earth, and Moon are in perfect alignment. This doesn't happen every time there is a full moon because the Moon's orbit is almost in line with Earth's orbit, but a tiny bit different.

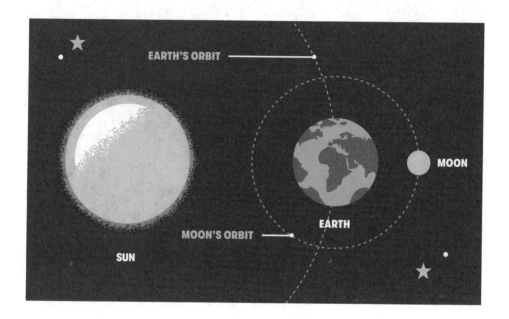

UMBRA AND PENUMBRA

TRY THIS!

Stick your hand underneath a bright light. What do you notice? You have a darker inner shadow and a lighter outer shadow! This is just like what happens with Earth's shadow—there is a darker inner shadow and a lighter outer shadow. The Moon turns red when it fully passes into the darker inner shadow, which is called the umbra. When this happens, it is a total lunar eclipse.

However, sometimes the Moon passes partially into both the umbra, and the penumbra, which is the lighter outer shadow. When this happens, the Moon doesn't turn red, but it looks like a big bite is taken out of it. This phenomenon is called a partial lunar eclipse.

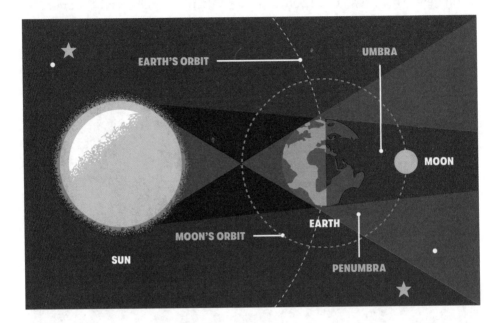

So Earth's shadow causes the Moon to turn red. But the Moon also has a shadow. Do you think the Moon's shadow turns Earth red? It's probably a good thing that it doesn't. But let's see what happens when the Moon moves from one side of Earth to the other, creating a perfect line, with the Sun on one side and Earth on the other.

RINGS OF FIRE

Where did the Sun go?! It didn't go anywhere! It is still here, hiding behind the Moon. But isn't the Moon much smaller than the Sun? Yes, it is. Let's see how that works.

A QUESTION OF PERSPECTIVE

Have you heard of the word perspective? This means that what you are looking at can change appearances by moving closer, farther away, or off to the side. Think of looking down at a house from an airplane. The house hasn't changed in size since you left the ground, but it sure looks smaller. The difference is that now you're a few thousand feet in the air.

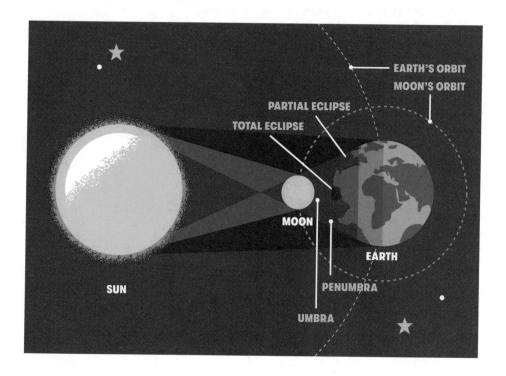

A case of perspective is going on between the Sun and Moon too. The Sun is so much larger than the Moon, but it is so much farther away that it actually looks like it is the same size. This phenomenon is unique to the Earth–Moon–Sun system.

The Moon is traveling along its orbit and then moves perfectly between the Sun and Earth. Because of perspective, the Moon covers up the Sun—a solar eclipse. Usually, there is a thin ring of the Sun remaining. That ring is actually the atmosphere of the Sun, which is called the corona, sometimes called the "ring of fire."

Here's a cool tidbit—astronomers create their own solar eclipses using special equipment to study the corona. If they don't, the super bright light from the Sun will make the corona almost impossible to observe.

 Never look directly at the Sun! If you are lucky enough to be in an area where there will be a solar eclipse, make sure you use special eye protection and filters for any telescopes or binoculars. Looking directly at the Sun, even if most of it is blocked, can still seriously damage your eyes.

 Think back to the question from the beginning of your adventure, and use all of the knowledge you have gathered so far to help you explain it. Why does the Moon's appearance keep changing?

_____

_____

_____

_____

_____

Mystery solved! Time to go into your tent and turn in for the night. On your next adventure, you will zoom in on Earth to explore what it's really made of.

CHAPTER 1
VOCABULARY

asteroids: small, rocky objects that orbit the Sun and are often potato-shaped.

asteroid belt: the region between Mars and Jupiter that contains many asteroids. Unlike what you typically see in movies, the asteroids within the asteroid belt are actually very far apart and very rarely collide.

comets: small objects made of ice, dust, and/or rock that orbit the Sun. When comets approach the Sun, they develop a tail of particles that point directly away from the Sun.

corona: the outermost layer of the Sun's atmosphere. It can be seen as the ring around the Sun during a solar eclipse.

gravity: a force that attracts objects toward the center of mass. For example, gravity pulls objects such as humans and airplanes toward the center of Earth, and gravity pulls Earth toward the center of the Sun.

lunar eclipse: the alignment of the Sun, Earth, and Moon where the Moon passes through Earth's shadow. A partial lunar eclipse occurs when only part of the Moon passes through Earth's shadow and looks like a cookie with a bite taken out of it. A total lunar eclipse occurs when the entire Moon enters Earth's shadow and appears to be dark red.

Milky Way galaxy: a collection of millions or even billions of stars with gas, dust, planets, and much more held together by gravity. Earth belongs to one of many solar systems within the Milky Way galaxy.

orbit: the path one object takes around another. For example, the Earth orbits the Sun.

penumbra: the lighter, outer region of a shadow that surrounds the umbra.

perspective: the changing of an object's appearance by moving closer, farther away, or from a different angle.

proportion: the comparison of objects in terms of their size, mass, or other physical property. For example, the Moon's diameter is a little more than a quarter of Earth's diameter and the Sun's mass is about 333,000 times the mass of Earth.

rotation: the spin of an object around its axis. For example, Earth rotates around the axis running from the North Pole to the South Pole. One rotation on Earth is called a day.

scale: the relationship between sizes of objects—a representation of large objects in a size that makes them easier to study and understand.

scientific notation: a method for writing really large numbers in a way to make them easier to read and work with. For example, one million (1,000,000) is written as 1×10^6 or just 10^6.

solar eclipse: the alignment of the Sun, Moon, and Earth in which the Moon blocks the light between the Sun and Earth. A partial solar eclipse occurs when the Moon covers part of the Sun's disk. A total solar eclipse occurs when the Moon completely covers the Sun's disk, leaving the corona visible in what is often called the "ring of fire."

solar system: a collection of planets, moons, asteroids, comets, and more in orbit around a central star. Our solar system consists of the Sun, Mercury, Venus, Earth, Mars, Jupiter, Saturn, Uranus, and Neptune as well as several dwarf planets, dozens of moons, and thousands of asteroids, comets, and meteoroids.

umbra: the inner, darker region of a shadow. The umbra is surrounded by the lighter penumbra.

CHAPTER 1 ANSWER KEY

PAGE 16

MILKY WAY GALAXY OBJECT	DISTANCE TO EARTH IN KILOMETERS	
	STANDARD NOTATION	SCIENTIFIC NOTATION
Moon	384,400	3.844×10^5
Sun	148,000,000	1.48×10^8
Proxima Centauri (the closest star other than the Sun)	39,740,000,000,000	3.974×10^{13}
Sirius (the brightest star in the night sky)	81,500,000,000,000	8.15×10^{13}
The center of the Milky Way	247,000,000,000,000,000	2.47×10^{17}

PAGE 19

SMALLEST					LARGEST
Asteroid	Moon	Earth	Sun	Solar System	Galaxy

PAGE 27

The axis of rotation stays exactly the same as Earth travels around the Sun.

PAGE 28

EARTH DURING NORTHERN SUMMER	EARTH DURING NORTHERN WINTER
The Northern Hemisphere is tilted toward the Sun, so it receives more sunlight to warm it up—summer.	The Northern Hemisphere is tilted away from the Sun, so it receives less sunlight and cools—winter.

When the Northern Hemisphere is tilted toward the Sun, the Southern Hemisphere is pointed away. This causes summer to occur in the Northern Hemisphere and winter to occur in the Southern Hemisphere. When the Northern Hemisphere is tilted away from the Sun, the Southern Hemisphere is tilted toward the Sun. This causes winter in the Northern Hemisphere and summer in the Southern Hemisphere.

PAGE 30

OUR LUNAR ORBIT TRAVEL LOG

LUNAR LOCATION	LUNAR PHASE NAME	LUNAR OBSERVATIONS	YOUR NEW MOON DRAWING
	New moon	All of the sunlight falls on the side of the Moon that is facing away from Earth.	

OUR LUNAR ORBIT TRAVEL LOG, CONTINUED

LUNAR LOCATION	LUNAR PHASE NAME	LUNAR OBSERVATIONS	YOUR LUNAR PHASE DRAWING
	Waxing crescent	You can see a sliver of the lit side of the Moon from Earth. The Sun is barely hitting the right side of the Moon.	
	First quarter	You can see the right half of the lit side of the Moon from Earth.	
	Waxing gibbous	The lit side of the Moon keeps moving left, and you can now see more than half of the Moon's face.	
	Full moon	The entire lit side of the Moon faces Earth. You can see the whole face lit up.	

OUR LUNAR ORBIT TRAVEL LOG, CONTINUED AGAIN

LUNAR LOCATION	LUNAR PHASE NAME	LUNAR OBSERVATIONS	YOUR LUNAR PHASE DRAWING
	Waning gibbous	More than half of the Moon is lit up, and it is on the opposite side as before.	
	Third quarter	Half of the Moon is lit up, the opposite half that was visible during the first quarter.	
	Waning crescent	There is a thin sliver of the Moon visible.	
	New moon	The Moon is completely dark because the entire lit side is facing away from Earth.	

PAGE 33

The Sun lights up half of the Moon, but you can't always see the entire lit side from Earth. As the lit side turns toward Earth, you can see the Moon grow from a new moon, through crescent, first quarter, and gibbous before the entire lit side is facing Earth and you see a full moon. Then, the lit side turns away from Earth and the Moon shrinks in the reverse pattern.

PAGE 34

The answer is **choice D**, behind you.

PAGE 38

In addition to going through phases, the Moon's appearance also changes during lunar eclipses. Sometimes, when the full moon passes into Earth's shadow, it turns bright red.

THE HISTORY OF PLANET EARTH

On a stretch of coastline in southern England, you can see 185 million years of history if you know what to look for! The formation shown here is part of the "Jurassic Coast," a World Heritage site located on the English Channel in Dorset. But how do you learn about history from a *cliff*? And how do you *know* that this cliff shows 185 million years of history? Read on to find out.

How do humans know when the events on the geologic time scale occurred?

A STROLL THROUGH THE EARTH'S PAST

It isn't just England where you can see millions of years of history with your own eyes. In fact, there are places all over the world. Places where unusual, or even catastrophic, things happened can give clues about Earth's history. Let's take a look at a few.

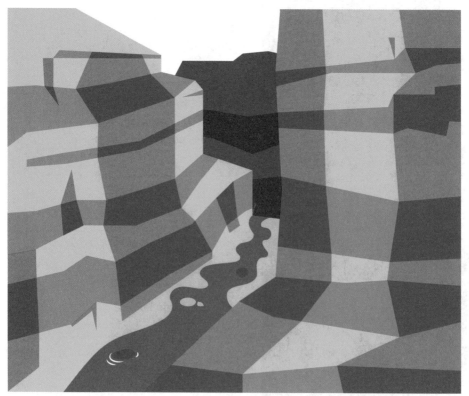

The layers of rocks in the Grand Canyon in Arizona show about 1.8 billion years of history.

The asteroid that crashed into Earth in what is now Mexico and wiped out the dinosaurs occurred 66 million years ago, forming the Chicxulub Crater.

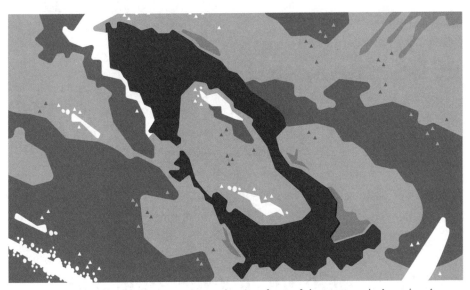

Now a lake, Mount Toba, in Indonesia, was the site of one of the most explosive volcanic eruptions in history, which occurred 74,000 years ago—it may have even caused a "volcanic winter" that lasted for up to ten years!

And the more you look, the more history you unravel. Let's make a timeline and fill it in as we go through the history of Earth.

THE GEOLOGIC TIME SCALE

Ready to discover more about Earth's history? Grab a piece of paper and something to write with. Draw a line across the middle of the paper all the way from one side to the other. Label the left side "Beginning of Earth" with a date of 4.6 billion years (4,600 millions years ago, or 4,600 MYA on the timeline below) and label the right side "Today."

BEGINNING OF EARTH   **TODAY**

| 4600 MYA | 1,800 MYA
Grand Canyon
began forming | 800 MYA
Animal life
began to
evolve in
the oceans | 700 MYA
Plant life
began to
evolve | 2.4 MYA
Earliest
relatives to
humans
evolved | 200,000 YEARS AGO
Earliest homo sapiens
(modern humans)
evolved |

YEARS IN MILLIONS

EONS, ERAS, AND PERIODS

We mentioned earlier that Earth was formed about 4.6 billion years ago. It came into existence at the same time the Sun and the rest of the solar system formed. Now you are going to take your timeline and break it into eons (the largest spans of time) and then break those eons into eras, which are still incredibly long, but shorter than eons. From Earth's beginning until today, there have been 4 eons and 3 eras.

PALEOZOIC, MESOZOIC, AND CENOZOIC ERAS

The first span of time is sometimes called the Precambrian Era, but only because scientists decided on the term—it's actually the length of three eons. On many geologic time scales, though, you'll see it named in the era category.

Each of these eras is broken up into periods, which are still pretty large chunks of time but smaller than eras. Let's skip the Precambrian and start with the Paleozoic Era. The Paleozoic Era is split into seven periods, the Mesozoic Era is divided into three, and the era that we currently live in, the Cenozoic Era, is broken into two periods. Put those on your timeline with some years.

EON	ERA	PERIOD	YEARS AGO (IN MILLIONS)
PHANEROZOIC	Cenozoic	Quaternary	1.6 – Today
		Tertiary	65.5 – 1.6
	Mesozoic	Cretaceous	144 – 65.5
		Jurassic	201 – 145
		Triassic	252 – 201
	Paleozoic	Permian	299 – 252
		Pennsylvanian	323 – 299
		Mississippian	359 – 323
		Devonian	419 – 359
		Silurian	444 – 419
		Ordovician	485 – 444
		Cambrian	541 – 485
PROTERAZOIC	Precambrian		2500 – 541
ARCHEAN			4000 – 2500
HADEAN			4600 – 4000

To break it down even more, each period can be broken into even smaller time periods called epochs. But even epochs are several thousands to millions of years long!

If you are following along in building your own timeline, make sure to leave some space for some super cool events, which you'll add along the way. Now give your timeline a proper name: the geologic time scale.

EON	ERA	PERIOD	EPOCH	YEAR (IN MILLIONS)
PHANEROZOIC	Cenozoic	Quaternary	Holocene	0.1 – Today
			Pleistocene	1.6 – 0.01
		Tertiary	Pliocene	5.3 – 1.6
			Miocene	23.7 – 5.3
			Oligocene	36.6 – 23.7
			Eocene	57.8 – 36.6
			Paleocene	65.5 – 57.8
	Mesozoic	Cretaceous	Extinction of dinosaurs	144 – 65.5
		Jurassic		201 – 145
		Triassic	First dinosaurs	252 – 201
	Paleozoic	Permian	Age of Amphibians	299 – 252
		Pennsylvanian		323 – 299
		Mississippian		359 – 323
		Devonian	Age of Fishes	419 – 359
		Silurian		444 – 419
		Ordovician	Age of Invertebrates	485 – 444
		Cambrian		541 – 485
PROTEROZOIC	Precambrian			2500 – 541
ARCHEAN				4000 – 2500
HADEAN				4600 – 4000

The name for the geologic time scale comes from the word "geology." Geology is the branch of science that means the study of Earth and the rocks it is made of.

There are all kinds of different timescales you can use for measuring different things. For example, cookies that just came out of the oven may have a lifespan of just a few minutes. Whereas the carrot sticks sitting next to them may have a lifespan of a few hours. However, when it comes to Earth, important stages in its history were so large that they have to be measured in *millions* or even *billions* of years!

TRANSITIONS BETWEEN PERIODS AND ERAS

Did these periods and eras turn from one to the next overnight, like what happens between New Year's Eve and New Year's Day? Nope, the transitions between time periods could take thousands of years. But how did these transitions start? Well, some transitions were the cause of a major geologic event, like an asteroid hitting Earth or a major volcanic eruption. The initial event may have lasted only moments, but it took time for the full force of the event to cause enough change to transition from one period to the next. Other transitions were due to biological changes as different types of life began to flourish, and even the changing of Earth's orbit around the Sun. Each period and era is defined by a unique climate, life forms, and events.

So how were scientists able to break up the whole history of Earth into periods and eras? And how do they know what the climate conditions were like? That you can sum up in one word—rocks!

BUILDING THE GEOLOGIC TIME SCALE WITH ROCKS

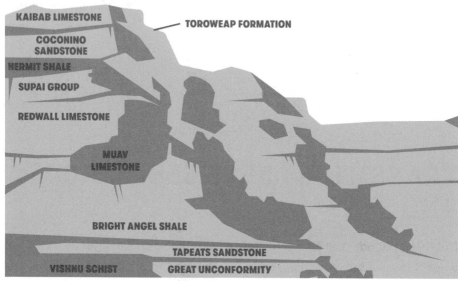

Layers of rock from the Grand Canyon

See all of those different layers of rock that make up that mountain? Each rock layer, or stratum (plural is strata), tells you a different chapter in Earth's history book. The topmost layer is the first chapter, which explains the youngest rock in the mountain. Each layer as you move down the mountain takes you farther back in time and provides more clues that allow you to figure out the history of Earth—kind of like a who-done-it mystery novel where all the clues come together to make sense at the end. Only, Earth's history isn't a story you can read in an afternoon. Humans have been gathering the clues to the story for hundreds of years. And each chapter that humans are combing through contains thousands of years of history.

THE LAW OF SUPERPOSITION

The understanding that rock layers are youngest at the top and oldest at the bottom is called the law of superposition. This allows scientists to compare the ages of rocks, minerals, and any other clues they find within the rock layers, or strata.

Sometimes, nature conveniently exposes all of these rock layers on its own. How nice! We don't even have to dig! Take another look at the exposed strata from the Grand Canyon on the previous page.

RELATIVE DATING

You can use the law of superposition to determine that the layers on the top are younger and the layers on the bottom are older. This is an example of relative dating. Relative dating doesn't give exact ages of the rocks or other objects, but it gives you an idea for how the ages of certain groups relate to each other. For example, you are younger than your parents. Your parents' parents, so your grandparents, are older than your parents, and so on.

CLUES FROM FOSSILS

Well, scientists don't look for family members or friends in the rock layers! But they do look for fossils. Fossils are the remains of animal and plant life that lived millions of years ago. Fossils get buried in the rock layers as those rock layers form, one on top of the other. Fossils can be relatively dated based on the rock layers they were discovered in.

 You searched around your local area and found that there was a mountain near your hometown where a few types of fossils were found. How cool! On the next page, you look at the picture of the strata where the fossils were found. Which fossil is the youngest? Put the fossils in order from youngest to oldest—youngest at the top.

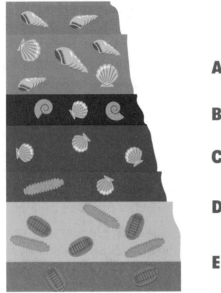

FOSSILS **RELATIVE AGE**
(Youngest at Top)

A _____

B _____

C _____

D _____

E _____

Congratulations, you just relatively dated the fossils!

So now you can determine which fossils and rock layers are older or younger than others, but can you determine their actual ages? For example, how do you know that the *Stegosaurus* lived about 150 million years ago and the *Tyrannosaurus rex* lived about 65 million years ago?

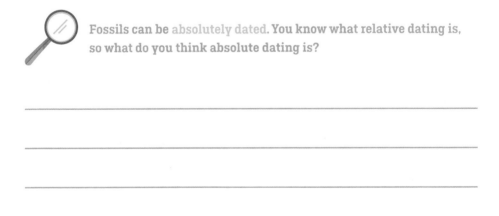

Fossils can be absolutely dated. You know what relative dating is, so what do you think absolute dating is?

_____

_____

_____

_____

_____

VOLCANIC ASH LAYER

○ **507 MILLION YEARS OLD** ▪

ABSOLUTE DATING

Absolute dating is finding the absolute or exact age of a fossil or other object. What clues do scientists look for in order to tell that a fossil is 65 million or 150 million years old?

CLUES FROM VOLCANIC ASH

One way that absolute dates can be found is by studying the layers of volcanic ash in the strata. When volcanoes erupt, ash gets sent out over hundreds or even thousands of miles. Ash contains radioactive material.

Radioactive material breaks down on very predictable time scales. Uranium, for example, breaks down on a very specific time scale. Every 250,000 years, half of the uranium turns into lead. Uranium is one of the several different radioactive materials that may be found in volcanic ash and some types of rocks. There are many different radioactive materials. Each one breaks down into a different material within a specific time period. By comparing the different materials within the strata, you can give them a "birthday."

So let's take a look at your geologic time scale timeline. So far, you have Earth's **4.6 billion year** history broken into eras, periods, and epochs. Add the *Stegosaurus* and *Tyrannosaurus rex* fossils that have been absolutely dated to your timeline.

USING MAJOR EVENTS TO UNDERSTAND EARTH'S HISTORY

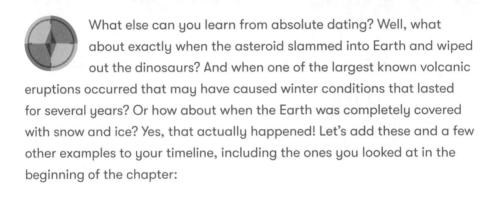

What else can you learn from absolute dating? Well, what about exactly when the asteroid slammed into Earth and wiped out the dinosaurs? And when one of the largest known volcanic eruptions occurred that may have caused winter conditions that lasted for several years? Or how about when the Earth was completely covered with snow and ice? Yes, that actually happened! Let's add these and a few other examples to your timeline, including the ones you looked at in the beginning of the chapter:

EON	ERA	PERIOD	EPOCH	EVENT	YEAR (IN MILLIONS)
PHANEROZOIC	Cenozoic	Quaternary	Holocene	Toba supervolcano	.74
				Humans began to migrate out of Africa	1.8
				Yellowstone supervolcano	2.1
				Earliest bipeds evolve	4
			Pleistocene		23
		Tertiary	Pliocene		
			Miocene		
			Oligocene		
			Eocene		
			Paleocene	Chicxulub impact	66
	Mesozoic	Cretaceous	Extinction of dinosaurs		145
		Jurassic		Pangea breaking	201
					245
		Triassic	First dinosaurs	Dinosaurs evolve	250
	Paleozoic	Permian	Age of Amphibians		299
		Pennsylvanian			323
		Mississippian			359
		Devonian	Age of Fishes		419
		Silurian			444
		Ordovician	Age of Invertebrates		485
		Cambrian			541
PROTEROZOIC	Precambrian			First multicell organisms	600
					2500
ARCHEAN				First single-celled organisms	3500
					4000
HADEAN					4600

THE BOUNDARIES BETWEEN ERAS AND PERIODS

So you know that the geologic time scale is broken down into all of these smaller time periods, but how can you pinpoint exactly where the boundaries are for each of the eras and periods? Sometimes, it's a mass extinction. For example, the extinction of the dinosaurs marks the boundary between the Mesozoic and Cenozoic Eras. Changing climate conditions define other boundaries, such as between the Triassic and Jurassic Periods. The rise of a species has also caused a transition, such as the rise of the reptiles, marking the beginning of the Pennsylvanian Period.

TIME SPAN	MILLIONS OF YEARS AGO	WHAT WE KNOW FROM THE CLUES
Hadean Eon	4600–4000	Heavy bombardment of Earth by large space rocks. Earth was inhospitable to life.
Archean Eon	4000–2500	Earliest known single-celled life forms began to evolve, such as bacteria and algae. The amount of oxygen in the atmosphere greatly increased.
Proterozoic Eon	2500–541	Multicellular organisms evolved.
Cambrian Period	541–485	Huge number of animal and plant life forms evolved, known as the "Cambrian Explosion."
Ordovician Period	485–444	The age of invertebrates. Most of North America was under water.
Silurian Period	444–419	Plants began to grow on land.
Devonian Period	419–359	The age of the fishes. Trees flourished further away from the coast.

Mississippian Period	359–323	More species of amphibians began to thrive. Large coal swamps began to form.
Pennsylvanian Period	323–299	The age of reptiles. Large tropical swamps spread over North America and Europe.
Permian Period	299–252	A large number of animal species became extinct. There is evidence of extreme seasons while all land was stuck together in one land mass known as Pangaea.
Triassic Period	252–201	Dinosaurs and mammals began to thrive.
Jurassic Period	201–145	Pangaea began to split up. Dinosaurs and reptiles were dominant. First evidence of birds.
Cretaceous Period	145–66	Flowering plants developed. Dinosaurs and about half of all species became extinct at the end of this period after the Chicxulub impact.
Tertiary Period	66–1.8	The age of mammals.
Quaternary Period	1.8–today	Humans began to evolve and thrive.

Let's take a quick break and think about what clues you can begin to piece together. How can you use the clues you found in building your geologic timeline to help you answer the question from the beginning of the chapter?

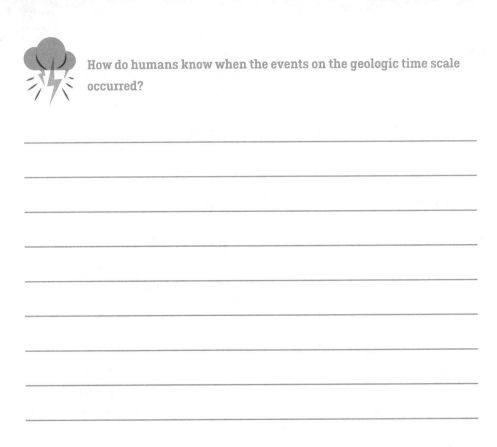

How do humans know when the events on the geologic time scale occurred?

_____

_____

_____

_____

_____

_____

_____

_____

_____

THE LIVES OF ROCKS

You take a walk around your neighborhood to see if you can spot any clues to understanding the geologic time scale. Maybe you see lots of tall buildings, maybe you see wide-open fields, or even anything in between. No matter where you are, you can probably find a rock. Any rock will do.

Did you find one? Where did you find it? Can you describe it?

_____

_____

_____

IDENTIFYING ROCK TYPES

Now let's take a look at the area of the Grand Canyon you looked at earlier. Wow, that's a lot of different kinds of rocks!

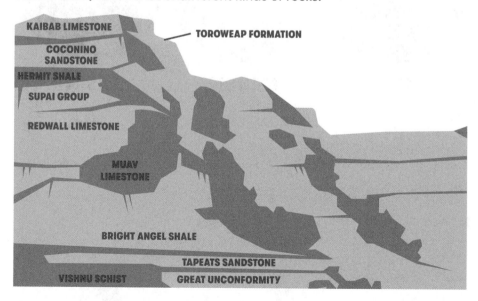

KAIBAB LIMESTONE

TOROWEAP FORMATION

COCONINO SANDSTONE

HERMIT SHALE

SUPAI GROUP

REDWALL LIMESTONE

MUAV LIMESTONE

BRIGHT ANGEL SHALE

TAPEATS SANDSTONE

VISHNU SCHIST

GREAT UNCONFORMITY

On the face of it, they may not look like much, but these rocks have a rich history spanning millions of years! And rocks like these are never really "finished"—they are constantly, very slowly, being transformed.

Let's look at an example of three rocks found in three different locations and look for clues to determine how they are related:

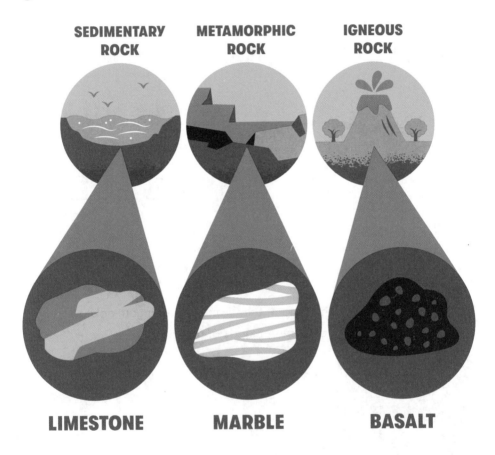

SEDIMENTARY ROCK

METAMORPHIC ROCK

IGNEOUS ROCK

LIMESTONE

MARBLE

BASALT

The limestone on the left can actually turn into the marble in the middle, which can then transform into the basalt on the right. But how?

THE ROCK CYCLE

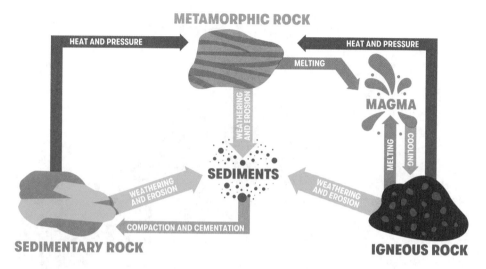

METAMORPHIC ROCK

HEAT AND PRESSURE

HEAT AND PRESSURE

MELTING

MAGMA

WEATHERING AND EROSION

MELTING

COOLING

SEDIMENTS

WEATHERING AND EROSION

WEATHERING AND EROSION

COMPACTION AND CEMENTATION

SEDIMENTARY ROCK

IGNEOUS ROCK

Oh dear, there are so many arrows going in different directions! Where do we start? Eenie, meenie, miney, moe. . . . Let's begin with igneous rocks.

IGNEOUS ROCKS

The word "igneous" literally means "from fire." And that is exactly how igneous rocks form. Igneous rocks form when liquid magma cools. How quickly the magma cools, and what other minerals and bits of stuff are around, determine what type of igneous rock will be formed. Let's take a closer look.

Sometimes when magma cools and solidifies into igneous rock, a process called crystallization takes place. This means that the magma forms into rock crystals as it cools and solidifies. But magma doesn't always need to be above ground to cool into igneous rock. In fact, magma can also cool underground! Away from the original magma chamber of course!

Igneous rocks that are formed underground are called intrusive. Intrusive rocks cool slowly, giving crystals a long time to grow. These igneous rocks are called coarse-grained, because you can see large bits of different types of crystals that have formed inside them.

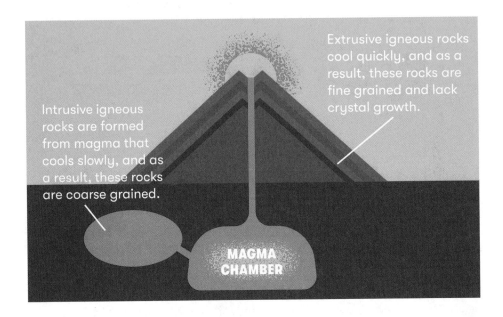

Intrusive igneous rocks are formed from magma that cools slowly, and as a result, these rocks are coarse grained.

Extrusive igneous rocks cool quickly, and as a result, these rocks are fine grained and lack crystal growth.

MAGMA CHAMBER

Igneous rocks that formed above ground are called extrusive. Extrusive rocks cool very quickly, giving crystals little to no time to grow. These igneous rocks are called fine-grained because the crystals are so tiny, if they are even there at all.

WEATHERING, EROSION, AND DEPOSITION

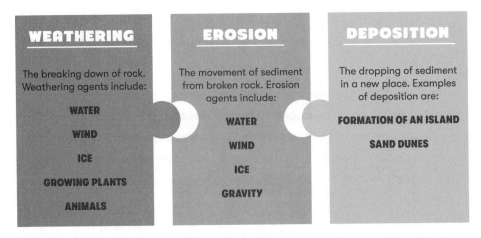

WEATHERING

The breaking down of rock. Weathering agents include:

WATER

WIND

ICE

GROWING PLANTS

ANIMALS

EROSION

The movement of sediment from broken rock. Erosion agents include:

WATER

WIND

ICE

GRAVITY

DEPOSITION

The dropping of sediment in a new place. Examples of deposition are:

FORMATION OF AN ISLAND

SAND DUNES

When rocks are exposed, like in those mountain and canyon examples you saw earlier, they are also exposed to processes like wind and rain. Wind and rain break off tiny little pieces of the igneous rocks. This is called weathering. Weathering can also occur from plants that are growing out of the rocks, the grinding of two rocks together, or water cooling and expanding into ice within the cracks of the rocks.

So what happens to these teeny bits of rock (which are called sediment)? They get swept away in a process called erosion. Wind, water, gravity, and even ice can carry the rock particles from one place to another. For example, wind can carry bits of sediment from a mountain into a river.

That river can then carry the sediment downstream. But then what happens to it? The sediment at some point reaches the end of its journey and settles down in a process called deposition. Deposition can happen either on land or underneath the water. Over long periods of time, sometimes thousands or maybe millions of years, more and more layers of deposited sediments get built up and push down more on the layers on the bottom. Have you ever swum down to the bottom of the pool and felt the change of the water pressure in your ears? This is the same idea. More stuff on top = more pressure = more compaction of the sediments. At some point, the sediments become cemented together to form an actual solid piece of rock instead of lots of bits of sediment.

Before we move on to study this type of rock, let's summarize the process of the breaking down of igneous rocks:

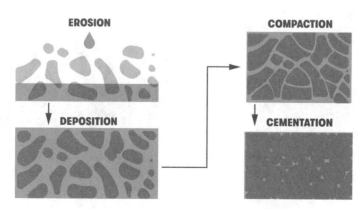

EROSION

COMPACTION

DEPOSITION

CEMENTATION

So what type of rock is made after sediment has been compacted and cemented together? If you take a look at the rock cycle diagram, can you figure it out based on the word "sediment"?

SEDIMENTARY ROCKS

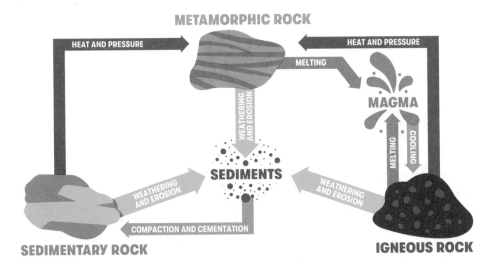

The name sedimentary rock comes from the word "sediment," which means "stuff that settles to the bottom of a liquid," such as a lake, sea, or ocean. It can even happen on land! Over thousands or millions of years, these bits of sediment slowly become compressed and cemented together.

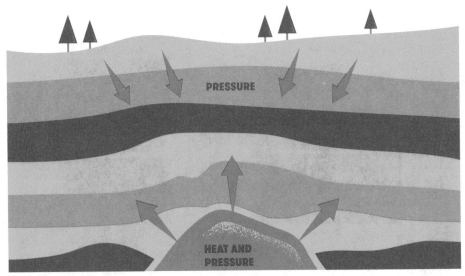

This means that if you look closely at a sedimentary rock, you are likely to notice spots of different colors or textures or possibly whole different layers within the rock.

Now let's say that sedimentary rock kept getting buried under more and more stuff. Eventually, it may even get pushed really deep underground, more than 12 kilometers (7.5 miles) where it can be exposed to high temperatures and pressures.

Predict what you think might happen to that sedimentary rock.

_____

_____

_____

_____

_____

_____

_____

_____

METAMORPHIC ROCKS

When sedimentary rocks are exposed to high heat and pressure, they turn into metamorphic rock. In fact, the word "metamorphic" means "transformed." Some metamorphic rocks make their way back up to the surface when mountains or canyons are formed. But more often, these rocks, like marble, are specifically dug up and mined.

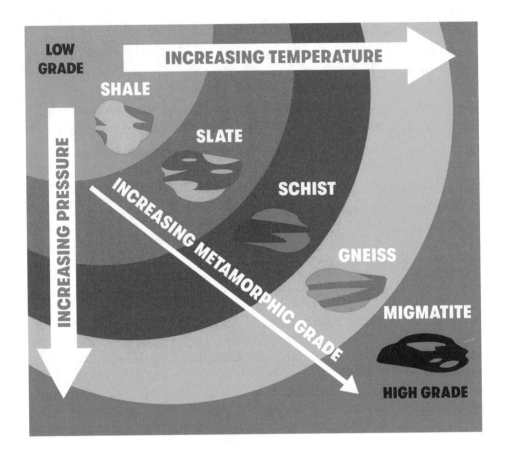

The temperature and amount of pressure the rock experiences determines what type of metamorphic rock it will become. The higher the temperature and pressure, the more the rock can be changed (also known as the metamorphic grade).

Now let's say the heat was actually hot enough to melt the rocks. Now, this heat has to be *super hot*. Like about 1,300 degrees Celsius or 2,400 degrees Fahrenheit. This is about 4 times hotter than the hottest part of a campfire. These hot temperatures melt metamorphic rocks and turn them into magma.

So what happens when the magma cools? Have you ever tried to refreeze a melted ice cream cake?

Don't try this at home unless you want to waste a perfectly good cake.

A ONE-WAY STREET

Once the cake has melted, there is no going back to the nice shape and orderly layers it had before. Instead, it's going to refreeze as a murky-colored lump, taking the shape of whatever container it's in at the time. That's kind of how it is with magma. Once it cools, it doesn't go back to being metamorphic rock. Instead, it solidifies into igneous rock.

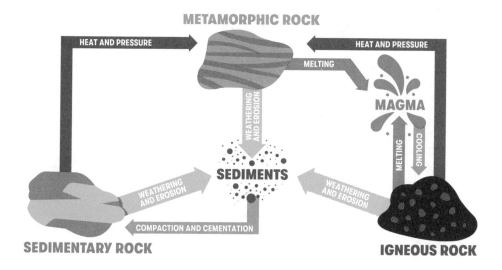

But there is a reason this whole thing is called the rock *cycle*: rocks keep cycling around and around and around! And not necessarily in any particular order.

Remember that rock you found earlier in this section? Go back to your description and see if you can determine what type of rock it is by examining it further. Based on what you know about the rock cycle, circle the type of rock you think it is.

Igneous   **Sedimentary**   **Metamorphic**

For example, let's say that the rock you found was an igneous piece of granite. Use the rock cycle to describe a path that rock could take as it turns into other types of rocks and eventually back into igneous rock. We discussed one path already here, so see if you can find a different one!

_____

_____

_____

_____

Now let's think back to the question from the beginning of the chapter. How can you incorporate your knowledge of the rock cycle into understanding the geologic time scale?

How do humans know when the events on the geologic time scale occurred?

_____

_____

_____

_____

CHAPTER 2 VOCABULARY

absolute dating: finding the absolute or exact age of a fossil or other object.

cemented: the process of sediments becoming stuck together to form a solid piece of rock.

compaction: the process of becoming more tightly packed together.

crystallization: the formation of magma into rock crystals as the magma cools and solidifies.

deposition: the process of sediment settling in a new location. Deposition is the opposite of erosion.

eons: the largest spans of categorized time. See also eras and epochs.

epoch: the smallest spans of categorized time. Eons are broken down into eras, which are broken down into periods, which are broken down into epochs.

eras: long spans of time, shorter than eons and longer than periods. Eons are broken down into eras, which are broken down into periods, which are broken down into epochs.

erosion: the process of transporting sediment from one place to another by wind, water, or gravity.

extrusive igneous rocks: igneous rocks that formed above ground that typically have very small to no grains and crystals.

fossil: the remains of animal and plant life that lived millions to billions of years ago.

geologic time scale: the dating and chronological organization of geological events.

geology: the branch of science that studies Earth: what it's made up of, how it works, and its history.

igneous rock: form when liquid magma cools. They can either be extrusive or intrusive. Granite, obsidian, and pumice are examples of igneous rocks.

intrusive igneous rocks: igneous rocks that formed underground that typically contain large grains and crystals.

law of superposition: the understanding that rock layers at the top of a rock formation are youngest and the rock layers at the bottom of a rock formation are the oldest.

magma: a very hot liquid made from melted rock below Earth's surface.

melt: the phase change when a solid object becomes a liquid.

metamorphic rock: a rock that has undergone significant heat and pressure. Marble, quartzite, and slate are examples of metamorphic rock.

periods: spans of time that are shorter than eras and longer than epochs. See also eons, eras, and epochs.

radioactive: material that emits radiation or particles due to unstable atomic nuclei.

relative dating: the ages of objects in relation to other objects. For example, you are younger than your parents.

sediment: teeny, tiny pieces of rock.

sedimentary rock: rock made from sediment that slowly become compressed and cemented together. Limestone, shale, and sandstone are examples of sedimentary rocks.

stratum: a layer of rock in a formation. The plural of stratum is strata.

weathering: rock that is broken into smaller and smaller pieces due to other rocks, water, wind, plants, or animals.

uranium: a chemical element that undergoes radioactive decay by slowly breaking down on its own and releasing energy and particles.

CHAPTER 2 ANSWER KEY

PAGES 55–56

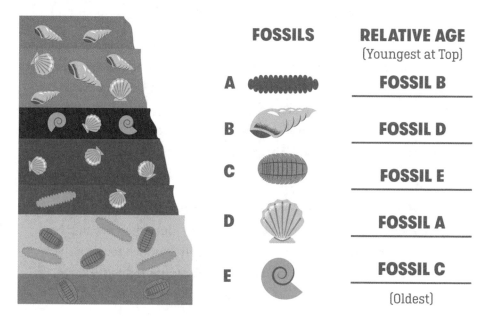

	FOSSILS	RELATIVE AGE (Youngest at Top)
A		FOSSIL B
B		FOSSIL D
C		FOSSIL E
D		FOSSIL A
E		FOSSIL C (Oldest)

Relative dating gives the ages of objects in terms of older than or younger than. Absolute dating determines the exact ages for things like fossils and rocks.

PAGE 62

Humans have been able to determine where objects and events are on the geologic time scale by looking at the layers of rock and fossils and by using different techniques to relatively and absolutely date them. This has allowed scientists to make a timeline of events in Earth's history.

PAGE 63

Any description of your rock will do.

PAGE 69

The sedimentary rock is going to get further compressed and squished together.

PAGE 72

(Top) Any answer is acceptable based on your description of your rock.

(Middle) Try this one out: The igneous rock is subjected to intense heat and pressure and becomes a metamorphic rock. The metamorphic rock rounds its way to the surface and becomes weathered. The eroded particles are deposited, compressed, and cemented together to form sedimentary rock. The sedimentary rock then makes its way back underground where it is turned into metamorphic rock. The metamorphic rock melts into magma and is cooled back into igneous rock.

(Bottom) Humans can study the types of rocks that were found in different rock layers to determine what types of rocks they are and how they formed. The age of rocks could then give indications to what the landscape and climate were like when that rock layer formed. These clues could then provide more information for the events on the geologic time scale.

NOTES

3 THE FORCES THAT SHAPE THE EARTH

No humans were involved in the making of the beautiful arch at the beginning of Chapter 2 or this colorful cliff in the Zhangye Danxia Landform Geological Park in China that almost looks like it's broken. But did you know that the arch on the Jurassic Coast was formed over millions of years, while this cliff's broken appearance occurred over just a few seconds? Really? How did that happen? Read on to find out more.

CHAPTER CONTENTS

Why do some landscapes form very quickly, while others form very slowly?

THE SLOW AND STEADY EARTH

FORMATION OF THE GRAND CANYON

1.7 BILLION YEARS AGO

1.25 BILLION YEARS AGO

500 MILLION YEARS AGO

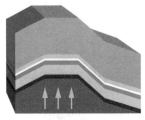

60 MILLION YEARS AGO

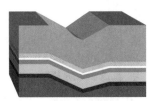

1.25 MILLION YEARS AGO

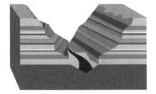

TODAY

Some processes on Earth take their sweet time, much like you dragging your feet when your parents are trying to take you somewhere you don't want to go.

Geologic wonders such as the Grand Canyon actually took almost *60 million* years to form! And that's after almost *2 billion* years of building up the rock layers that you can see today. A combination of weathering and erosion slowly created the canyon after periods of plate tectonics moved the landscape. Wait, what are plate tectonics? Don't worry, we will get to that shortly! Let's review weathering and erosion first, which you began to learn about in the previous chapter.

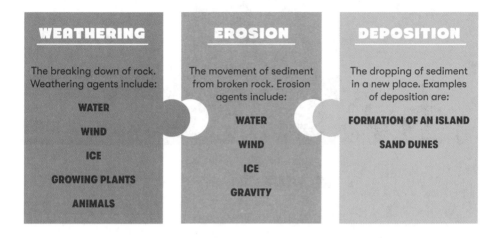

WEATHERING

The breaking down of rock. Weathering agents include:

WATER

WIND

ICE

GROWING PLANTS

ANIMALS

EROSION

The movement of sediment from broken rock. Erosion agents include:

WATER

WIND

ICE

GRAVITY

DEPOSITION

The dropping of sediment in a new place. Examples of deposition are:

FORMATION OF AN ISLAND

SAND DUNES

WEATHERING: A DEEPER DIVE

 In the last chapter, you learned that weathering was the breaking down of rock. There are actually three different kinds of weathering: mechanical, chemical, and organic.

MECHANICAL WEATHERING

Mechanical weathering is the physical breaking up of a rock. Let's say you took a hammer and started carefully pounding on a rock with it. That is an example of mechanical weathering. In nature, it is often wind and water-carrying particles that scrape against rocks and slowly wear them down. Another example of mechanical weathering happens through the freezing and melting of water. When water gets into the little cracks and crevices of a rock and freezes, that water expands and pushes the rock apart. This process repeats over and over again, breaking the rock into smaller and smaller pieces.

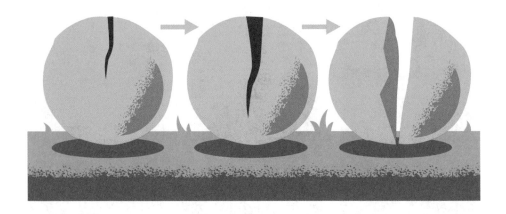

WATER SEEPS INTO CRACKS IN THE ROCK

WHEN WATER FREEZES, IT EXPANDS IN VOLUME, ENLARGING CRACKS

THIS PROCESS REPEATS: WATER FREEZES AND THAWS AGAIN AND AGAIN, EVENTUALLY ROCK BREAKS

CHEMICAL WEATHERING

Chemical weathering is the chemical breakdown of rock. For example, the carbon dioxide in acid rain reacts with the minerals that are found in some rocks. That reaction causes those minerals to break down and then wash away, leaving the non-reacting rock behind. This is a common way that caves are dug out, especially those made out of limestone, which is a sedimentary rock that reacts with the carbon dioxide in acid rain.

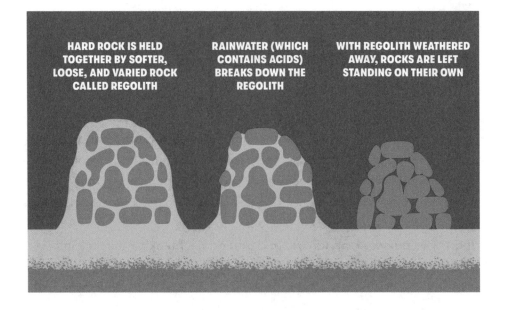

HARD ROCK IS HELD TOGETHER BY SOFTER, LOOSE, AND VARIED ROCK CALLED REGOLITH

RAINWATER (WHICH CONTAINS ACIDS) BREAKS DOWN THE REGOLITH

WITH REGOLITH WEATHERED AWAY, ROCKS ARE LEFT STANDING ON THEIR OWN

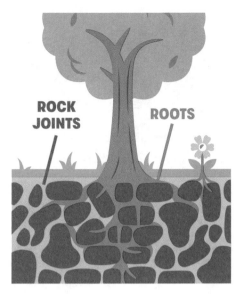

ROCK JOINTS

ROOTS

ORGANIC WEATHERING

Organic weathering is the breaking down of rocks by things that are alive, like trees and animals. Tree roots grow deep into rocks, breaking the rocks up and moving them out of the way. Some plants actually contain acid that helps weaken and break down rocks even further. So, organic weathering is kind of like both mechanical and chemical weathering combined, just with living things.

After the rock and other stuff have been weathered, the little pieces (also called sediment) are swept away through the process of erosion. Erosion can move the bits of rock with the help of water, wind, or even gravity! The process of actually moving the sediment is called transportation. The rock bits travel away and eventually are deposited somewhere else. The process of deposition (recall from Chapter 2) can build up new geologic structures, such as dunes or even islands!

The processes of weathering and erosion often take thousands or millions of years. These processes are usually so slow that you won't see any changes day to day. But if you hop into your time machine and either go forward or backward in time thousands of years, chances are you won't recognize the landscape! But sometimes, some geological processes are sudden and dramatic.

EARTH'S DRAMATIC SIDE

While some processes on Earth take hundreds of thousands of years to shape the landscape, other events can change the landscape in mere seconds.

VOLCANOES, HURRICANES, AND EARTHQUAKES

VOLCANOES

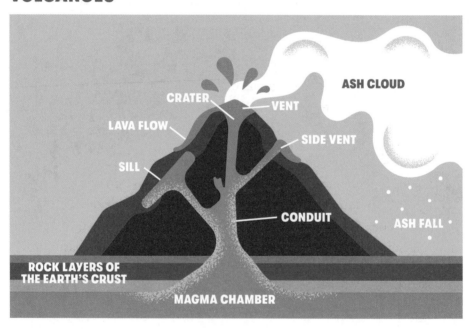

Volcanic eruptions are actually a combination of fast and slow processes. Before a volcano erupts, magma brews for hundreds or thousands of years in an underground "pocket" inside the volcano called a magma chamber. Eventually, the pressure from the hot magma builds up, travels upward, and bursts through the vent either at the top (the crater) or the side of the volcano.

For example, in 1980, in just mere *seconds*, Mount Saint Helens in Washington blew off the top one-third of itself and destroyed *everything else* within an 8-mile (13-kilometer) radius. Boom! Then gone. Volcanoes are just one example of how the landscape can be changed in a matter of moments. What are some other examples of processes that can quickly shape Earth's landscape? Other than volcanic eruptions, the major players are hurricanes and earthquakes.

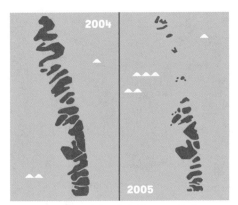

The Chandeleur Islands before and after Hurricane Katrina

HURRICANES

Hurricanes, with their incredibly high winds and heavy precipitation, can completely alter landscapes. For example, Hurricane Katrina greatly reduced the amount of land in the Chandeleur Islands off the coast of Louisiana over the course of a week. The hurricane dropped a lot of water, picked up excess sediment, and transported it.

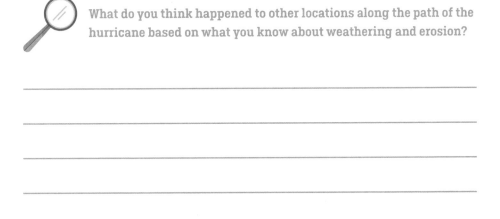

What do you think happened to other locations along the path of the hurricane based on what you know about weathering and erosion?

_____

_____

_____

_____

_____

The sediment that was picked up had to go somewhere! Just as places like the Chandeleur Islands lost land, other locations gained more land where the sediment was deposited.

EARTHQUAKES

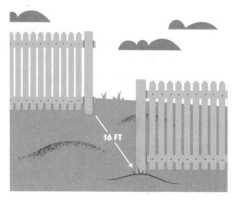

Earthquakes can also change the landscape in mere moments. See that fence in the image? That fence has an opening about 16 feet (5 meters) wide. But the fence was not built that way. In fact, both of those fences were once a single fence. A massive earthquake struck San Francisco in 1906. During the 42-second span of the earthquake, the ground underneath the fence broke apart and moved one side of fence 16 feet away from the other.

Earthquakes, like volcanic eruptions, are the result of hundreds, thousands, and even millions of years of slow processes.

So now you have figured out some of the ways that Earth's landscape can change.

How does the knowledge you have collected so far help you answer the question from the beginning of the chapter?

 Why do some landscapes form very quickly, while others form very slowly?

_____

_____

_____

_____

_____

ONCE UPON A TIME ON OUR PLANET: PANGAEA

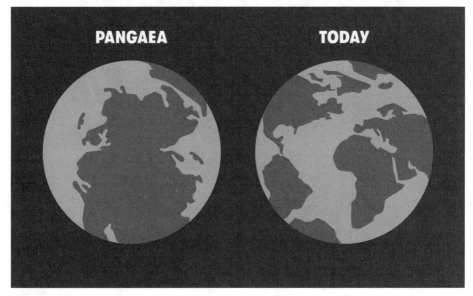

That image on the left doesn't look like the Earth we know. Did we travel to a different planet in a spaceship? Nope! That is Earth! Instead of a spaceship, we used our time machine to travel backward in time about 300 million years. But where are North and South America? Antarctica? Africa? Asia, Australia, and Europe? They are all there, as you will see soon. Instead of the seven continents we have today, 300 million years ago, Earth had one supercontinent named Pangaea.

Pangaea was a huge landmass with all the continents as you know them today clumped together. In fact, the word "Pangaea" means "all-Earth" in Greek. Pangaea was known as a supercontinent. The ~29% of Earth's surface that is land was pretty much all in one place, like a ginormous island.

That's right, continents can move! The continents are moving even now, taking us along for a very slow ride. Let's take a closer look at how Pangaea transformed into the continents you know today.

Can you put the movement of the following continents in order from oldest to youngest? Try to use the labels underneath each map to put them in order. Using the blank boxes next to each image, assign each map a number between 1 and 5, using "1" for the oldest and "5" for the most recent. Use the image on the previous page to help guide you.

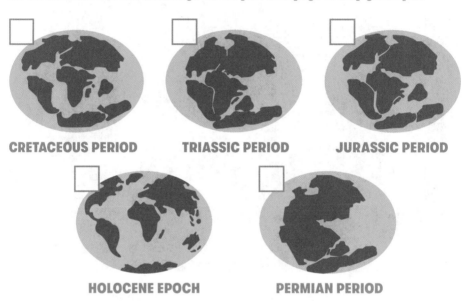

CRETACEOUS PERIOD   **TRIASSIC PERIOD**   **JURASSIC PERIOD**

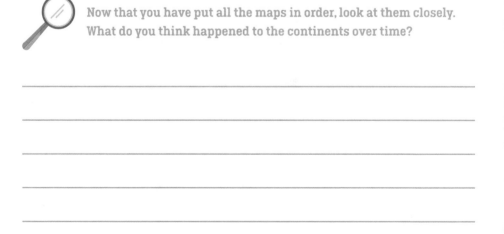

HOLOCENE EPOCH   **PERMIAN PERIOD**

Now that you have put all the maps in order, look at them closely. What do you think happened to the continents over time?

_____

_____

_____

_____

_____

ALFRED WEGENER AND THE THEORY OF CONTINENTAL DRIFT

Of course, no humans were around to draw the map of the world in those days. The first person to propose that the Earth once contained one huge supercontinent was German scientist Alfred Wegener (1880–1930). And most people thought he was crazy.

Wegener got his idea by looking at a map of the world. He noticed that the continents seemed to fit together like the pieces of a jigsaw puzzle.

Let's test out Wegener's idea. Print out a world map showing the continents, or feel free to trace the map from this page onto a blank sheet of paper. Then cut out just the continents and play around with them. Can you get them to fit together like a puzzle?

Wegener proposed the name continental drift to explain the movement of the continents. But he didn't leave his theory with only a name. He found evidence to back up his claims. Let's take a closer look at what he found.

CLUE #1: FOSSILS

Fossils provided major clues to Wegener's theory of continental drift. Take a look at these plant fossils found on three different continents. The plant fossils are believed to show leaves from the same type of ancient tree, *Glossopteris*. This type of tree was very common during the Permian period (299–252 million years ago).

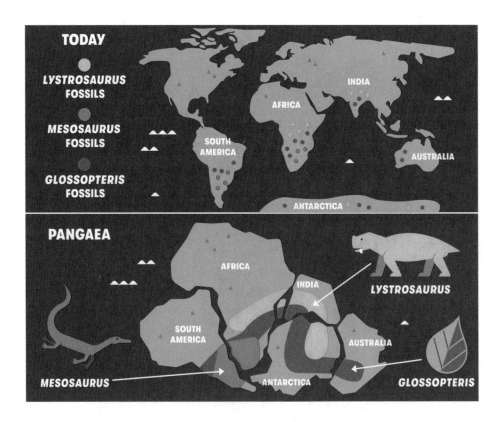

Why is this so important? Well, Wegener reasoned that finding fossils of this tree in such different parts of the world suggested that this tree was once common all over the world. Not only that, but that the tree was common when the continents were still connected. Let's check out another example of fossil evidence that Wegener used to state his claims.

Wegener studied the fossils of two prehistoric animals, the *Mesosaurus* (which looked like a cross between a fish and a crocodile) and the *Lystrosaurus* (a small plant-eating dinosaur) and where they have been found.

On which continents have these three fossils been found?

Mesosaurus: _____

Lystrosaurus: _____

Glossopteris: _____

The plant and animal fossils seemed spread out with no rhyme or reason, but drawing the continents pushed together revealed a pattern. However, Wegener had many critics. Geologists around the world argued that there could be other explanations for Wegener's evidence.

Can you think of another explanation for Wegener's fossil evidence?

_____

_____

_____

_____

_____

_____

_____

_____

_____

OTHER POSSIBLE EXPLANATIONS

FOSSIL	ALTERNATIVE EXPLANATION	LIKELINESS?
 **GLOSSOPTERIS TREE**	Wind carried the seed of the *Glossopteris* tree from Australia to Antarctica.	Unlikely. The seed is large, and the wind wouldn't have been able to carry it very far.
LYSTROSAURUS **MESOSAURUS**	The animals swam or crossed land bridges to get from one continent to another.	While the *Mesosaurus* was an aquatic animal, its body wasn't built for long distance swims, and it definitely couldn't swim between continents. *Lystrosaurus* was a land animal that couldn't swim, and there were no land bridges that connected Antarctica, India, and South Africa. And no fossils were found in between those continents.

Wegener firmly believed in his evidence and chose not to let the other scientists talk him out of his theory. He continued publishing more evidence to support continental drift. Let's look at some more evidence.

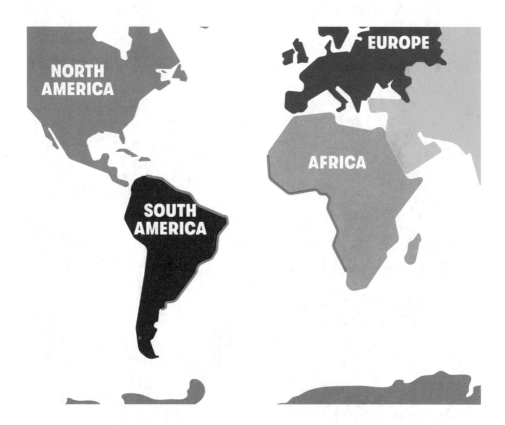

CLUE #2: ROCKS (AGAIN!)

Let's go back to these coastlines and take a deeper look. Wegener noticed that rocks along the east coast of South America matched the rocks along the west coast of Africa. Not only that, but mountain ranges on different continents looked like they were once connected!

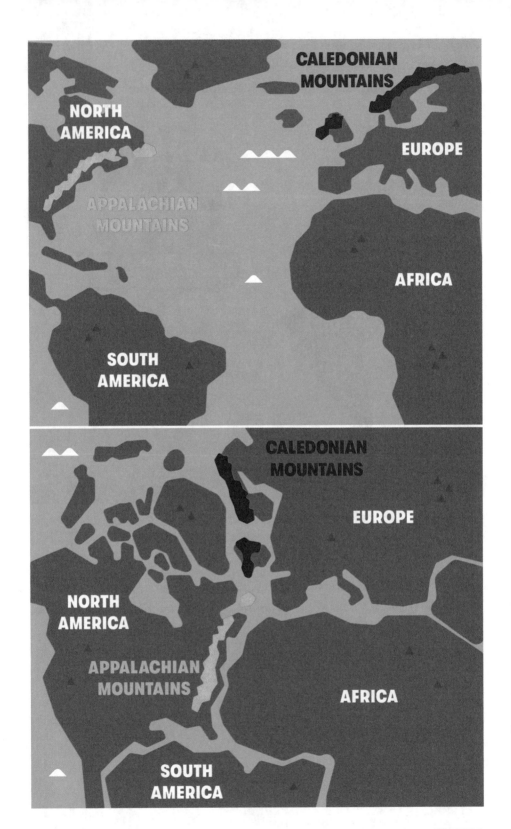

_____

_____

_____

_____

_____

Were these massive mountains once connected? If so, what geological events could rip enormous mountains apart like that? Because Wegener could not explain what caused the mountains to move, again, no one believed him. Unfortunately, Wegener died on a scientific expedition to Greenland before his theory became widely accepted. But after his death, scientists found more and more evidence to support continental drift, including why continental drift happens. In fact, researchers later discovered that Pangaea was only one of several supercontinents that have existed since Earth formed.

CONTINENTS ON THE MOVE

Actually, the next piece of evidence that you are going to look at was discovered accidentally. An American scientist Harry Hess (1906–1969) was a navy captain who commanded a ship that transported soldiers during World War II. He also just happened to have been a geology professor before the war began. So how did he accidentally discover a key piece of continental drift? He was testing out some awesome new technology.

SHEDDING LIGHT ON THE MYSTERIOUS DEEP DARK SEA

Hess's ship was equipped with new sonar technology to help detect danger underwater, such as hidden rocks or enemy submarines. Being a curious scientist, Hess also used this technology to create a map of the ocean floor as the ship glided above it.

SONAR TECHNOLOGY

Sonar stands for **so**und **na**vigation **r**anging. Sonar technology helps ships and submarines navigate through water in a similar way to how bats navigate in the dark. Bats are mostly active at night, when there isn't enough light for them to get around safely just using their eyes. That's why bats produce high-pitched squeals as they fly. When the sounds hit something, like the wall of a cave, they bounce back as an echo that the bat's ears can catch. The bat's brain uses the echoes to figure out where objects are located in the dark so it doesn't accidentally collide with a wall.

Similarly, not much sunlight reaches deep into the ocean, so a submarine captain can't rely on vision to guide her vessel. Instead, a sonar device sends sounds out into the water and then waits for the sounds to hit something and for the echoes to bounce back. The sonar device then uses the time it took for the echo to return to calculate how far away objects must be in the water. In this way, a submarine or a ship can map out the locations of underwater obstacles or detect an enemy submarine.

Have you ever seen pictures or videos of what the bottom of the ocean looks like? At the time, most people thought it looked like the desert: smooth and flat for miles on end. To everyone's surprise, Hess discovered that instead, some parts of the ocean floor looked to have mountains and canyons, similar to what you may see on land. Let's take a look at a very important underwater mountain range that Hess found as he was mapping the ocean floor.

AN UNDERWATER MOUNTAIN RANGE

This range is now called the Mid-Atlantic Ridge. As more of the ocean floor was mapped with sonar technology, the Mid-Atlantic Ridge was found to stretch almost all the way from one end of the globe to the other. So what is a ridge anyway? A ridge is essentially a chain of mountains that are similar in height. Hess's discovery of an underwater ridge proved to be an important key to Wegener's theory.

SEAFLOOR SPREADING

A rift, or a break, runs along the entire underwater ridge. Hess speculated that the ocean floor is actually spreading apart. You read that correctly— the western side of the Mid-Atlantic Ridge gradually moves away from the eastern side, causing the rift along the middle to widen.

MID-ATLANTIC RIDGE

This idea became known as seafloor spreading. Yes, the floor at the bottom of the Atlantic Ocean is actually getting bigger.

SEA FLOOR SPREADING

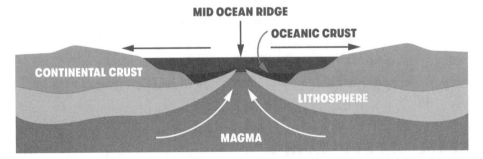

Magma underneath the ocean floor pushes up through the rift in the Mid-Atlantic Ridge. As the magma comes up, it pushes the ocean floor to the side. The magma cools and forms new ocean floor. In turn, that pushes the continents on both sides of the Atlantic Ocean apart.

Rock samples have been taken from several locations across the floor of the Atlantic Ocean.

VIEWING THE MID-ATLANTIC RIDGE

It's pretty difficult to see the rift in the Mid-Atlantic Ridge unless you happen to have a submarine handy—that is, except in one place on Earth. If you ever go to Iceland, you can see the part of the Mid-Atlantic Ridge that crosses dry land. There, you can clearly observe the gap between the western and eastern sides of the ridge. Scientists estimate that this gap is widening at a rate of about one inch, or 2.5 cm, per year. Have you ever tried to watch your fingernails grow? Let's put it this way: it's not very exciting. But if you didn't cut your nails for a year, the result would be pretty dramatic. It's like that with the seafloor. Even if you go to Iceland, you won't be able to see the rift widening before your eyes. It's spreading just a little slower than the speed your fingernails grow, but by the end of a year, the continents will be about an inch farther apart!

A diver explores the Mid-Atlantic Ridge off Iceland, near where the ridge extends to dry land.

SUBDUCTION ZONES

If **mid-ocean ridges** are places where rock is coming up from the Earth's interior, will Earth keep getting bigger and bigger? Nope. Because what comes up also goes down. As new magma is coming up to form new ocean floor, old ocean floor goes back down deep into Earth.

These areas are called **subduction zones**. This is where the old ocean floor goes back down into the Earth, where it is recycled. Let's look at the parts of a subduction zone:

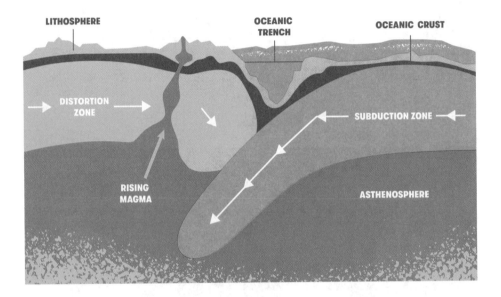

Remember, Earth is constantly recycling all its materials—rocks, water, carbon, and now ocean floors. Ocean trenches are the deepest places found on the ocean floor. They are formed over these subduction zones where one piece of ocean floor goes underneath another.

PLATE TECTONICS

Building on the work of Wegener and Hess, scientists have uncovered a lot of evidence that helps explain Wegener's continental drift theory. Today we know that the Earth's crust is composed of a bunch of tectonic plates, which are solid sections that move as one piece. Tectonic plates are made up of lighter rock that floats on top of the heavier rock like paper floats on top of water. There are seven large tectonic plates as well as many smaller plates.

Just as Wegener predicted, the tectonic plates are always moving, just veeeery sloooowly.

You can see that some of the plates are moving apart, while others are moving closer together. So far you've seen how tectonic plates can move apart and one example of where tectonic plates can move together. But there are other ways that tectonic plates can interact. Let's check them out.

THE FORMATION OF MOUNTAINS

When two tectonic plates move toward each other, one does not always go down and underneath another one. Sometimes, two plates crash head on—in very slow motion. These collisions are the interactions that build mountain ranges, like the Himalayas. In fact, the Himalayas are still growing today!

SLIP FAULTS

There are also places where two tectonic plates slide sideways past each other. These are called slip faults.

Remember this fence from earlier in the chapter? That fence was built across the San Andreas Fault in California. The San Andreas Fault is an example of a slip fault. Slip faults are

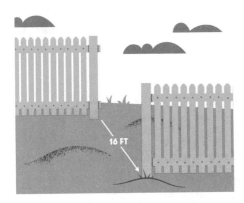

prime locations for earthquakes, like the 1906 one that split this fence apart.

Wow, our planet is amazing! It can take its time changing slowly over millions of years, and yet it can change in an instant. How can you incorporate all the knowledge you have gained to help answer the question from the beginning of the chapter?

Why do some landscapes form very quickly, while others form very slowly?

_____

_____

_____

_____

_____

_____

_____

CHAPTER 3 VOCABULARY

chemical weathering: the breakdown of rock due to the reaction of the rock with substances in water or air. For example, limestone reacts with carbon dioxide in acid rain and breaks down.

collisions: the process of two tectonic plates slowly moving toward each other where one does not subduct under the other. Collisions of this type form mountain ranges.

continental drift: the theory that continents gradually move across Earth's surface.

magma chamber: an underground "pocket" inside a volcano that is filled with magma.

mechanical weathering: the breakdown of rock due to processes such as pounding, grinding, and the expansion of ice.

mid-ocean ridge: locations in the oceans where rock is coming up from Earth's interior and causing the ocean floor to spread.

organic weathering: the breakdown of rock due to things that are alive such as tree roots and animals.

Pangaea: a supercontinent that existed 300 million years ago.

seafloor spreading: the process of the bottom of the ocean spreading due to new rock coming up from underneath Earth's surface and pushing either side of the ocean floor away from the other.

slip fault: locations where two tectonic plates slide past each other in opposite directions.

sonar: technology that utilizes sound waves to map the ocean floor and other obstacles to allow ships and submarines to navigate safely through the water.

subduction zones: locations where old, dense ocean crust moves underneath less dense continental crust and back down inside Earth.

supercontinent: a single, large continent that is made up of most or all of Earth's land.

tectonic plates: solid sections of Earth's crust that move as one piece.

transportation: the process of moving sediment from one place to another.

CHAPTER 3 ANSWER KEY

PAGE 85

After the hurricane picked up sediment from those islands, it was transported and deposited in other locations, building up new land.

PAGE 86

Some landscapes, like the arch on the Dinosaur Coast and the Grand Canyon, were formed over millions of years due to processes like weathering and erosion. Other landscapes, like the broken cliff in China at the beginning of this chapter and Mount Saint Helens, were formed over seconds or minutes due to processes like earthquakes and volcanic eruptions.

PAGE 88

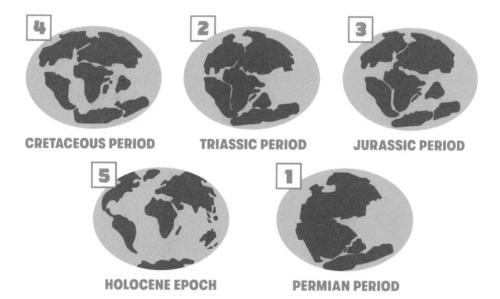

CRETACEOUS PERIOD   **TRIASSIC PERIOD**   **JURASSIC PERIOD**

HOLOCENE EPOCH   **PERMIAN PERIOD**

The large continent on map #1 broke apart, with the pieces gradually moving farther apart. They separate more and more on each map. Eventually, these pieces became the continents you know today.

PAGE 91

Mesosaurus: South America and Africa

Lystrosaurus: Antarctica, India, and Africa

Glossopteris: South America, Africa, India, Antarctica, and Australia

One alternative explanation is that the seeds of the tree were transported from one continent to another by wind or by the ocean and then began growing in the new location. The animals could have swum between the continents or crossed land bridges.

PAGE 95

If the mountains were similar heights and formed out of the same type of rock, like the rock found on the coasts of South America and Africa, then it would be pretty good evidence that the mountain ranges formed when the continents were all squished together.

PAGE 102

There is no one correct answer here! Scientists have many different models based on the current movement of the tectonic plates for both gradual changes on a grand scale (like perhaps the formation of a new supercontinent) and for sudden changes on a smaller scale. Here is one such example:

There are also many different models of what the next supercontinent may look like. Here is one such example:

The Earth is constantly changing very slowly over millions and billions of years through processes like plate tectonics, continental drift, weathering, and erosion. These processes can move continents, build up mountains, and carve out canyons and rock arches. Sometimes, these same processes that are millions of years in the making cause a sudden and dramatic change that can alter the landscape in just seconds, like an earthquake or volcanic eruption.

WATER, WEATHER, AND CLIMATE

Tomorrow, you'll be heading out on a long hike up a mountain to take in the view, and then back down to set up your tent in the river valley before sunset. You need to pack food, water, and the right gear for whatever adventures—and weather—may come. How do you determine what gear to bring? Read on to find out.

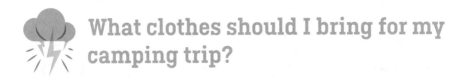

What clothes should I bring for my camping trip?

THE WATER CYCLE

Peeking outside might give you some clues for how to dress for tomorrow. There are still a few puddles on the ground from yesterday's rain. The Sun has started to break through the clouds. The air is humid, like a bathroom after someone took a long shower. Why is that?

Let's start with the rain that fell yesterday. Rain is a type of **precipitation**, which simply means some form of water that falls to the ground from the sky.

Go ahead and list any other types of precipitation you can think of.

_____

_____

_____

PRECIPITATION

You already know that rain falls down from the clouds in the sky. Find the large cloud over the ocean. That looks like a perfect rain cloud. Let's draw some rain coming down from that cloud.

RAIN
PRECIPITATION

Did you list snow as another type of precipitation? Don't worry, it won't be cold enough to snow where you are headed to camp.

While we're at it, let's draw some snow coming down from the large cloud over the mountain, and label that too.

Why is the air so humid? You also notice that the Sun is starting to break through the clouds and that the temperature is rising.

EVAPORATION

As the Sun warms the Earth, some water turns into vapor. Vapor is the gaseous form of water. The process of water turning into vapor is called evaporation. Evaporation is what will eventually dry out all the puddles after a heavy rain.

Let's go ahead and add evaporation to our diagram. Evaporation occurs over every body of water, from huge oceans to tiny puddles.

MEASURING EVAPORATION

Let's do a little experiment to see how evaporation works.

Find a shallow bowl, plastic container, or pot that no one is going to need for a few days. Fill it with water from the tap, and leave some room at the top so that you don't have to worry about spills.

Place the water-filled container in a safe spot where it won't be in anybody's way or get bumped accidentally. Take a ruler and place one end in the deepest or flattest part of the bowl or container, holding it as straight as you can. If you can, use a metric ruler, which is in centimeters. This is what scientists use.

Record how high the water level is on the table below, next to Day 1. Check back around the same time every day and measure the height of the water. Be sure to put the ruler in exactly the same spot and hold it as straight as you can. Keep a record of your observations over the next week.

DAY	WATER LEVEL (CM)
1 (Start)	
2	
3	
4	
5	
6	
7	

What were your observations over the course of the week?

_____

_____

_____

_____

Evaporation is just one of the ways that water can get back into the sky. Let's do one more little experiment to learn about a different way water gets back into the sky. Don't worry, this experiment will only take an hour or so!

TRANSPIRATION

Any potted plant you might have at home will be perfect for this experiment. If you don't have any, a flowering plant or bush outside will do the trick. Just make sure that it has leaves. Find a clear plastic bag and hold it upside down so that the opening is facing the ground. Then pull the bag over a large branch or section of the plant that contains leaves.

Tie the opening of the bag with a string or tape it shut. Make sure the opening of the bag is closed off as much as possible without injuring the plant. Check back on your plant after an hour.

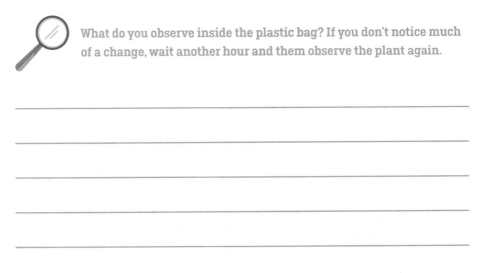

What do you observe inside the plastic bag? If you don't notice much of a change, wait another hour and them observe the plant again.

_____

_____

_____

_____

_____

_____

Don't forget to remove the plastic bag after you have recorded your observations!

This experiment showed how water can get back into the sky through transpiration. Plants need water, just like humans do, and they drink it up from the soil. However, when plants "breathe," or transpire, they release small amounts of water vapor and oxygen. That explains the water droplets that you saw inside that plastic bag!

Actually, humans do the same thing—that's why on a cold day, you can see your breath.

Let's go ahead and add transpiration to that large tree next to the lake seems like a logical place to put it, and no need to add the plastic bag.

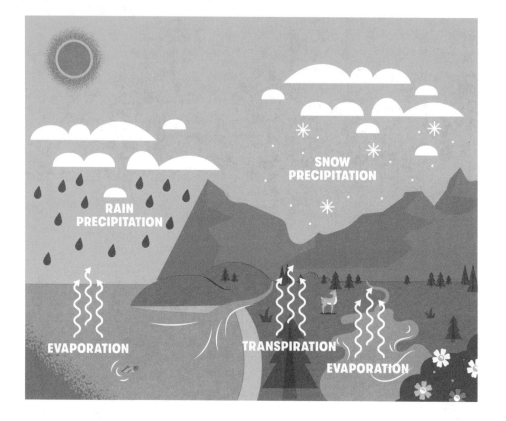

Let's see. . . you know that rain falls from the sky and that water can make its way back into the sky as vapor. But what happens to it next?

CONDENSATION

Think back to the plastic bag over the plant. You probably saw some water droplets on the inside of the bag. The water droplets are formed through a process called condensation. Condensation occurs when water vapor cools and transforms back into liquid water. You can often see condensation on the bathroom mirror after a shower, as the steamy bathroom starts to cool down. Condensation also explains how rain comes from clouds.

Notice that the condensation you see usually occurs on a surface: the plastic bag and the bathroom mirror. Hmm. Predict what you think happens with the condensation that forms clouds.

_____

_____

_____

_____

Water vapor rises up into the atmosphere. It cools as it rises upward.
Eventually, the water vapor meets a bit of dust. The water vapor then
condenses onto that dust particle, just like the water vapor condenses
onto the bathroom mirror after your shower. More and more water vapor
particles condense onto that piece of dust and others nearby. This process
continues, and that bit of dust grows larger and larger, eventually creating
a fluffy cloud!

Now let's add condensation to our water cycle diagram. We'll just pick a
cloud and label the process of condensation.

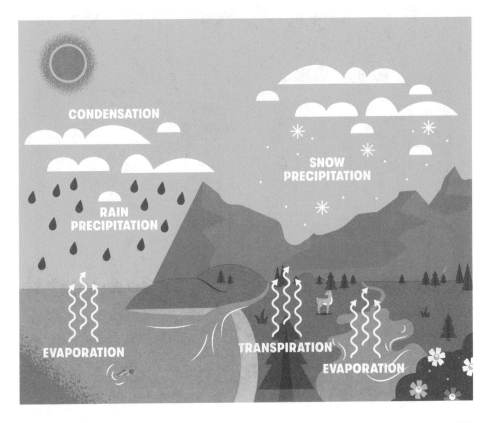

CRYSTALLIZATION

On really cold days, precipitation often involves another process: crystallization. As condensed water droplets fall from the sky, the freezing temperature turns them into little ice crystals called snowflakes.

You have already learned about crystallization in the rock cycle, and it's really the same idea here, just with water instead of magma.

FLOW AND RUNOFF

How does the weather cycle affect the processes of weathering and erosion? Let's think about it! If the rain pours down on a mountain, what happens? It runs down the slope. This is called a downhill flow, also known as surface runoff.

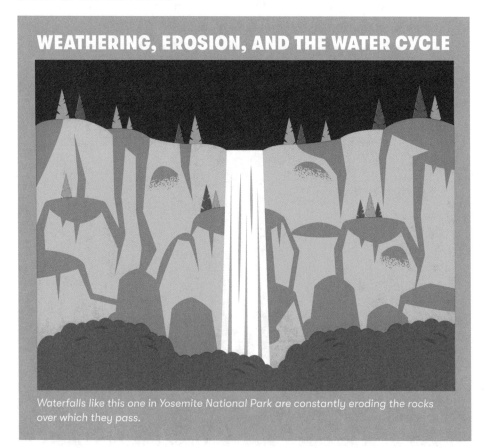

WEATHERING, EROSION, AND THE WATER CYCLE

Waterfalls like this one in Yosemite National Park are constantly eroding the rocks over which they pass.

Downhill flows, which are part of the water cycle, also play a part in the rock cycle. In the previous two chapters, you learned that flowing water can gradually wear away rocks, breaking and carrying off little bits as sediment. This is called weathering and erosion of rocks. Downhill flows contribute to this process by wearing down the slopes that they move along.

Where do you think this occurs on your diagram of the water cycle? Let's draw an example of surface runoff on our diagram in a place where the process might occur.

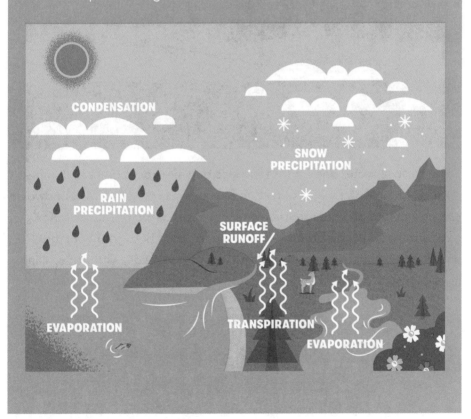

GROUND WATER AND AQUIFERS

Did you know that part of the water cycle is actually underground? Let's add some of this underground water cycle stuff to our water cycle diagram.

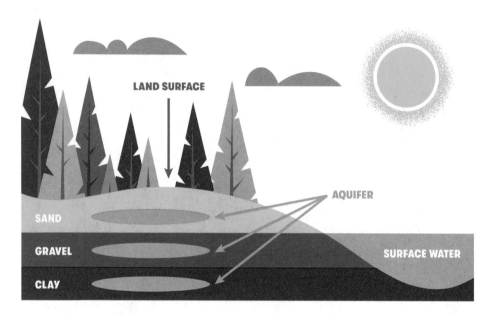

Some surface water and rainwater seeps between rocks and soil. It moves downward through layers of Earth to become groundwater. Groundwater can collect into an underground water reservoir called an aquifer. An aquifer is not an underground river; it's more like a backyard pool that no one has cleaned in years, so it's full of rocks and soil, with water filling in any spaces it can find.

WELLS

If you are ever stranded in a remote location without drinking water, remember: you can always count on groundwater! If you dig a hole deep enough in the ground, you will eventually find water while creating a basic well. Throughout history, humans have relied on wells for drinking water and for watering their crops. Today, wells are still the main source of fresh water in many places.

Water sure travels a lot! It's exhausting just to think about the trip that the water in your drinking glass took just to get there. But how does water relate to the question from the beginning of the chapter?

Does this help you figure out what clothes to bring for your camping trip?

_____

_____

_____

_____

MOVEMENT OF WATER IN THE ATMOSPHERE

What does water have to do with the weather? Well, there can't be any rain or snow without water—that's why there is no precipitation on the Moon. But the water cycle can't explain everything about the weather. For example, peeking outside again as you pack for your trip, you notice that a brisk wind has picked up. Where did that wind come from?

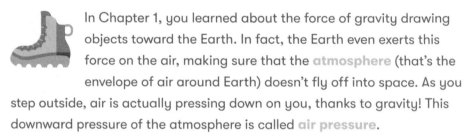

In Chapter 1, you learned about the force of gravity drawing objects toward the Earth. In fact, the Earth even exerts this force on the air, making sure that the **atmosphere** (that's the envelope of air around Earth) doesn't fly off into space. As you step outside, air is actually pressing down on you, thanks to gravity! This downward pressure of the atmosphere is called **air pressure**.

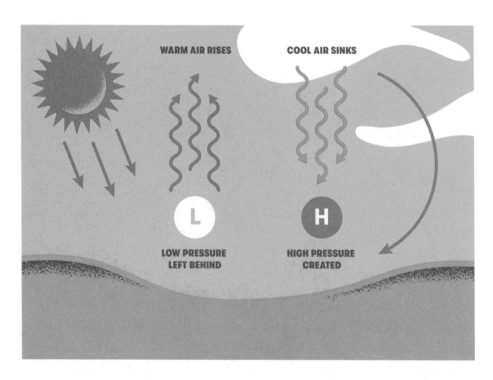

WARM AIR RISES   COOL AIR SINKS

L LOW PRESSURE LEFT BEHIND

H HIGH PRESSURE CREATED

AIR PRESSURE

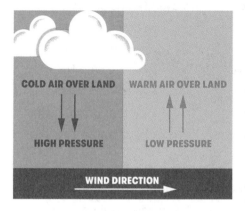

COLD AIR OVER LAND   **WARM AIR OVER LAND**

HIGH PRESSURE   **LOW PRESSURE**

WIND DIRECTION

Air in the atmosphere acts the same way—moving from areas of high air pressure to areas of low air pressure.

And if you think about it, something very similar happens when a person "passes wind": gas that is under high pressure in the intestine escapes to an area of low pressure. As you know all too well, the smell tends to be less pleasant than a cool breeze.

Air pressure can change for a number of reasons. For example, the ground in your neighborhood warms up on a sunny day. The heat from the ground also warms up the air. Warm air is less dense than cooler air. This means that warm air rises up into the atmosphere, while cool air sinks down. So, on a warm day, you may experience less air pressure than on a cool day.

Air naturally moves from high pressure areas to low pressure areas. That movement of air is— you guessed it—wind.

Let's think about a can of soda. When you open a can of soda, you hear a "pop!" That's because the gas inside the can is under high pressure. When you open the can, the gas escapes to the lower pressure outside the can.

Birds and some insects can detect changes in air pressure, but humans are not so good at this. We need a device called a barometer. A traditional barometer measures air pressure by measuring how much air pushes down on the liquid mercury inside the device. That explains the units typically used for air pressure—millimeters of mercury (mm Hg). There are a lot of different units you may hear when listening to the weather report. Just like miles and kilometers are used for distance, mm Hg is just one of many units scientists use to measure air pressure.

PREDICTING THE WEATHER

In that "prehistoric" era before the Internet and even television, ship captains (and pirates!) out at sea depended on barometers to help them predict when a storm was coming. If they noticed a rapid drop in air pressure, they immediately ordered the crew to prepare the ship for a storm. Hopefully they beat the winds that might rush toward them, as those types of winds often bring rainclouds. On the other hand, if they noticed air pressure rising, they relaxed and prepared for smooth sailing and clear skies.

Today, there are more than 100,000 weather stations just in the United States alone. These weather stations take continual measurements of air pressure. Meteorologists (people who use science to forecast the weather) use those measurements to create detailed pressure maps. A map like this allows us to make some educated guesses about weather phenomena like wind.

 Take a stab at being a meteorologist. Draw some arrows on the air pressure map. Start the arrow where you think the wind may start and point it in the direction you think it will blow.

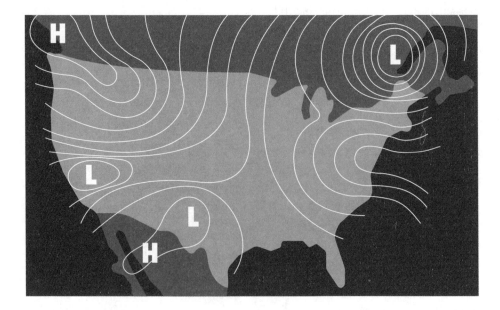

Hmm, what are those wavy lines on the map? Those are called isobars.

Those lines show where air pressure is the same, kind of like a border. The closer the isobars are to each other, the faster the pressure is changing.

Based on the isobars, at which one of your arrows do you think the wind is blowing the fastest?

_____

_____

_____

_____

Maybe checking a weather app can help you decide how to dress for tomorrow.

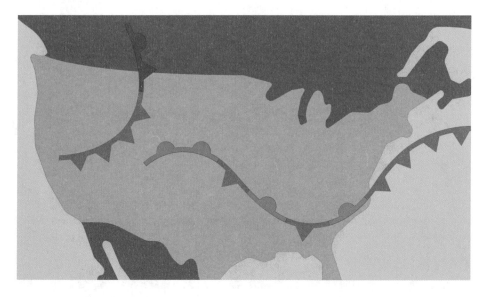

Unfortunately, the weather app is showing a weird-looking map. You know the symbols for pressure and isobars, but what are those lines with little triangles and semicircles on them?

AIR MASSES AND FRONTS

Have you ever walked by an air-conditioned store on a hot day and gotten a blast of cold air as you passed the door? Now imagine that amount of air times a million! Just like the air that comes rushing out at you from the store is cold throughout, an air mass is a bunch of air in one place that is the same temperature throughout. Air masses are huge and can go on for hundreds of miles.

What happens when you get to the border between air masses? Well, the temperature, humidity, and other conditions that were consistent across one air mass would change very quickly. Maybe even significantly.

The boundary between air masses is called a front. The conditions in a weather front are often turbulent. You may experience gusting winds, thunderstorms, or dramatic changes in temperature. It all depends on the type of front.

That map on the weather app shows air masses and fronts with colors and symbols instead of words. Can you crack the code?

WEATHER MAP SYMBOLS

Try to use the information in the table below to fill in the missing text.

SYMBOLS ON MAP	COLOR AND SHAPE = AIR TEMPERATURE	DIRECTION THE SYMBOLS ARE POINTING = DIRECTION OF MOVEMENT	NAME
	Red circles = warm air	Moving up/north	Warm front
	Blue triangles = cold air	Moving _____	Cold front

	Red circles = _____ air Blue triangles = _____ air	Not moving ("undecided" between moving up/north and moving down/south)	Stationary front
	Purple (Blue mixed with red) circles and triangles = _____ air	Moving _____	Occluded front

Now we're on to something! Each of these four types of fronts brings predictable changes in weather. Let's investigate further.

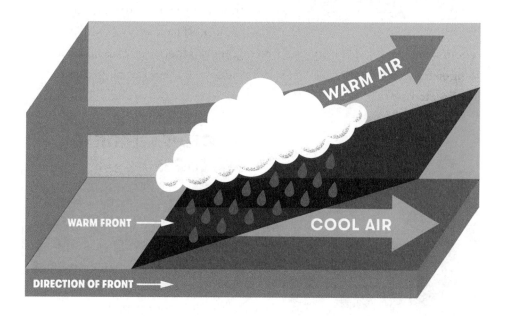

In a warm front, a warm air mass moves above a cold air mass. Moisture in the warm air condenses, creating clouds. This can result in rain and sometimes thunderstorms.

If you had to guess whether a warm front is likely to be coming from a high-pressure or low-pressure area, what would you guess and why?

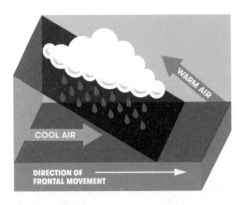

In a cold front, the opposite occurs: a cold air mass comes in and pushes warm air upward. Thunderstorms are common in cold fronts. However, cold air moves more quickly than warm air. This means that the change in weather conditions is more rapid than when compared to a warm front. When a cold front passes through your area, you may feel a rapid drop in air temperature and gusting winds; a barometer will show the air pressure starting to rise.

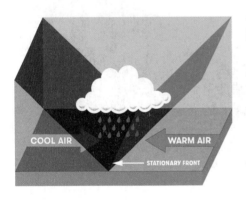

AN OLD-FASHIONED STANDOFF

Sometimes, a warm air mass and a cold air mass rush at each other and neither will budge, like that pile of dirty socks on your bedroom floor. That creates a stationary front. Huh, that explains the symbol for a stationary front!

A stationary front can stay in place for days, marking a boundary between colder and warmer temperatures. Sometimes, winds blow parallel to the boundary line, and there is usually precipitation where the two air masses meet. Eventually, one of the air masses will move when the winds begin to change.

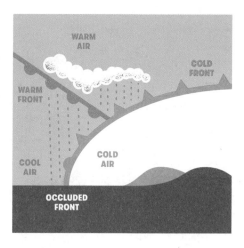

An **occluded front** is basically a traffic jam involving a cold air mass and a warm air mass. In an occluded front, a warm air mass moves slowly toward a cool air mass. Then, in the plot twist, a faster-moving cold air mass catches up. The warm and cold air mix together, usually bringing precipitation and unstable temperatures. However, unlike a stationary front, an occluded front is moving. And when it passes, the sky will clear up.

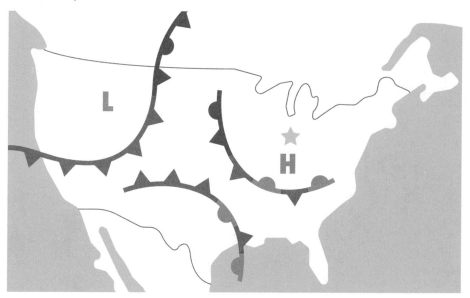

 Try your hand at interpreting the weather map shown above. If you were in western Indiana (indicated by the star), what weather might you expect in the next day or so?

_____

_____

_____

Have you ever heard or read a weather forecast that said "50% chance of rain"? Weather forecasts are actually based on the movement of air masses and the interactions between fronts. Meteorologists study weather patterns to estimate the *probability* of events like rain or snow. But, there are a lot more factors in understanding the weather than just the movement of air masses.

 Let's see if your improved understanding of meteorology can help you with your packing quandary. How can you use what you have learned to figure out what clothes to bring for this camping trip?

_____

_____

_____

WHAT'S LAND GOT TO DO WITH IT?

Wait, there's more to understanding the weather than just the water cycle and all that stuff about the atmosphere? Believe it or not, landforms make a big difference in weather conditions too. Mountains can block the passage of a weather front, forcing an air mass to rise or to be squeezed in between its peaks. Wide, flat areas like the prairies can allow wind to gather force, allowing tornadoes to form. Elevation also makes a big difference: generally speaking, the higher above sea level you go, the cooler the air temperature will be.

And then there's water, like lakes, seas, and oceans. These bodies of water also play a large role in the weather. Compared to land, water is slower to warm up and also slower to cool down again. Therefore, areas of land that are near water tend to have *less* extreme temperatures: cooler in the summer and warmer in the winter.

The differences in temperature between land and water on the coast create those delightfully cool sea breezes during the summer. The warmer land is an area of low pressure. The cooler air above the water is an area of higher pressure. And you know what happens between areas of low pressure and high pressure—wind.

Let's compare two very different locations in California. One location is on the Pacific Ocean, on the western edge of the state. The other location is high up in the Sierra Nevada Mountain range, on the eastern edge of the state. Based on what you know so far, how would you compare these two locations?

_____

_____

_____

Let's note that the two locations lie along the same latitude—in other words, the two locations lie along the same horizontal line on the globe. Latitude tells you how far a point on the globe is from the equator. Generally speaking, conditions are warm near the equator and get colder as you move toward the North or South Pole. Areas along the same line of latitude may experience similar weather conditions.

Does this new information change how you might describe the conditions between these two locations in California?

_____

_____

_____

However, relying on latitude alone could get you into trouble and have you packing for the wrong type of weather conditions. Another piece of the puzzle is altitude, or elevation above sea level. The higher up you go in the mountains, the colder it gets. Some mountains are so tall that they are covered in snow throughout the entire year.

Remember that for your trip tomorrow, you will be hiking up a mountain and then heading back down to pitch a tent in the river valley. How does this knowledge about how landforms affect the weather help you figure out what to pack?

_____

_____

_____

_____

_____

_____

STAYING CURRENT WITH THE CURRENTS

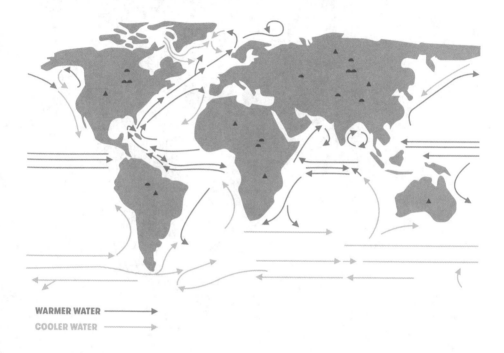

WARMER WATER ⟶
COOLER WATER ⟶

You already know some information about how large bodies of water can affect conditions near the coastlines. Let's surf the currents to find out more!

Just like air masses move around in the atmosphere in predictable ways, water moves throughout the ocean in predictable ways. This movement of the water is called an ocean current. Depending on their temperature, currents can either have a warming or cooling effect on the land near which they pass.

THE GREAT RUBBER DUCKY

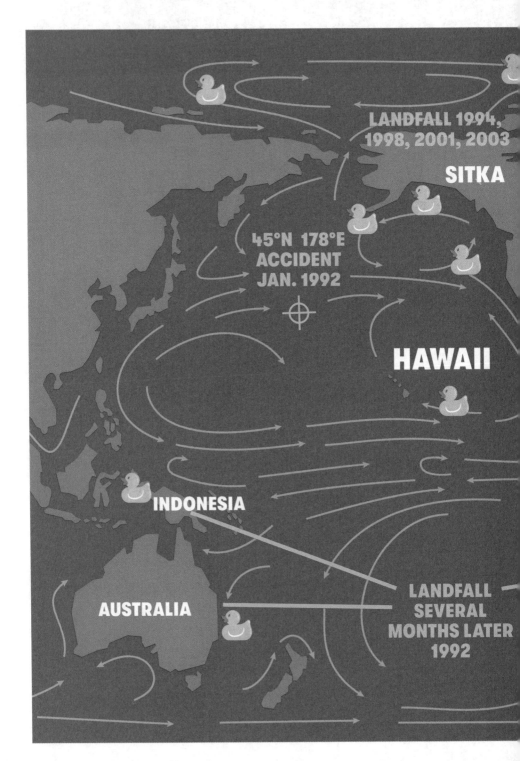

LANDFALL 1994, 1998, 2001, 2003

SITKA

45°N 178°E
ACCIDENT
JAN. 1992

HAWAII

INDONESIA

AUSTRALIA

LANDFALL
SEVERAL
MONTHS LATER
1992

ACCIDENT OF 1992

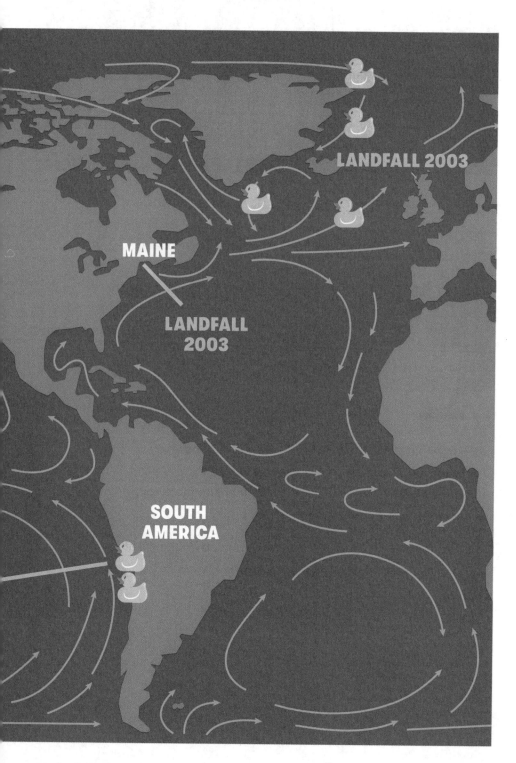

Ocean currents are a rather slow process. Let's look at an example. In January 1992, a shipping container filled with rubber ducks fell off a ship into the Pacific Ocean on its way from Hong Kong to the United States. Seriously! Oceanographers, scientists who study the ocean, tracked the movement of some of the rubber ducks as they landed on beaches around the world. It took eleven years for one rubber duck to travel from near the middle of the Pacific Ocean to the UK, and more kept showing up for several years!

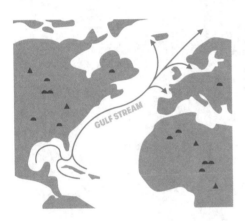

For example, the Gulf Stream, a huge, warm ocean current that begins in the Gulf of Mexico and flows northward through the Atlantic Ocean, is one reason why northern Europe is not quite as cold as you would expect it to be based on its latitude and altitude.

So what makes these ocean currents flow? There are lots of reasons within the complex system that moves water all over the world. One of the most important reasons is sunlight. More sunlight falls in the regions nearest to the equator, warming them up more so than areas farther away from the equator.

Do you remember what happens with warm and cold air? Let's compare it to what happens with warm and cold ocean water:

AIR	WATER
Warm air rises; cool air sinks.	Warm water floats; cold water sinks.
Cold air flows underneath the area with warm air.	Cold water flows underneath the area with warm water.

Take another look at the ocean current map on page 133.

What do you notice about the currents between the Northern and Southern Hemisphere?

_____

_____

_____

_____

_____

_____

It looks like the currents in the Northern Hemisphere move in an opposite direction than the currents in the Southern Hemisphere. But why?

Let's perform a little experiment. If you happen to have an old globe that you don't mind drawing on, you can join in and follow along in this experiment together. Otherwise, just make it a thought experiment.

Imagining that the Earth is rotating around its axis, just like it does every single day, spin your imaginary globe. Imagine taking a marker and trying to draw a straight line from north to south *while* the globe is spinning. Let's say you place your marker tip on the west coast of the United States. Spin the globe as you draw a line heading straight down toward the equator.

Can you describe what might happen?

_____

_____

_____

_____

Congratulations! You have just observed the Coriolis effect! The Coriolis effect influences the direction that ocean currents travel. Not only that, but the Coriolis effect also influences how air masses move across the planet. Water and air don't travel along a straight line. Instead, they move along a curve. The curves tend to be clockwise in the Northern Hemisphere and counterclockwise in the Southern Hemisphere.

WEATHER VERSUS CLIMATE

 We've talked about **weather** quite a bit. If you had to define the word "weather" to a student who is a year or two younger than you, what would your definition be?

_____

_____

_____

Perhaps your definition mentioned that weather is something that can change on a day-to-day basis. So what is **climate**? Sometimes, you may hear some people use those terms interchangeably, thinking that both words have the same meaning. But actually, climate refers to the typical weather in a region over a long period of time.

 Determine if each statement below is an example of weather or climate by circling the correct word.

YOU CHOOSE: WEATHER OR CLIMATE?

CIRCLE ONE		DESCRIPTION
weather	climate	**75% chance of rain in your town**
weather	climate	**Snow likely in the northeastern corner of the United States in January**
weather	climate	**Overnight lows of 38 degrees and clear skies**
weather	climate	**A high of 68 degrees with a gentle breeze**
weather	climate	**Mild winters and summers along the California coastline**

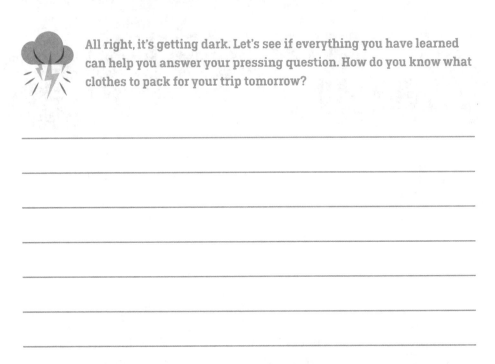

All right, it's getting dark. Let's see if everything you have learned can help you answer your pressing question. How do you know what clothes to pack for your trip tomorrow?

_____

_____

_____

_____

_____

_____

_____

CHAPTER 4 VOCABULARY

air mass: a large mass of air that is in one place and is the same temperature throughout.

air pressure: the downward pressure of the atmosphere by gravity.

altitude: the elevation of a point above sea level.

aquifer: an underground water reservoir.

atmosphere: the envelope of air around Earth.

barometer: a device that measures air pressure.

bodies of water: an accumulation of water in an area such as a lake, sea, or ocean.

climate: the typical weather in a region over a long period of time.

cold front: a location where a cold air mass pushes a warm air mass upward.

condensation: the process of water vapor cooling and transforming back into liquid water.

Coriolis effect: the rotation of Earth influences the direction that the ocean currents and air masses travel.

crystallization: the formation of ice crystals from the freezing of liquid water.

current: the movement of water in a body of water.

downhill flow: the flow of water and/or debris down a slope. Also known as surface runoff.

evaporation: the process of liquid water turning into vapor.

front: the boundary between air masses.

groundwater: water that travels underground through little cracks in the soil and spaces between rocks.

isobars: lines on a weather map that indicate where air pressure is the same. The closer the isobars are to each other on the map, the faster the pressure is changing.

landforms: a significant feature of the Earth's terrain such as a mountain or canyon.

latitude: the distance between a point on the globe and the equator.

meteorologist: a scientist who utilizes known patterns and technology to forecast the weather.

occluded front: the location where a cold air mass overtakes a slower moving warm air mass and mixes together while moving in the same direction.

oceanographer: a scientist who studies the ocean and the life in it.

precipitation: any form of water that falls to the ground from the sky.

stationary front: the location where a warm air mass and cold air mass move toward each other and neither moves out of the way.

surface runoff: the flow of water and/or debris down a slope. Also known as downhill flow.

transpiration: the process of plants releasing water vapor into the air.

vapor: the gaseous form of water.

warm front: the location where a warm air mass moves above a cold air mass.

weather: the state of the atmosphere in a specific place at a specific time, which includes air temperature, air pressure, humidity, precipitation, and wind.

wind: the movement of air.

CHAPTER 4 ANSWER KEY

PAGE 111

Snow, hail, sleet, freezing rain. . .

PAGES 113–114

Your numbers will vary, but you should see the water level decreasing over time due to evaporation. It may decrease more on some days than on others, depending on the temperature and humidity of your home.

PAGE 115

The inside of the bag is fogged up and/or covered in water droplets.

PAGES 116–117

The condensation that forms clouds needs something solid to "stick" to, like maybe a dust particle or other solid bit floating in the air.

PAGE 121

What you have learned so far helps explain why precipitation occurs and also why the air may feel damp after a heavy rainfall the day before. The cycling of water in the environment is the reason behind these phenomena. However, you still don't know how to predict whether it might rain, snow, or be damp tomorrow, which would help you decide what to pack for your trip.

PAGE 124

Your arrows may look slightly different, but the key is that you should have wind arrows going from high-pressure areas to low-pressure areas.

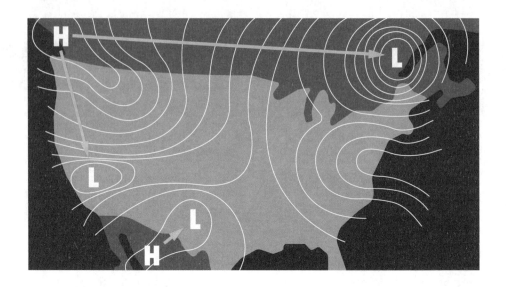

PAGE 125

The wind may be blowing the fastest toward the low pressure system in the upper right because the isobars are scrunched together.

PAGES 126–127

SYMBOLS ON MAP	COLOR AND SHAPE = AIR TEMPERATURE	DIRECTION THE SYMBOLS ARE POINTING = DIRECTION OF MOVEMENT	NAME
	Red circles = warm air	Moving up/north	Warm front
	Blue triangles = cold air	Moving down/south	Cold front
	Red circles = warm air Blue triangles = cold air	Not moving ("undecided" between moving up/north and moving down/south)	Stationary front

	Purple (Blue mixed with red) circles and triangles = mixed warm and cold air	Moving up/north	Occluded front

PAGE 128

A warm front is likely to come from a low-pressure area, because warm air masses tend to go hand-in-hand with low air pressure. That's why a warm front on a weather map is often pointing away from an area with the L (low pressure) symbol.

PAGE 129

A warm front is approaching western Indiana from the west, so you might expect a shift to higher temperatures and some precipitation.

PAGE 130

By understanding the properties of air masses and what happens when they interact, you can determine the current weather conditions. And by understanding how air masses move, you can determine how the weather may change over the next few days. This will allow you to determine what type of clothes and gear to bring on your camping trip.

PAGE 131

The location in the mountains will be colder than the location on the coast of California because the coast is at sea level and the mountains have a high elevation. The location on the coast is also warmer because it is right next to the ocean, which creates moderate conditions.

PAGE 132

Because the two locations are along the same latitude, maybe the mountains won't be as cold or the coast won't be as warm.

Even though the two locations are along the same latitude, they are at different altitudes, so it will be colder high up in the mountains and warmer at sea level. You can expect the air temperature to be cooler as you ascend the mountain and warmer in the valley down below because it tends to be colder at higher altitudes. Therefore, it makes sense to bring layers of clothing. If you consulted a map to determine if there was a large body of water near your campsite or hiking location, you would be able to determine if the weather would potentially be more mild near a large body of water or more drastic farther away from the water. In addition, since precipitation is common on mountain slopes, you might want to pack some waterproof items.

PAGE 137

The ocean currents in the Northern Hemisphere generally go clockwise, and the ocean currents in the Southern Hemisphere generally go counterclockwise or straight toward the east.

The marker line will end up curved instead of straight.

PAGE 139

Technically, weather is the state of the atmosphere (air) in a specific place at a specific time. This includes the air temperature, air pressure, the amount of moisture in the air (humidity), precipitation, and wind. If your definition covered most of these points, even if you used different words, you've got it!

weather	climate	75% chance of rain in your town
weather	**climate**	Snow likely in the northeastern corner of the United States in January
weather	climate	Overnight lows of 38 degrees and clear skies
weather	climate	A high of 68 degrees with a gentle breeze
weather	**climate**	Mild winters and summers along the California coastline

PAGE 140

You can consult a weather map to make predictions about possible upcoming changes in the weather in the area where you will be hiking and camping. The direction of moving weather fronts and the location of areas of high and low pressure can give you a general idea what to expect. An understanding of the climate this time of year can also help by giving you a probable range of weather conditions. By taking into account all of the information from meteorology forecasts as well as your knowledge of the landscape, you can determine what type of clothes and gear to pack for your trip.

5 EARTH AND HUMAN ACTIVITY

Today, you need to pack for a day at the beach, and you'll definitely need something to protect your skin from the Sun (hate to say it, but your parents were right about this one). Did you know that sunscreen is more important today than it was only thirty years ago? Why is that? The picture on this page is a clue. Read on if you are curious.

CHAPTER CONTENTS

Why did the hole in the ozone layer of the atmosphere change?

THE SPHERES OF EARTH

ATMOSPHERE
ATMO: AIR

HYDROSPHERE
HYDRO: WATER

EARTH

GEOSPHERE
GEO: GROUND

BIOSPHERE
BIO: LIFE

THE FOUR SPHERES OF THE EARTH

The atmosphere is one of the four spheres of Earth. Everything on Earth exists in one of these spheres: atmosphere, biosphere, geosphere, and hydrosphere.

EARTH SPHERE	WHAT DO WE FIND THERE?
Atmosphere	The air that you breathe and that you feel as wind—it is mostly nitrogen with supporting players of oxygen, carbon dioxide, and some other stuff.
Biosphere	All of the living things—all humans, animals, plants, and yes even insects and spiders. Everything that is alive is part of the biosphere.
Geosphere	The ground, the insides of Earth, the mountains, and other rocky parts of Earth.
Hydrosphere	All of the water on Earth including liquid, frozen, and vapor.

All of these spheres work together. Take a look at this growing plant. How do the spheres interact here? Label each part in the scene below with the name of its sphere.

So the plant lives in the biosphere. It's home is in the soil, which is part of the geosphere. It also uses the minerals within the soil to flourish. The plant drinks up water, the hydrosphere, from its roots underneath the soil in order to grow. And the plant takes in carbon dioxide through its leaves and lets out oxygen, both part of the atmosphere. All of these things that the plant uses to grow and thrive are called natural resources.

EARTH'S OWN SUPPLIES: NATURAL RESOURCES

Humans, along with all other living creatures, depend on natural resources (supplies) from the Earth in order to build things, to grow things, and even to simply breathe!

STONES, METALS, AND MORE

There are many natural resources that are found in the geosphere. Humans mine all sorts of stones and metals for various uses. Some examples include granite, marble, aluminum, copper, iron, silver, and gold. The stones are usually taken from the ground, cut into specific shapes, and polished. Metals are often found in metal ores, which are rocks that contain enough of a valuable metal to make it worth mining.

You can also mine sand, gravel, and gypsum for construction, talc for making rubber, paper, and paint. Gemstones are mined because people value their appearance, although some have practical uses as well.

FOSSIL FUELS

Besides all these minerals, the geosphere is the source for fossil fuels. Fuels are things that are burned for energy, and the word "fossil" in their name means that these fuels formed from the fossils of living things over millions of years. Fossil fuels include coal, oil (the kind that is buried deep underground, not the kind used for baking and frying), and natural gas. In this adventure, you will get to know them really well and learn some unsavory facts about them.

RESOURCES FROM THE EARTH'S SPHERES

 Can you think of one resource that you may use from each of Earth's spheres? Try to think of at least one example that hasn't been discussed already.

EARTH SPHERE	EXAMPLES THAT I USE IN EVERYDAY LIFE:
Atmosphere	
Biosphere	
Geosphere	
Hydrosphere	

RENEWABLE RESOURCES

Some of the natural resources that come from these four spheres are renewable. Renewable resources are a bit like a rechargeable gift card: after you spend the money on it, you can reload the card and continue using it. Likewise, nature can produce renewable resources again and again, replacing what has been used up within your lifetime.

NON-RENEWABLE RESOURCES

However, most natural resources are non-renewable resources. These types of resources can be replaced in theory, but the process takes so long that you won't be around to see it happen. Many of these types of resources need many thousands or even many millions of years to replenish. Do you think you can wait that long for your rechargeable gift card to be reloaded?

RENEWABLE VS. NON-RENEWABLE RESOURCES

 Now try to complete this table by placing check marks where appropriate.

	RENEWABLE RESOURCE	NON-RENEWABLE RESOURCE
Can be replaced in our lifetimes		
Used up faster than it is replaced		
Coal		
Air		
Metals		
Wind		
Water		
Natural gas		

WATER CYCLES AROUND AGAIN

What did you put down for water? Well, when it comes to water, things are not so clear-cut.

 Remember when we learned that the Earth's water cycles through the atmosphere, the land, and large bodies of water? In other words, nature "recycles" water all the time. Humans are also part of the water cycle, which means that the water you drink today will soon find its way back into the environment. However, humans use water in many other ways besides drinking it: they wash things in it with soap and detergent, dispose of chemicals in it, contaminate it with pesticides, and sometimes spill huge amounts of oil into it. Many of these activities **pollute** water by adding harmful substances to it that are difficult or impossible to remove. You will take a closer look at pollution later in this adventure. For now, keep in mind that while water in general is a renewable resource, clean water is not. This is because you cannot always replace the clean water you have used up within a lifetime.

THE CARBON MERRY-GO-ROUND

 As you may have noticed, nature is really into recycling. It recycles rocks, water, and it even recycles a fundamental element found in all living things: carbon.

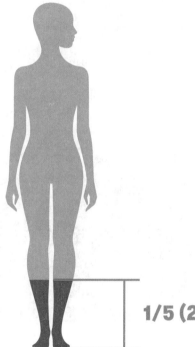

1/5 (20%) CARBON

In fact, carbon makes up almost one-fifth of your body mass. But what you have inside you is not pure carbon. Carbon actually bonds (sticks closely) with other stuff to make stuff like proteins, fats, and carbohydrates. Because of that little fact, humans are known as carbon-based life forms. Pretty much all life on Earth is carbon-based!

So where does all that carbon come from? Well, allow us to introduce. . . the carbon cycle!

THE CARBON CYCLE

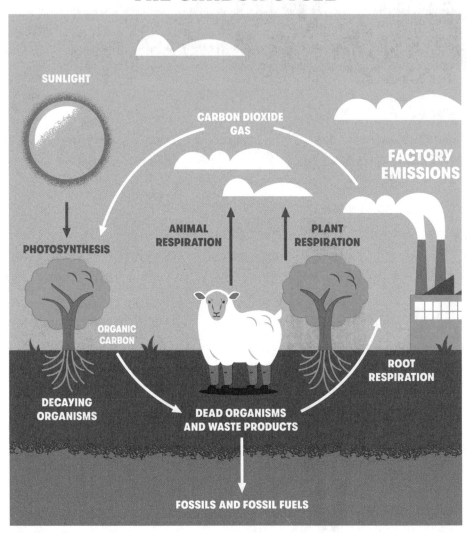

SUNLIGHT

CARBON DIOXIDE GAS

FACTORY EMISSIONS

PHOTOSYNTHESIS

ANIMAL RESPIRATION

PLANT RESPIRATION

ORGANIC CARBON

ROOT RESPIRATION

DECAYING ORGANISMS

DEAD ORGANISMS AND WASTE PRODUCTS

FOSSILS AND FOSSIL FUELS

Does this look familiar? It kind of looks like the water cycle from the previous chapter, right? The carbon cycle follows the same idea as the water cycle—carbon circles through all of Earth's spheres. The total amount of carbon stays the same, but it moves from place to place, just like water.

Humans breathe out carbon dioxide. Most animals do too. And you may have heard that plants breathe in carbon dioxide. Well, they don't actually breathe like we do because plants don't have lungs, but they do absorb carbon dioxide from the atmosphere.

PHOTOSYNTHESIS

With the help of sunlight, plants use carbon dioxide to convert it into sugars and starches that allow the plant to grow. This process is called photosynthesis.

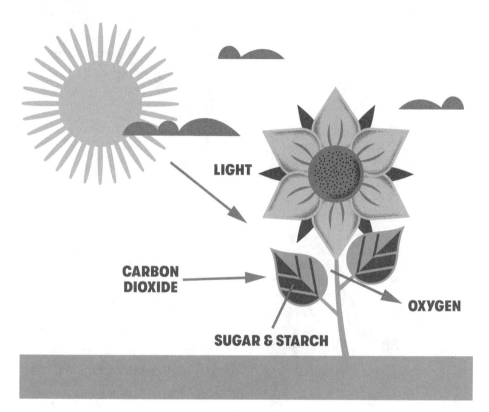

CONSUMING CARBON (LITERALLY!)

In turn, animals, including humans, can eat the plants (or eat other animals that have eaten plants). When you consume plant- or animal-based food, carbon can be used to grow and power your body.

However, some of the carbon escapes back into the atmosphere when you breathe. You breathe *in* oxygen and breathe *out* carbon dioxide. In other words, because of respiration (breathing), you lose carbon every few seconds!

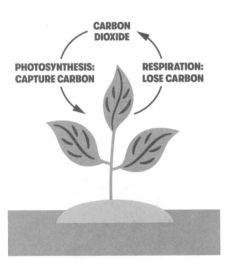

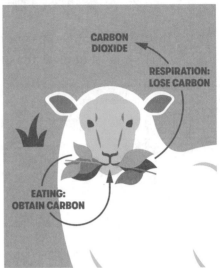

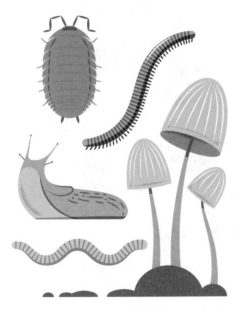

Even with all this loss of carbon going on every day, living things are still like massive carbon storage units. What happens to all that carbon when living things die? Decomposers, which are various creatures that break down dead organisms, release carbon into the atmosphere, soil, and water.

Tiny, prehistoric sea plants and animals died and settled on the ocean floor. Over time, they were covered by layers of silt and sand.

Over millions of years, the remains of these plants and animals were buried deeper. Tremendous heat and pressure transformed them into oil and gas.

In order to extract oil and gas deposits from the deeply buried formations, humans have to drill down through layers of sand, silt, and rock.

PETROLEUM & NATURAL GAS FORMATION

SAND & SILT ROCK

SAND & SILT

PLANT & ANIMAL REMAINS

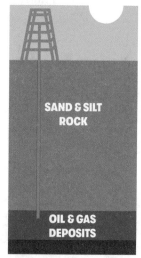

OIL & GAS DEPOSITS

Tiny, prehistoric sea plants and animals died and settled on the ocean floor. Over time, they were covered by layers of silt and sand.

Over millions of years, the remains of these plants and animals were buried deeper. Tremendous heat and pressure transformed them into oil and gas.

In order to extract oil and gas deposits from the deeply buried formations, humans have to drill down through layers of sand, silt, and rock.

FOSSIL FUELS

Here is where something incredible happens in the carbon cycle: some dead organisms do not decompose immediately. Instead, they end up trapped in areas with no air, such as under rocks at the bottom of the ocean. Over millions of years, these remnants of organisms turn into fossils and get buried deeper and deeper underground.

Draw on your knowledge from Chapter 2: the deeper you go into the Earth's interior, the more heat and pressure you find there. Heat and pressure compress the fossils, gradually transforming them into fossil fuels (coal, natural gas, and crude oil, from which gasoline is made to power cars).

Did you know it takes 98 tons of prehistoric plants to produce just one gallon of gasoline? That's 196,000 pounds of plants that lived back when dinosaurs still walked the Earth! You can imagine why you can't replace fossil fuels in a hurry. On the other hand, you can burn them pretty quickly, releasing a whole lot of carbon dioxide into the atmosphere. This is a big problem, as you will see shortly.

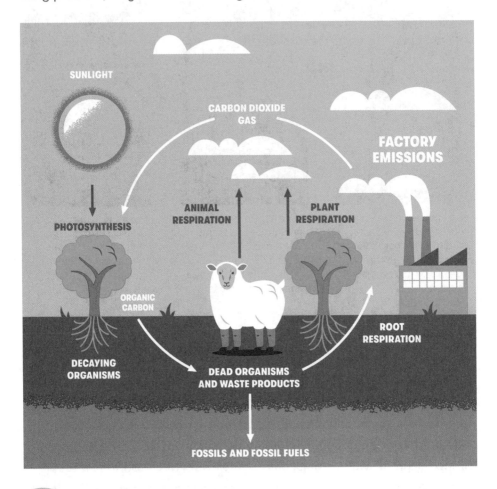

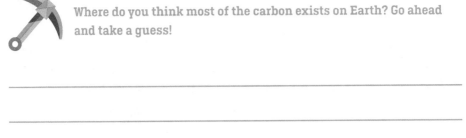

Where do you think most of the carbon exists on Earth? Go ahead and take a guess!

Now check out these diagrams to see if you were right:

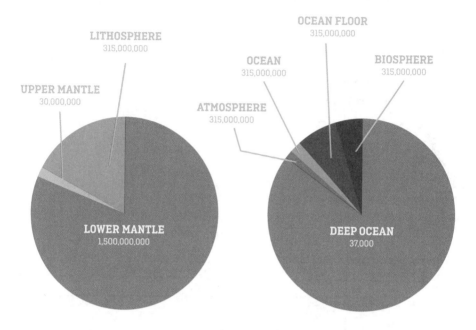

TOTAL CARBON BELOW EARTH'S SURFACE
1,845,000,000 billion metric tons

LITHOSPHERE
315,000,000

UPPER MANTLE
30,000,000

LOWER MANTLE
1,500,000,000

TOTAL CARBON ABOVE EARTH'S SURFACE
43,500 billion metric tons

OCEAN FLOOR
315,000,000

OCEAN
315,000,000

BIOSPHERE
315,000,000

ATMOSPHERE
315,000,000

DEEP OCEAN
37,000

As you can see, there is *far* more carbon underneath the ground than up in the atmosphere. In fact, there is more than 3 million times more carbon underneath the ground than just what is in the atmosphere. And there is 63 times more carbon in the deep ocean than in the atmosphere.

Now that you've learned a lot about carbon dioxide in the atmosphere, are you starting to develop some theories about what might have caused the ozone layer in the atmosphere to change? We haven't specifically defined "ozone" yet, so work with what you already know to start developing your theory.

_____

_____

_____

_____

HUMAN IMPACTS ON EARTH SYSTEMS

Humans have played a large part in altering the natural systems that have been in place for millions of years on Earth. Burning fossil fuels faster than they can be replenished is one such example.

What do you think will happen if humans keep burning fossil fuels?

_____

_____

_____

_____

POPULATION GROWTH

Now let's take a look at how the world's human population has changed over the last few centuries. The following table shows how the world's human population has grown over the past 600 years. Complete the third column of the table by following the example given for the years 1500 and 1600. Your calculations will tell you by what percentage the world's population increased in each century compared to the century before.

HUMAN POPULATION GROWTH BY CENTURY

YEAR	ESTIMATED WORLD POPULATION	% OF POPULATION GROWTH PER CENTURY
1400	400,000,000 (400 million)	
1500	450,000,000	$\frac{450{,}000{,}000 \text{ (population in this century)}}{400{,}000{,}000 \text{ (population in last century)}} \times 100\%$ $\approx 113\%$
1600	550,000,000	$\frac{550{,}000{,}000}{450{,}000{,}000} \times 100\% \approx 122\%$
1700	550,000,000	
1800	600,000,000	
1900	1,000,000,000 (1 billion)	
2000	?	

Now take a look at your numbers. If you had been a scientist looking at this table in the year 1900, approximately how large would you have predicted the world's population to become in the year 2000? Feel free to make some calculations to explain your answer.

_____

_____

_____

_____

_____

Well, the imaginary scientist from the past is in for quite a surprise! In 2000, the world's population was 6 billion (6,000,000,000), and only 20 years later, it's already at 7.8 billion.

That's great! The more the merrier, right? Well, it's not that simple. More people on the Earth means more demand for clean water, energy, soil for growing food, and other natural resources.

H2-UH-OH

Let's take a closer look at water. Remember that water is a renewable source, but fresh (not salty ocean) water is not. The graph below shows how much fresh water humans have used every year since 1901 for drinking, watering crops, and in factories.

GLOBAL FRESH WATER USAGE SINCE 1901

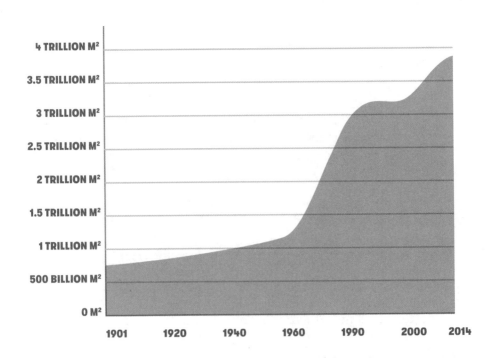

LEARNING FROM PLACES WITH DRY CLIMATES

This can really become a problem for the future if the population grows so much that humans start using up fresh water faster than it is replaced. In fact, because fresh water is not easily found in all places on Earth, some places already struggle to keep up with the demand for water. For example, several countries in the hot, dry climates of North Africa and the Middle East use up all of their renewable fresh water supply every year from local rivers, lakes, and even rainwater.

People in these countries often have to dip into other sources of water, such as taking ocean water and *desalinating* it (removing salt) or removing water from aquifers. Aquifers take much longer to refill than it takes for humans to drain them, so they are considered a non-renewable source of water.

LAND AND PEOPLE

And what about land? As the population grows, people will need more space to build their homes. More importantly, we'll need a lot more space for farms to grow enough food for everyone.

HOW WE USE LAND

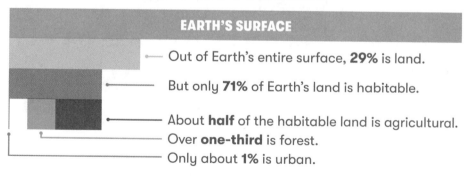

EARTH'S SURFACE

Out of Earth's entire surface, **29%** is land.

But only **71%** of Earth's land is habitable.

About **half** of the habitable land is agricultural.
Over **one-third** is forest.
Only about **1%** is urban.

Out of the 29% of Earth's surface covered in land (the rest is ocean), only 71% of that land was considered habitable in 2019. And of that habitable land, half was used for agriculture. And of the land that was used for agriculture, about 75% of it was used for livestock.

Is there anything about the numbers on this chart that might be cause for concern? Explain your answer.

_____

_____

_____

_____

_____

_____

_____

As you have seen, the human population keeps growing faster and faster. This puts a large strain on the Earth's natural resources, potentially resulting in shortages for people. However, humans are not the only ones on this planet who rely on natural resources: plants and animals also need fresh water, habitable land, and clean air. As humans take up more space and consume more resources, there is less and less available for wildlife.

THE CHANGING CLIMATE

We haven't discussed much about clean air since we mentioned carbon dioxide and the carbon cycle. How has human growth affected the atmosphere?

IS IT GETTING HOT IN HERE?

Do older people, like your teachers or parents, ever tell you that the climate was different when they were growing up?

Remember, climate refers to the typical weather in a region over a long period of time. Do they talk about how much colder winters used to be, or how it never got as hot in the summer as it does now?

Maybe their memory is playing a trick on them? To find out, take a look at the graph on the following page that shows how the average temperature on Earth has changed over the past century and a half:

AVERAGE TEMPERATURE ON EARTH

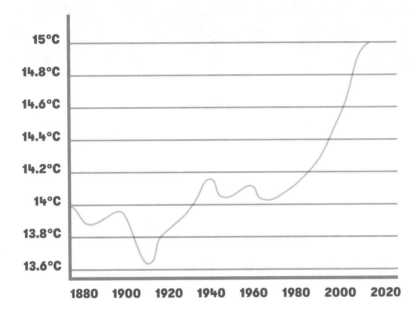

The graph starts at 1880, back when your great-great-great-great grandparents were probably about your age. To figure out the average temperature on Earth that year, scientists collected all the air temperature measurements they could find from all around the globe and calculated their average. They repeated the same thing for each year up to 2020.

 Fill in the blank: According to this graph, from 1880 to 2020, the average air temperature _____ creased by _____°C.

 Use the graph on the following page to predict what's going to happen to global temperatures in the future if the current trend continues. Notice how the temperatures from about 1970 onward seem to fall nearly on a straight line? Grab a writing utensil and any object with a straight edge.

Align your straight edge so that it passes through or close to most of the points on the curve from 1970 to 2020 in the incomplete graph on the next page. Draw a line along the edge of the straight edge, connecting 1970 to 2020.

PREDICTING FUTURE TEMPERATURES ON EARTH

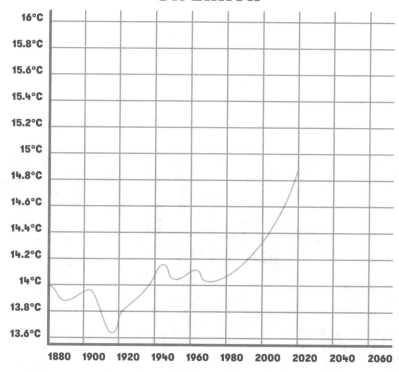

This is called a "line of best fit." Continue that line into the future, using your writing utensil and straight edge to continue the line of best fit past where the curve ends to the end of the graph paper.

 Look at where your line of best fit crosses the vertical line marked "2060." What is the average temperature reading?
_____°C

This is your prediction for what the average global temperature will be in 2060 if the current trend continues.

What you just did is something called a *linear regression*. It's a fancy way of saying you made a line of best fit and used it to make a prediction, which is actually a very powerful method scientists use to analyze measurements. In fact, climate scientists have done something very similar (except using expensive software on a computer) to estimate that the global average temperature in 2060 will be about 16°C. That's what scientists mean when they talk about global warming.

SO WHAT'S THE BIG DEAL?

Maybe you're wondering what the big deal is about the Earth being a couple of degrees warmer than it was in 1880. As it turns out, those 2 degrees Celsius (equal to 1.8 degrees Fahrenheit) make an enormous difference. Here are just a few of the things that scientists expect to happen if the Earth continues to warm up as predicted for the next 40 years. Fasten your seatbelts!

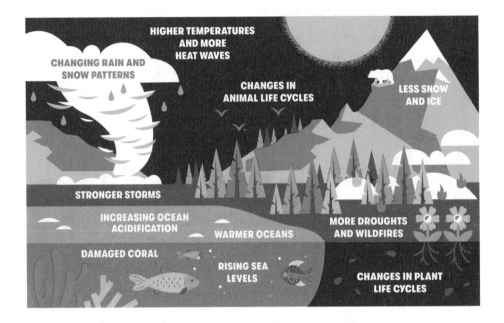

1. EXTREME TEMPERATURES, DROUGHTS, AND WILDFIRES WILL BECOME MORE COMMON.

While the average global temperature may only rise by those 2 degrees, the annual highest and lowest temperatures are expected to change more drastically. For example, the average of 4 and 6 is 5. But the average of 0 and 10 is also 5.

HEAT WAVES AND DROUGHTS

Over the past several years, many places around the world have already seen record high temperatures during the summer months. These heat waves are considered a health hazard. Scientists predict that if the average global temperature does rise to 16°C, over one-third of the world's population will have to deal with dangerous heat waves more often.

Extreme high temperatures can also cause droughts (long periods without rain or other precipitation). This means that crops will not get the water they need, which will result in food shortages.

WILDFIRES

When unusually high temperatures and droughts occur in the same place, they can result in destructive wildfires, like the ones that have raged in California nearly every summer for the past two decades. It is not a coincidence that six of the twenty largest fires in California's history all happened in the year 2020 alone. These fires, besides burning down huge areas of forest, also killed wildlife, destroyed homes and other buildings, and damaged the air quality so much that people living nearby had to wear special masks and/or stay indoors to avoid inhaling dangerous amounts of smoke.

 Maybe you are thinking, "Wait a minute! But you mentioned higher highs and lower lows. Does that mean global warming isn't really happening?" In a word, no. One region could be experiencing an unusual heat spell while another is experiencing an unusual cold spell. The term "global warming" takes into account that there will be hotter summers and harsher winters. Rain and wind patterns will also change, causing extreme drought in some locations and heavier rainfall in others. Extreme weather events like tropical cyclones (also known as hurricanes) may become more intense, with their effects felt farther from the tropics than in the past. For example, the fact that Hurricane Sandy, which originated off the coast of Central America in 2012, traveled so far north as to cause extensive flooding in New York City is likely, at least in part, due to global warming and rising sea levels. Climate change due to global warming is more complex than all the places on Earth getting warmer all the time.

2. DRINKING WATER WILL BECOME SCARCER.

More frequent droughts will mean less precipitation in many places. As a result, lakes and rivers will shrink in size, and in some places, dry up altogether, leaving millions of people without access to drinking water. And if people do not have enough water to drink, then they also won't have enough water for their crops and livestock. This means that water shortages will go hand-in-hand with food shortages. As the situation worsens, wars may even start over access to rivers.

3. SEA LEVELS WILL RISE, FLOODING COASTAL AREAS.

As the world gets warmer, ice sheets at the Earth's poles and ice caps on mountaintops will melt faster. This will lead to a rise in sea levels, which are already at least 21 cm (about 8 inches) higher than they were in the time of your great-great-great-great grandparents, and they are expected to keep rising.

Historically, humans have built cities by the water; in fact, eight of the world's ten largest cities are near the coast. These coastal cities are now at increased risk of flooding. When dangerous storms hit, water is likely to surge farther inland than it has in the past, causing death as well as damage to homes and other structures. For example, scientists estimate that Hurricane Katrina, which killed approximately 1,200 people in 2005, would have caused much less extensive flooding if it had happened in 1900, when sea levels were lower.

4. CORAL REEFS AND OTHER SEA LIFE WILL BECOME INCREASINGLY THREATENED.

Global warming has been gradually "bleaching" the world's coral reefs. Bleaching is what happens when a beautifully colored coral reef expels all the tiny creatures living in it and turns white because of stress, such as unusual heat. Chemical sunscreen has also caused bleaching of reefs. A coral reef can gradually recover from bleaching, unless the temperature stress continues, causing the reef to die. Coral reefs provide a home for fish and other sea life, so their death means a shrinking habitat for sea creatures, and the loss of a natural wonder for human snorkelers and scuba divers. About 30% of the world's coral reefs have died due to heat stress between 2014 and 2017.

Global warming can threaten ocean life in another way as well. Some of the gases that cause global warming, as you will learn shortly, also mix with ocean water, making it more acidic. This will make the ocean less and less habitable for a lot of sea life.

5. THE CHANGING CLIMATE WILL THREATEN WILDLIFE.

Most plants and animals have evolved to survive in a specific geographic range and have adapted to the typical climate in those areas. As the climate continues to change, some species may no longer be able to survive in their former habitats. Others will see the areas where they can survive shrink significantly. Combined with the growing human population encroaching on natural habitats, wildlife may be increasingly "squeezed out," resulting in more species becoming endangered and ultimately even extinct.

IS HUMAN ACTIVITY CAUSING GLOBAL WARMING?

By now, you're probably convinced that global warming is real and problematic. But is it our fault? To answer this question, we need to talk about something called the greenhouse effect.

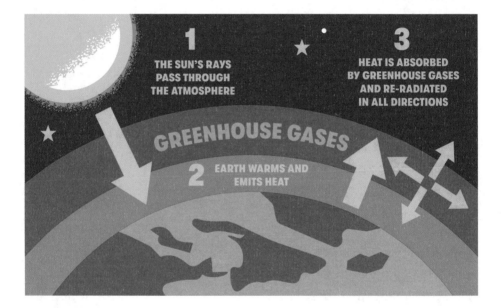

1 THE SUN'S RAYS PASS THROUGH THE ATMOSPHERE

3 HEAT IS ABSORBED BY GREENHOUSE GASES AND RE-RADIATED IN ALL DIRECTIONS

GREENHOUSE GASES

2 EARTH WARMS AND EMITS HEAT

Have you ever seen a greenhouse that is used for growing plants and food? It's a simple structure, with walls and ceiling made of transparent plastic or glass. These structures are very useful for growing food or other plants in climates that are a bit too cold. The greenhouse traps heat, faking a warmer climate for the plants inside. The clear plastic or glass lets sunlight in but prevents air from escaping once it's been warmed up.

THE GREENHOUSE EFFECT

What if we told you that the Earth is a bit like a greenhouse? Instead of having plastic wrap around the planet, there is an atmosphere. The atmosphere contains a few gases that are especially good at trapping heat. That's why they are called greenhouse gases.

Remember the discussion about carbon dioxide in the atmosphere? It is one of the main greenhouse gases. Others include ozone (ah, finally we get to ozone!), methane, nitrous oxide, and even water vapor. These gases are the reason the Earth's surface remains at a comfortable temperature at night. The Moon, which has no atmosphere, plummets to –130°C (–208°F, and that's in the warmest areas) at night despite being about the same distance from the Sun as Earth.

Clearly, greenhouse gases are needed to keep the Earth at a habitable temperature. The problem is that lately, there have been more and more of these gases in the atmosphere. And more of these gases in the atmosphere trap more heat near Earth's surface.

RELEASE OF GREENHOUSE GASES SINCE 1850

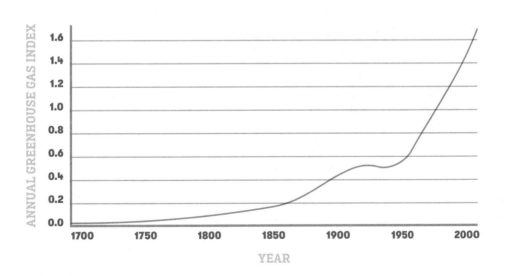

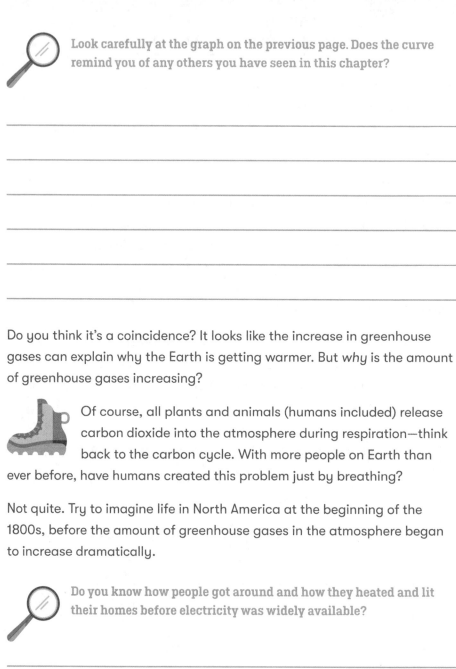

Look carefully at the graph on the previous page. Does the curve remind you of any others you have seen in this chapter?

_____

_____

_____

_____

_____

_____

Do you think it's a coincidence? It looks like the increase in greenhouse gases can explain why the Earth is getting warmer. But *why* is the amount of greenhouse gases increasing?

Of course, all plants and animals (humans included) release carbon dioxide into the atmosphere during respiration—think back to the carbon cycle. With more people on Earth than ever before, have humans created this problem just by breathing?

Not quite. Try to imagine life in North America at the beginning of the 1800s, before the amount of greenhouse gases in the atmosphere began to increase dramatically.

Do you know how people got around and how they heated and lit their homes before electricity was widely available?

_____

_____

_____

_____

Compare that to today. Today, most people get around by car, bus, train, airplane, and even boat. Almost all of these vehicles run on fossil fuels. To heat your home, you may burn natural gas (another fossil fuel) or use electricity, which often lights your home as well. Where does that electricity come from? A lot of it comes from burning fossil fuels. In other words, humans burn a lot of fossil fuels just for their normal daily activities.

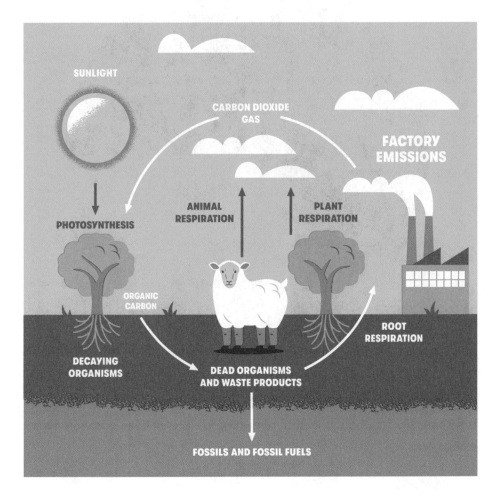

 As mentioned earlier, fossil fuels took millions of years to form, creating an underground store of carbon. Now, by quickly digging up and burning these fossil fuels, humans have unbalanced the carbon cycle, releasing an unprecedented amount of carbon dioxide into the atmosphere. Carbon emissions from burning fossil fuels are the largest source of greenhouse gases.

SOURCES OF GREENHOUSE GASES, WORLDWIDE

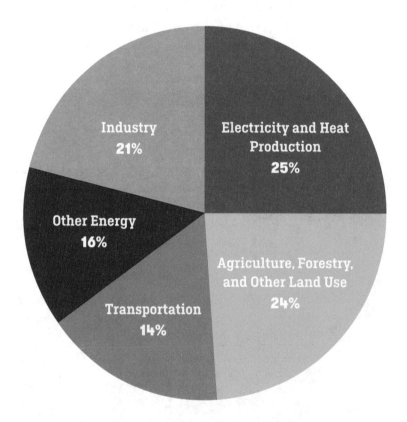

Of course, individual people are far from the only culprits in the rising carbon emissions. Industry also heavily relies on burning fossil fuels and is responsible for about one-fifth of the world's greenhouse gas emissions every year.

NATURAL CAUSES OF CLIMATE CHANGE

 So what about natural causes like volcanoes? When a volcano erupts, it emits a huge amount of smoke that contains carbon dioxide. But even active volcanoes that are not currently erupting are *degassing* (emitting gas) a little bit every day. Scientists estimate that all this volcanic activity contributes 645 million tons of carbon dioxide gas into the atmosphere every year. That's an enormous amount of greenhouse gas! By comparison, humans produce about 30 billion tons of carbon dioxide a year.

 To get a sense of the relative magnitude of these numbers, let's write them out in expanded form:

645 million = 645,000,000

30 billion = _____

COULD IT BE THE SUN?

Another possibility is that the Sun itself is warming the Earth more strongly than before. Could it be causing our planet to heat up independently of the greenhouse gases? Scientists have built models to see whether natural causes like these could explain global warming.

These models show with a high degree of certainty that "natural" causes alone could not cause the climate change we have seen in the past 120 years. Human activity, scientists believe, is a primary contributor to global warming.

WHAT ABOUT WATER VAPOR?

Carbon dioxide isn't the only greenhouse gas. Another culprit is water vapor.

 We learned in the previous chapter that water evaporates into the atmosphere as part of the water cycle. If global temperatures increase, more water will evaporate. This will lead to more water vapor in the atmosphere, increasing the amount of greenhouse gases even more.

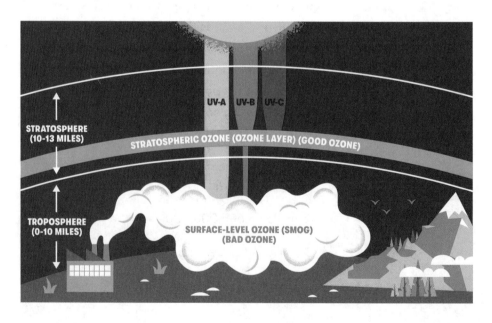

OZONE

 Now let's take a look at ozone. Ozone naturally occurs in the atmosphere. Think of it as Earth's sunscreen—it blocks a lot of the harmful ultraviolet (UV) rays coming from the Sun. These are the rays that cause sunburn and even skin cancer, which is why it is very important to wear sunscreen!

But ozone also occurs near the surface, driven by the burning of fossil fuels. So what's the difference? Ozone high up in the atmosphere is the good kind of ozone because it blocks harmful radiation. Ozone near the surface is the bad kind of ozone and can lead to health problems, especially lung issues like asthma.

Bad ozone increases with more and more burning of fossil fuels. Does this affect the ozone higher in the atmosphere? In a way, yes. Certain chemicals that were used a lot in industry in the 1900s emitted gases known as CFCs into the atmosphere. Many of those gases destroyed ozone particles.

 What do you think happened when the ozone particles were destroyed?

_____

_____

_____

_____

_____

WHAT CAN WE DO ABOUT IT?

 The good news is that being aware of the problem gives us a chance to fix it, or at least prepare for some of the consequences that we may be unable to prevent.

In fact, people began to realize that those CFCs were causing trouble in the atmosphere in the 1970s, and many industries changed the chemicals they used. And I bet you have heard that it is better for the environment to walk or ride a bike rather than drive somewhere. Let's dive a bit deeper.

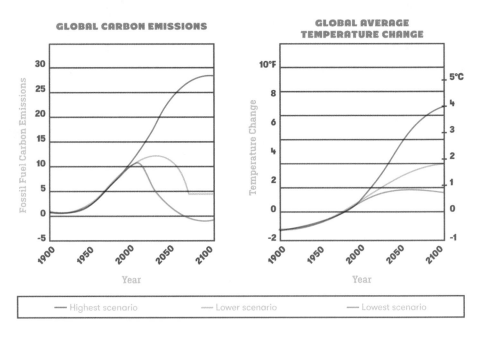

GLOBAL CARBON EMISSIONS

Fossil Fuel Carbon Emissions

30
25
20
15
10
5
0
-5

1900   1950   2000   2050   2100

Year

GLOBAL AVERAGE TEMPERATURE CHANGE

Temperature Change

10°F — 5°C
8 — 4
6 — 3
4 — 2
2 — 1
0 — 0
-2 — -1

1900   1950   2000   2050   2100

Year

— Highest scenario   — Lower scenario   — Lowest scenario

These graphs show three possible scenarios for greenhouse gas emissions from fossil fuel burning during the remainder of the twenty-first century (the 2000s). For each potential level of emissions, you can see the predicted rise in global temperatures.

CLEAN ENERGY

To limit the negative consequences of global warming, the best thing you can do is to reduce your use of fossil fuels as much as possible. In other words, humans need alternative forms of clean energy.

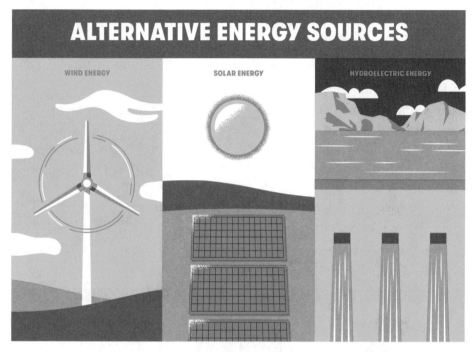

ALTERNATIVE ENERGY SOURCES

WIND ENERGY   SOLAR ENERGY   HYDROELECTRIC ENERGY

OTHER ALTERNATIVE ENERGY SOURCES: BIOENERGY AND GEOTHERMAL ENERGY

Clean energy doesn't release greenhouse gases—or any polluting gases—into the atmosphere. Renewable sources such as wind, sunlight, and running water can be used to generate electricity without polluting the atmosphere. While electricity from water needs to be set up in places with large rivers or waterfalls, energy from wind and the Sun can be gathered from any open piece of land or even on the roofs of buildings.

For example, the Sahara in Africa has been researched as a possible location to collect energy from wind and the Sun. Interestingly, climate researchers predict that the extra mixing of air created by wind farms would result in more clouds and rainfall, potentially turning the desert into a more livable place for people, plants, and animals. In an area of the world that struggles with water shortages, a wind or solar farm could really be a lifesaver!

OUR ACTIONS MATTER

You can try to conserve energy at home, including something as simple as choosing energy-efficient light bulbs for your desk lamp.

You can use public transportation or carpool whenever possible to reduce the number of vehicles on the road. These days, electric cars are also an option, and they will likely become more common and less expensive over time. If the weather permits, you can walk or ride a bike or scooter and feel great knowing that you're helping the environment and getting some exercise at the same time. You can also talk to adults about getting more involved in the future of the planet you will inherit.

Finally, you can look for ways to become a voice in your own community. For example, Greta Thunberg, a teenager from Sweden, has taken it upon herself to speak up to world leaders to fight for change. All of these small changes are part of *"reducing your carbon footprint,"* which simply means reducing your personal contribution to greenhouse gas emissions.

CHANGES TO THE OZONE LAYER OVER TIME

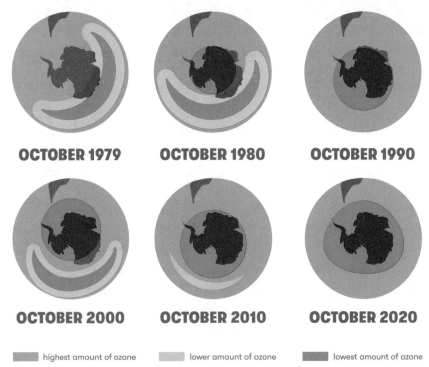

OCTOBER 1979   OCTOBER 1980   OCTOBER 1990

OCTOBER 2000   OCTOBER 2010   OCTOBER 2020

highest amount of ozone   lower amount of ozone   lowest amount of ozone

Now, let's circle back to that pesky ozone. Ozone exists in the stratospheric ozone layer all around Earth. But, for many reasons, the ozone over Antarctica has been more affected than most other locations. The opposite image shows the evolution of a large hole in the ozone layer above Antarctica over a period of nearly 40 years.

Can you use all of the knowledge you have gathered over the course of this chapter to explain why the hole in the ozone layer of the atmosphere changed? What do you think the ozone hole will look like in the future? Use the illustrations on the previous page to help form your opinion.

_____

_____

_____

_____

_____

_____

_____

CHAPTER 5 VOCABULARY

atmosphere: the envelope of air surrounding Earth.

biosphere: all of the living things on Earth.

clean energy: energy that comes from sources such as the Sun and wind. Also known as renewable energy.

climate change: significant changes in weather patterns and temperature over periods of time.

decomposers: various creatures that break down dead organisms and release carbon into the atmosphere, soil, and water.

drought: a long period without rain or other precipitation.

extreme weather events: very large and intense weather events such as tornados, tsunamis, and hurricanes.

fossil fuels: fuels that formed over millions of years from the remains of plants and animals under intense heat and pressure such as coal, petroleum or oil, and natural gas.

geosphere: the ground, the insides of Earth, the mountains, and other rocky parts of Earth.

global warming: the long-term increase of Earth's global surface temperature.

greenhouse effect: the process of Earth's atmosphere trapping heat and warming the planet.

greenhouse gases: gases in the atmosphere that are especially good at trapping heat inside of Earth's atmosphere, such as carbon dioxide and methane.

hydrosphere: all of the water on Earth including liquid, frozen, and vapor.

natural resources: resources such as water and oxygen that humans and other living organisms depend on that occur naturally.

non-renewable resource: natural resources that take an incredibly long time to replenish, such as coal and natural gas.

ores: rocks that contain enough of a valuable metal to make it worth mining.

photosynthesis: the process by which plants use carbon dioxide and convert it into sugars and starches that allow the plant to grow.

pollute: the addition of harmful substances that are difficult or impossible to remove.

renewable resources: natural resources that can be replaced in short periods of time, such as solar and wind.

respiration: the process of breathing.

CHAPTER 5 ANSWER KEY

PAGE 151

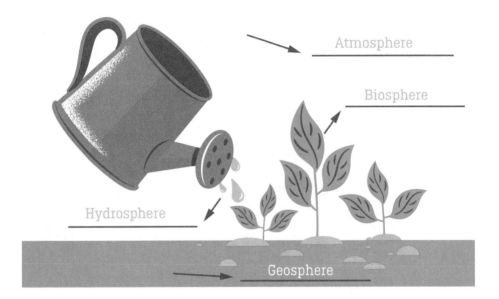

Atmosphere

Biosphere

Hydrosphere

Geosphere

PAGE 153

These are just a few examples; you may have thought of some other awesome ideas!

EARTH SPHERE	EXAMPLES THAT I USE IN EVERYDAY LIFE:
Atmosphere	Oxygen, sweat evaporates
Biosphere	What goes into your body also comes back out.
Geosphere	The battery in your smartphone relies on minerals that are mined
Hydrosphere	The water you drink comes back out again; you sweat when you exercise.

PAGE 154

	RENEWABLE RESOURCE	NON-RENEWABLE RESOURCE
Can be replaced in our lifetimes	X	
Used up faster than it is replaced		X
Coal		X
Air	X	
Metals		X
Wind	X	
Water	X	X (Clean water)
Natural gas		X

PAGE 162

Remember that you were supposed to guess! Therefore, [almost] any answer is acceptable. As you read on page 163, the vast majority of carbon exists below the Earth's surface.

PAGE 163

Burning of fossil fuels by humans increases the amount of carbon dioxide in the air. Therefore, maybe the ozone hole has something to do with the amount of carbon in the atmosphere, causing the hole to get bigger as more carbon goes into the atmosphere.

PAGE 164

More and more carbon will move from underground into the atmosphere, changing the balance of the carbon cycle.

YEAR	ESTIMATED WORLD POPULATION	% OF POPULATION GROWTH PER CENTURY
1400	400,000,000 (400 million)	You need the population for the year before to calculate this, but if you estimated 102%, you are pretty close based on population estimates in the year 1300.
1500	450,000,000	$\dfrac{450,000,000 \text{ (population in this century)}}{400,000,000 \text{ (population in last century)}} \times 100\%$ $\approx 113\%$
1600	550,000,000	$\dfrac{550,000,000}{450,000,000} \times 100\% \approx 122\%$
1700	550,000,000	109%
1800	600,000,000	167%
1900	1,000,000,000 (1 billion)	165%
2000	?	

From 1700 to 1800 and from 1800 to 1900, the world's population grew by about 165%. A scientist in 1900 might have expected this trend to continue, in which case he would predict the world's population in 2000 to be about 2.7 billion, because 1,650,000,000 (the population in 1900) × 165%/100= 2,722,500,000. The scientist might also have looked at earlier centuries and therefore predicted a smaller population increase. In any case, you would not expect the scientist's prediction for 2000 to be higher than 3 billion people based on the trends seen at the time—though in fact the world's population exceeded 6 billion in 2000!

PAGE 168

If the human population grows, even more land will be necessary for agriculture as well as built-up areas (cities, etc.). The only other habitable land available is already covered by lakes, rivers, forests, or shrubs. Humans need lakes and rivers, so this means cutting down forests or shrubs to expand agricultural areas. This will reduce habitats available for wild animals.

PAGE 170

According to this graph, from 1880 to 2020, the average air temperature increased by 1.1 degrees C. (It's also fine to round to 1°C.)

PAGE 171

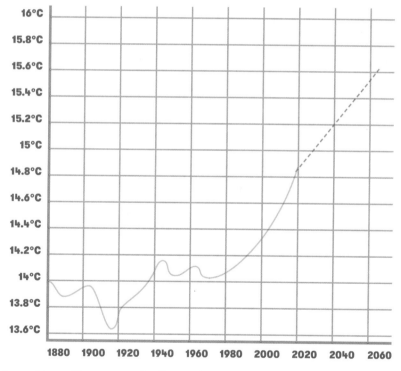

The line of best fit crosses the "2060" line between 15.8 and 16°C, or very close to that range. So this is the average predicted global temperature for that year. Your line of best fit may look slightly different and may cross the "2060" mark at a slightly different point.

PAGE 178

The shape of the curve from 1880 to 2020 is very similar to the global temperature curve. If you decided to graph the changes in global populations, you would also notice that it is very similar to that graph.

In the early 1800s, people mainly got around by horse or horse-drawn carriage, or by ship (powered by the wind) for long voyages. People used candles to light their homes and heated their houses primarily by burning wood. (People were beginning to also burn coal for heat, but mining coal was still a new and minor source of energy.)

PAGE 181

30 billion = 30,000,000,000

PAGE 183

Less ozone in the atmosphere means more dangerous ultraviolet (UV) radiation from the Sun reaches the surface.

PAGE 187

More ozone-harming gases that were pumped into the atmosphere caused more ozone to be destroyed, creating the hole in the atmosphere and allowing more dangerous UV radiation to reach Earth's surface. More ozone is being formed at the surface, but it doesn't affect the hole up in the atmosphere. Maybe as part of our efforts to reduce our carbon footprint, we can also figure out how to rebuild the ozone layer in the atmosphere to close the hole and protect all life from UV radiation.

NOTES

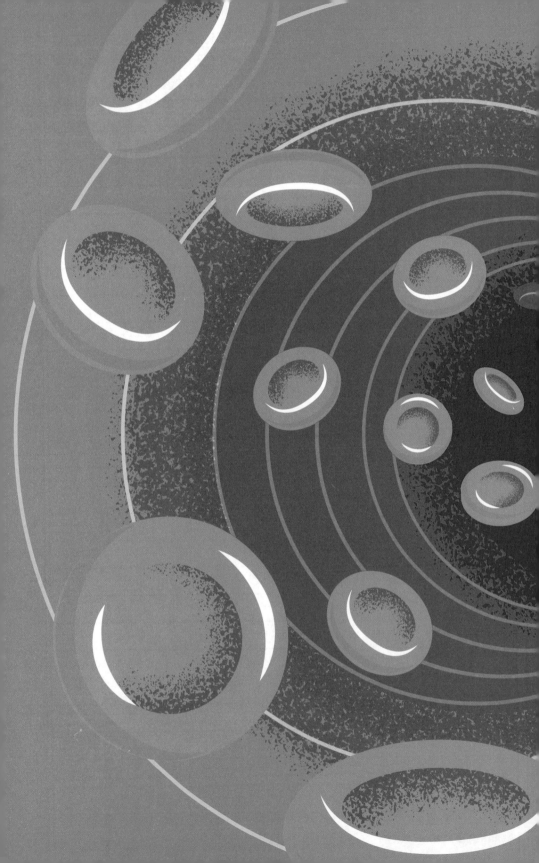

6 FROM CELLS TO ORGANISMS: STRUCTURES AND PROCESSES

Ouch! You got a cut on your leg. Did you know that the pain traveled through a nerve cell in your leg that can be a meter (about 36") long? And the blood that is slowly trickling out is made out of red blood cells, which are only about 6 micrometers in diameter—less than half the width of an average strand of human hair. Different as they are, those are not the only cells in the human body! All cells have specific functions. Let's find out more about them!

CHAPTER CONTENTS

How do all the different types of cells in your body help to heal that cut on your leg? Let's take a look!

EXPLORING THE LIVES OF CELLS

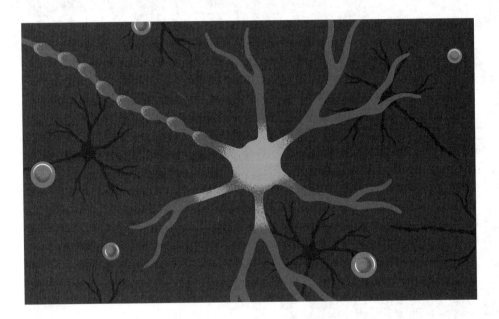

 Find the smallest object you can. If it looks like a speck of dust with your eyes, you might discover with a magnifying glass that it is a tiny living spider.

Four hundred years ago, people would not have known that humans and spiders have living cells in common! That all changed with the invention of the **microscope**.

THE INVENTION OF THE MICROSCOPE

The invention of the light microscope allowed scientists to see cells for the first time. English scientist Robert Hooke (1635–1703) built a microscope with three lenses. While considered cutting edge at the time, it is feeble compared to today's powerful tools. Now, scientists use electron microscopes to study cells at the molecular level.

Robert Hooke published a book of drawings he made while looking at living things through a microscope, such as insects and plants. One of the most sensational things in his book was, believe it or not, a picture of cork: the stuff used to plug wine bottles, which comes from tree bark. Under the microscope, Hooke could see that cork consisted of neat rows of tiny rectangles that he called "cells."

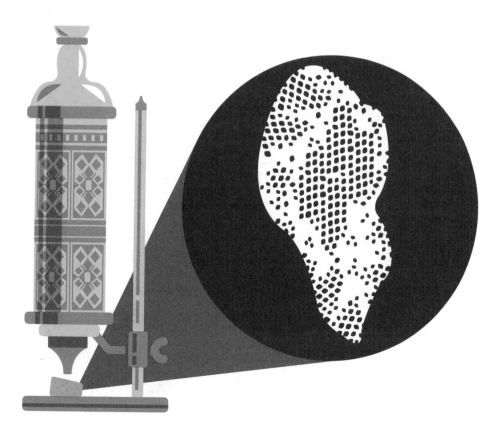

Hooke's book inspired other people to try looking at everyday stuff under a microscope. Antonie van Leeuwenhoek (1632–1723), a Dutch businessman who conducted science experiments as a hobby, even built his own microscope in his spare time. Van Leeuwenhoek was the first person to observe human red blood cells and bacteria under a microscope. The more organisms scientists observed, the stronger the evidence that all organisms were made up of these cells. The link between cells and life became clear to microscopists during the 1830s. This led to their conclusion that all living things are made up of one or more cells. Cells, then, are the basic units of life. You will see that cells come in many sizes and shapes and have specific structures to carry out their functions.

Further work by Rudolph Virchow (1821–1902) on living organisms showed that cells self-reproduce and that every cell comes from a cell that existed before it. Observations of living things under the microscope continued, until finally, plant biologist Matthias Schleiden (1804–1881) and animal biologist Theodor Schwann (1810–1882) proposed a far-reaching idea called Cell Theory. Let's take a look at its main points:

CELL THEORY

1. All living things are made up of one or more cells.
2. Cells are the basic unit of life.
3. All new cells are produced from existing cells.

Determine if the following statements are true or false.

_____ Some living creatures are made up of a single cell.

_____ All cells are basically identical in size and shape.

_____ Microscopes are made out of lenses.

_____ Virchow determined that cells contain DNA.

MICROSCOPE TECHNOLOGY

Improvements have vastly increased the range of visibility of microscopes and the preparation of the specimens to be studied. This in turn led to discoveries in science.

c. 1590	The first light microscope is invented in Europe.
1665	Hooke publishes drawings of living things seen under a light microscope.
1675	Leeuwenhoek makes his own microscope and observes animal cells and bacteria.
1678	Jan Swammerdam makes first known drawing of human red blood cells.
1830	Joseph Lister improves microscopes by placing two lenses at different distances.
1830	Matthias Schleiden and Theodor Schwann propose Cell Theory.
1938	Ernst Ruska invents the electron microscope.
1981	The invention of scanning technology makes 3-D images possible.
2017	Lawrence Berkeley National Laboratory builds the most powerful electron microscope to date.

ONE OR MANY?

It turns out that we have this in common with spiders and even grass: each of us is made up of lots of cells. That makes us multicellular organisms. On the other hand, the smallest organisms only contain one cell—in other words, they are unicellular. Look at the examples on the next page.

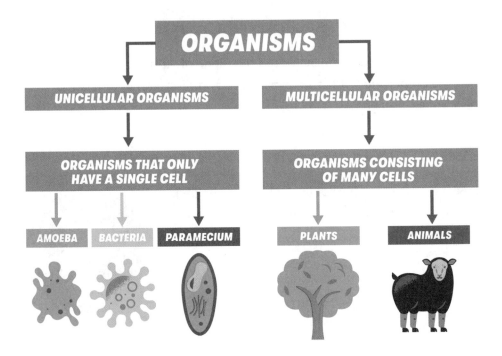

ORGANISMS

UNICELLULAR ORGANISMS

MULTICELLULAR ORGANISMS

ORGANISMS THAT ONLY HAVE A SINGLE CELL

ORGANISMS CONSISTING OF MANY CELLS

AMOEBA   BACTERIA   PARAMECIUM

PLANTS

ANIMALS

 For each item below, try to decide whether it describes a unicellular organism or a multicellular organism. Check the correct column for each item.

ITEM	UNICELLULAR ORGANISMS	MULTICELLULAR ORGANISMS
Can be seen with the naked eye		
An amoeba (a tiny creature that lives in pond water)		
A sunflower		
One cell performs all the functions that are necessary for life		
A fish		
Can only be seen with the aid of a microscope		

Streptococcus pneumoniae (a type of bacteria that can cause the illness pneumonia)		
Different cells perform different functions that are necessary for life		

THE BUSINESS OF BEING A CELL

All cells, no matter how big or small the organism they are part of, must perform many basic functions during their lives.

You might compare a cell to a busy restaurant that is open 24 hours a day, seven days a week. Raw materials are brought in to make food. Some food is eaten in the restaurant, and some is taken out. Sometimes food is prepared ahead of time. Wastes are removed or recycled. Similarly, your cells are taking in nutrients, secreting and storing chemicals, and making and breaking down substances.

Every good restaurant needs a good manager to organize operations and pass on information to employees. Likewise, a cell carries the instructions to direct all cell activities, including cell division, or reproduction. A cell also knows how to interact with other cells and how to remove unnecessary materials from within itself.

Cells are filled with a substance called cytoplasm. Within the cytoplasm of animal and plant cells are structures called organelles. Just like your internal organs, such as the heart and brain, perform different important functions inside your body, so do the organelles inside a cell. Some organelles process energy, while others manufacture substances needed by the cell or other cells. Certain organelles move materials, while others are storage sites. Animal and plant cells are surrounded by a membrane, and so are many of the organelles. Although all cells have functions in common, not all cells are the same.

Let's start by looking at animal cells (and that includes human cells as well).

A TOUR OF AN ANIMAL CELL

With one of the earliest microscopes, Leeuwenhoek was able to see a key feature of animal cells: their external boundary, which we now call the cell membrane.

CELL MEMBRANE

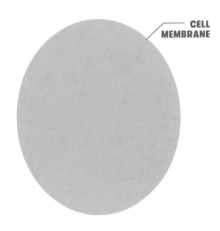

You can also think of a cell as a house. If you open a window to get some fresh air, there is usually a screen to keep the bugs out. For the cell, the cell membrane is its window screen, and its job is to control what gets into the cell as well as what gets out.

THE CYTOPLASM

The cytoplasm inside cells is a gelatin-like fluid in which the cell's organelles float. Many chemical reactions occur within the cytoplasm. The cytoplasm is also important because it gives the animal cell its shape.

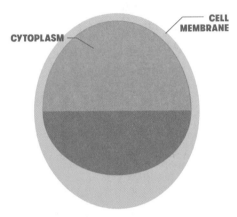

THE NUCLEUS

The nucleus is separated from the cytoplasm by a membrane. Materials enter and leave the nucleus through openings in this membrane. The genetic material (DNA) in the nucleus contains the instructions for everything the cell does. Basically, the nucleus is the control center of the cell.

MITOCHONDRIA

Mitochondria are organelles that release energy from the breakdown of food. This energy then gets used by the cell. Mitochondria are sometimes called "the powerhouse of the cell." You can compare them to a power plant that provides electricity for a city. The more active a cell is, the more mitochondria will be found in it. Your muscle cells have large numbers of mitochondria!

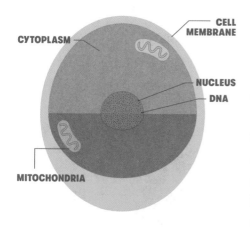

THE ENDOPLASMIC RETICULUM

The endoplasmic reticulum, or ER, looks like a bunch of tubes that extend from the nucleus to the cell membrane. Materials are processed and moved around within these tubes.

The ER may be "rough" or "smooth." When you look at the rough ER with an electron microscope, you can see that it has what looks like little black dots on it. These tiny organelles are called ribosomes, and they actually build proteins. The smooth ER has no attached ribosomes. It processes other substances such as lipids. You

can think of the ER as a large network of manufacturing plants.

THE GOLGI APPARATUS

The Golgi apparatus looks like a stack of membranes seen in profile, and it is usually found near the nucleus and the ER. It was named after Camillo Golgi (1843–1926), the Italian scientist who first discovered it. Its job is to sort, package, and deliver proteins and other cellular substances to areas inside the cell. It also carries substances to the cell membrane where they are released out of the cell. Like a warehouse, it ships packages and goods all over the body.

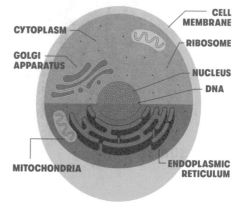

THE LYSOSOME

The lysosome looks like a small spherical object inside the animal cell. Its job is to break down or digest parts of the cell that no longer work. After the breakdown, the cell can use the pieces to build something new. In that way, the lysosome is like the cell's waste management and recycling facility.

Wow! Who knew there was so much going on inside our tiny cells? But if animal cells are that complex, what about plant cells? It turns out that they are just as busy.

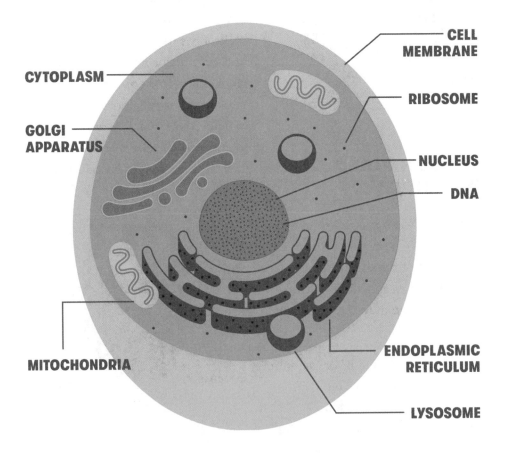

CELL MEMBRANE

CYTOPLASM

RIBOSOME

GOLGI APPARATUS

NUCLEUS

DNA

MITOCHONDRIA

ENDOPLASMIC RETICULUM

LYSOSOME

INSIDE A PLANT CELL

 Take a look at this plant cell. Do any organelles look familiar from the animal cell? Label as many as you can.

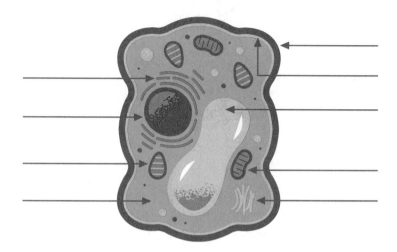

There are probably a few organelles that you can't label yet. Let's take a look at them one by one.

THE CELL WALL

You may have noticed that the plant cell has a different shape than the animal cell you saw before. That's due to the cell wall, a second, more rigid border outside the cell membrane. Think of it like the window frame holding a screen in place. The cell wall helps the plant cell to keep its shape, provides support, and like the cell membrane, helps control what gets in and out of the cell.

CHLOROPLASTS

In some plant cells, there are green organelles in the cytoplasm called chloroplasts. Chloroplasts contain chlorophyll, which gives many leaves and stems their green color. The chloroplast's job is to capture energy from the Sun's rays, which is then used to make food for the plant.

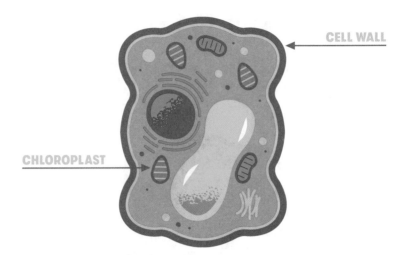

THE VACUOLE

That big empty-looking blob inside plant cells is called a vacuole. The vacuole, which has a large membrane-bound space filled with water, maintains water balance and pressure inside the plant cell. If the vacuole doesn't have enough water in it, it shrinks in size, making the plant cell "cave in," and if all the plant cells similarly cave, they make the whole plant droop.

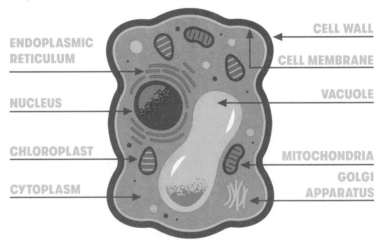

Imagine you're a biologist doing a presentation to a bunch of scientists, and your slides accidentally get mixed up. Can you put them in order just by looking at them under the microscope? See if you can label each as either plant or animal cells.

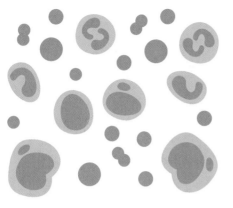

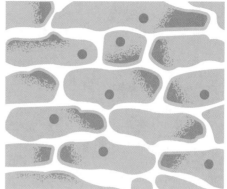

Label:_____

Label:_____

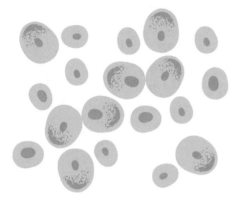

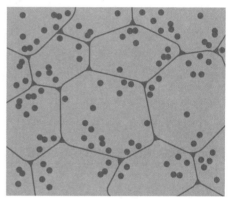

Label:_____

Label:_____

 The yellow cells at the top right are from an onion plant. Why do you think they might be missing chloroplasts?

_____

_____

_____

_____

_____

Which structures are NOT found in both animal and plant cells?

A. Mitochondria

B. Cell membranes

C. Chloroplasts

D. Golgi apparatus

COMPLETE THE CONCEPT MAP OF CELL ORGANELLES

A concept map shows how pieces of information are related to each other, such as a family tree. Check out this concept map about cell organelles. Organelles have several different functions. Fill in the blanks to complete the concept map of cell organelles.

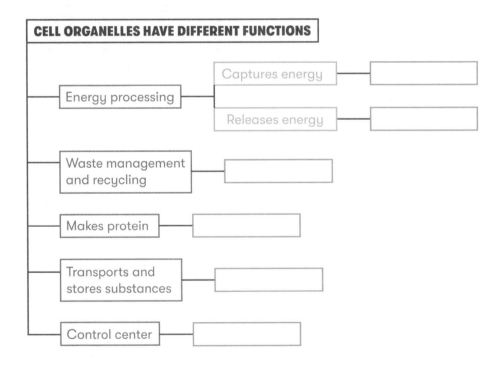

CELL ORGANELLES HAVE DIFFERENT FUNCTIONS

Energy processing
- Captures energy
- Releases energy

Waste management and recycling

Makes protein

Transports and stores substances

Control center

A BRIEF LOOK AT BACTERIAL CELLS

Back in the seventeenth century, Leeuwenhoek did something fun: he asked two old men who had never brushed their teeth in their lives to give him a sample of their saliva. He described what he saw under the microscope: ". . . an unbelievably great company of living animalcules, a-swimming more nimbly than any I had ever seen up to this time." Those were bacteria, having a blast in a mouth that had never seen toothpaste.

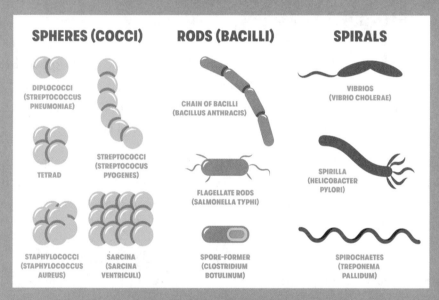

If you saw bacteria under the microscope, would you be able to tell? Here are a few clues that could tip you off that you're looking at bacteria rather than plant or animal cells:

- Bacteria have both a cell membrane and a cell wall.

- Bacteria have no nucleus.

- Bacteria are a lot smaller than plant or animal cells.

- Bacteria come in a few possible shapes: spheres (like a ball), rods (like a pill capsule), and spirals.

TRANSPORT ACROSS THE CELL MEMBRANE

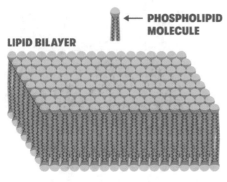

LIPID BILAYER

← **PHOSPHOLIPID MOLECULE**

STRUCTURE OF A CELL MEMBRANE

The cell membrane is like a window screen that keeps insects out. It will let some things through more easily than others.

The cell membrane is a strong yet flexible double layer of phospholipid molecules. Phospholipid molecules are molecules in which the head (the side pointing outward from the surface) is attracted to liquids, such as water, and the tail (the side pointing inward) avoids the same liquids. These properties make the cell membrane super picky about what substances to let through.

Substances can cross this structure by slipping between phospholipid molecules or through special passageways (not shown). Cells take in food, oxygen, and other substances from the environment and release waste back into the environment.

The cell membrane also protects the cell from foreign or harmful substances. If a virus or bacterium is present, the cell membrane may spot it as being harmful and block it from getting into the cell. Let's take a closer look at how things get in and out of a cell.

DIFFUSION

Diffusion is the simplest type of membrane transport, which works only for small molecules that can pass in between phospholipids, sort of like going through the gaps in a fence. Carbon dioxide and oxygen are two substances that can get across the cell membrane by diffusion. It is important to note that, in diffusion, substances only move from where their concentration is high to where their concentration is low. This is called traveling down their concentration gradient.

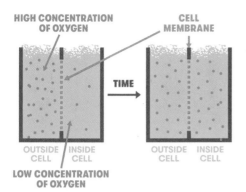

For example, if there is a lot of oxygen outside the cell and very little inside the cell, some oxygen will move into the cell. After a while, there will be an equal concentration of oxygen inside and outside of the cell.

OSMOSIS

The diffusion of water through a cell membrane is called osmosis. Water is just so special to living things that its transport across the membrane gets its own name. When water moves across the membrane, it also moves from a high concentration of water molecules to a low concentration of water molecules.

ACTIVE TRANSPORT

Sometimes, a substance is needed inside a cell even though the amount of that substance inside the cell is already greater than the amount outside the cell. For example, root cells need minerals like sodium, potassium, and calcium from soil. Mineral molecules tend to move out of the root by diffusion because there are more of them inside the root cells than outside. Active transport requires root cells to use up energy in order to move minerals back into the cell across the cell membrane.

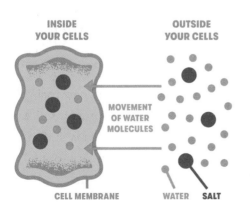

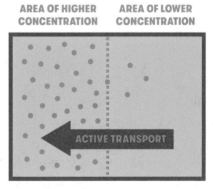

What could happen if an animal cell is placed in pure water?

A. It would swell and burst.

B. It would shrink.

What do you think happens after a plant has been watered?

_____

_____

What is it called when cells use energy to move molecules?

A. Diffusion

B. Osmosis

C. Active transport

D. Transfusion

HOMEOSTASIS: STAYING STABLE

Cells are always trying to stay stable in order to function properly. For example, a healthy root cell maintains the proper mineral and water content inside the cell. The ability of a cell (or organism) to keep stable conditions inside even when the conditions outside of the cell change, is called maintaining homeostasis. All living things maintain homeostasis, not just cells, but whole animals and plants too. Part of the homeostasis of your body is maintaining a normal body temperature and blood pressure. That's why they are some of the first things your doctor examines during a check up. If homeostasis is disrupted (like when you have a fever or your blood pressure is too low), that's a good indicator of something going wrong in your body—and that's also true for individual cells.

A cell's organelles work together to help it maintain homeostasis. The cell membrane has an especially important role in this, because it needs to make sure the amount of water in the cell and the concentrations of key minerals like sodium and potassium stay within a certain range. If a cell has too little water, it can shrivel up, while too much water can cause it to burst.

REGULATING WATER BALANCE IS PART OF MAINTAINING HOMEOSTASIS

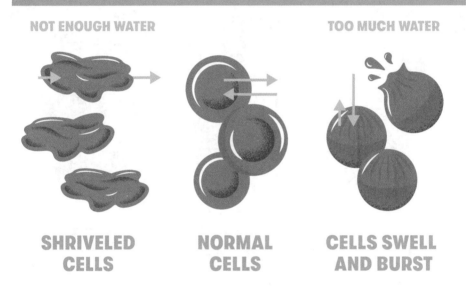

NOT ENOUGH WATER

TOO MUCH WATER

SHRIVELED CELLS

NORMAL CELLS

CELLS SWELL AND BURST

The wrong amounts of minerals can also cause cells to malfunction, particularly for cells with special jobs, like brain cells and heart cells.

SPECIALIZED CELLS

Your body contains trillions of cells, but they are not all the same. A cell in your skin, a cell in the muscle in your leg, and a cell in your brain all look very different, despite having a cell membrane and the organelles we have already discussed. That's because these cells are specialized for particular functions in your body.

For example, they differ in shape. A cell in your brain has to send electrical signals to other cells in your brain, so it has outgrowths like tiny wires reaching out to touch other brain cells. A muscle cell has to move your body by getting shorter (contracting) and longer (relaxing), so it is long and cylinder-shaped, like a bungee cord. A red blood cell needs to carry oxygen to every part of your body, so it is shaped like a caved-in disk that won't get stuck in narrow blood vessels.

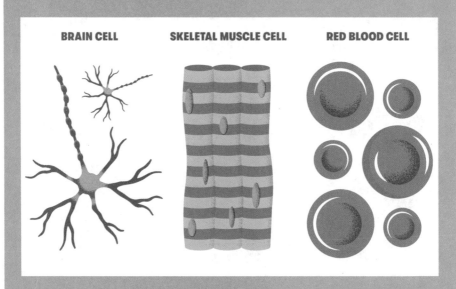

BRAIN CELL   **SKELETAL MUSCLE CELL**   **RED BLOOD CELL**

In addition, cells in your body differ in how many of each type of organelle they contain, and some cells even have key organelles missing on purpose. For example, a brain cell has one nucleus, just like you would expect. However, a muscle cell in your calf can run the whole length of your calf, so it has lots of nuclei (sometimes several hundred!) that control different segments of the cell. And finally, a red blood cell has no nucleus at all. That's how it can maintain that caved-in shape, because there is no nucleus taking up space in the middle. Of course, a cell without a nucleus to take charge of things can only survive so long, which is why red blood cells only live a few months before needing to be replaced with new cells.

Now that you have gained some knowledge about what cells are and how they work, can you start to answer the question from the beginning of the chapter?

How do all the different types of cells in your body help to heal that cut on your leg?

_____

_____

_____

_____

_____

_____

CELLULAR REPRODUCTION

One key function of a cell is reproduction, or making copies of itself. When a cell makes a copy of itself, it is called cell division. Before a cell can divide, it has to form two nuclei in a series of steps. Once the nucleus divides, the cytoplasm separates to form two new cells. There are two types of cell division: mitosis and meiosis.

MEIOSIS AND MITOSIS

In mitosis, two nuclei are formed that are identical to each other. Once the process of mitosis is complete, the cell divides into two identical new cells.

In meiosis, the nucleus of a special reproductive cell divides twice to produce four gametes. Gametes are special cells needed for reproduction.

As you know, the nucleus of a cell contains genetic material. Why is it important for a cell to copy its hereditary information before dividing?

_____

_____

_____

_____

Here is a summary of where mitosis and meiosis occur and what their purpose is:

UNICELLULAR ORGANISM	MULTICELLULAR ORGANISM
Mitosis followed by division is how it reproduces, making two organisms out of one.	Mitosis followed by cell division allows the organism to make new cells so it can grow larger and develop.
	Mitosis followed by cell division serves to replace cells that are old or damaged with new cells.
	Meiosis followed by cell division allows the organism to create gametes—sperm and egg cells that are necessary for the organism to reproduce.

Let's look at mitosis first to see how most cells manage the task of making a copy of themselves.

MITOSIS

In mitosis, a cell divides into two cells, making an identical copy of itself. The cell is filled with essential organelles, the most important one of which is the nucleus, containing the cell's genetic material. The cell must make a copy of everything and then neatly organize it and split it up equally between the two new cells. When the nucleus divides, chromosomes play the important part. A chromosome is a structure in the nucleus that actually contains the genetic material. Before mitosis begins, each chromosome duplicates. Then each chromosome coils tightly into two thick strands that are identical, called chromatids. It's not an easy task for a cell to divide, which is why the cell has a whole system consisting of five steps: interphase, prophase, metaphase, anaphase, and telophase.

MITOSIS

  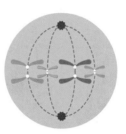 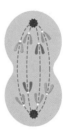 

1. INTERPHASE **2. PROPHASE** **3. METAPHASE** **4. ANAPHASE** **5. TELOPHASE**

 To help you remember the order of these phases, make up a creative mnemonic by starting each word with the first letter of a phase of mitosis. For example, you could use something like, **"I** p**r**efer **m**ilk **a**nd **t**ea."** Go ahead, make one of your own.

I _____

P _____

M _____

A _____

T _____

THE PHASES OF MITOSIS

INTERPHASE

Interphase is the phase between cell divisions. During this phase, the cell grows and prepares for mitosis by making sure it has the materials needed for the next phase. Toward the end of interphase, DNA (the genetic material) is copied and chromosomes duplicate.

PROPHASE

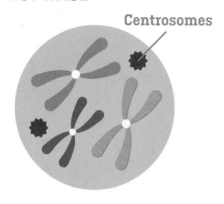

Centrosomes

This cell has six chromosomes. The cell gets ready to split up the duplicated genetic material equally. Since the DNA has been copied during interphase, each chromosome now has an identical copy. The copies are called chromatids. To keep track of the duplicates, the cell keeps each chromatid attached to its copy, forming an X-like shape.

consists of two organelles called centrosomes that migrate to opposite ends of the cell, kind of like a north and south pole. Between them, the cell sets up fibers running from one pole to the other. These are made of proteins. The paired sister chromatids, which are identical copies of the chromosome attached together at a point called a centromere, then attach to these fibers.

METAPHASE

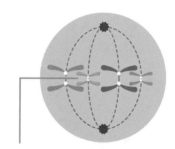

Lining up of chromosomes on the metaphase plate

In metaphase, the sister chromatids line up along the center of the cell, exactly midway between the two poles of the spindle apparatus. This imaginary line is called the metaphase plate.

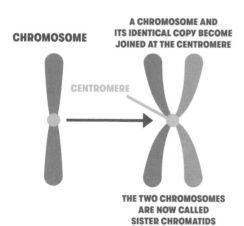

CHROMOSOME

A CHROMOSOME AND ITS IDENTICAL COPY BECOME JOINED AT THE CENTROMERE

CENTROMERE

THE TWO CHROMOSOMES ARE NOW CALLED SISTER CHROMATIDS

To organize splitting up the chromatids equally, the cell forms a so-called spindle apparatus. This

ANAPHASE

In anaphase, the sister chromatids separate and are pulled apart to opposite poles of the cell.

TELOPHASE

This is the final step of mitosis. The cell has divided the genetic material equally between the two ends of the cell. It can now take apart the spindle apparatus. The chromosomes loosen and uncoil,

and a nucleus starts to form around the genetic material at each end of the cell. At the same time, the cell is starting to split up into two cells. This process has its own name: cytokinesis.

CYTOKINESIS

Cytokinesis looks a little different depending on whether the cell is an animal or plant cell. That's because plant cells have a cell wall, while animal cells do not. In an animal cell, special proteins form a band across the middle of the cell (called a "furrow"), pinching it in two. Picture tying a string around the middle of a balloon and then slowly tightening the string, so that the balloon becomes like two joined spheres. That's what the proteins do to the animal cell.

In a plant cell, a new cell wall starts to form along the midline between the two poles. It starts forming from the middle of the cell, moving toward the sides until there is a complete cell wall separating the two new cells.

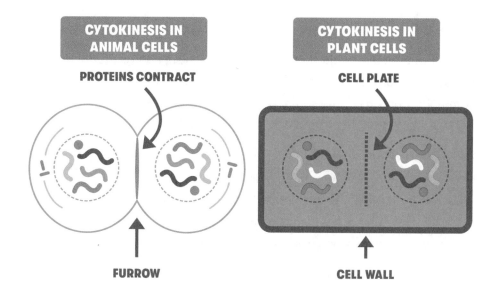

CYTOKINESIS IN ANIMAL CELLS

PROTEINS CONTRACT

FURROW

CYTOKINESIS IN PLANT CELLS

CELL PLATE

CELL WALL

There are now two identical new cells in place of the original cell.

Check-in questions:

True/False: Each cell produced by mitosis and cell division has the same number and type of chromosomes as the original cell.

When do chromosomes duplicate during a cell's life cycle?

A. Telophase

B. Interphase

C. Anaphase

D. Metaphase

When do chromatids separate during mitosis?

A. Telophase

B. Anaphase

C. Metaphase

D. Prophase

MEIOSIS

Sexual reproduction is another way a new organism can be produced. Two sex cells, also called an egg and a sperm, come together from two different organisms of the same species. A new organism grows from the cell that forms from the joined egg and sperm cell.

The human body forms two types of cells: body cells and sex cells. Body cells have 46 chromosomes, or 23 pairs of chromosomes. The chromosomes in each pair are similar to each other in size, shape, and genetic material (DNA). Sex cells do not have pairs of chromosomes. Human sex cells have only 23 chromosomes, one from each pair of similar chromosomes.

Each species of organism has a certain number of chromosomes.

This picture shows the number of chromosomes in body cells and sex cells of a mosquito:

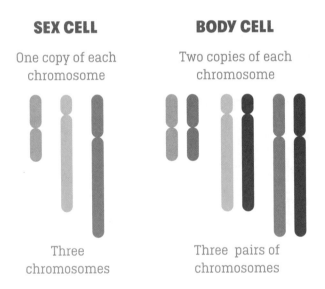

SEX CELL

One copy of each
chromosome

Three
chromosomes

BODY CELL

Two copies of each
chromosome

Three pairs of
chromosomes

After two sex cells combine, a cell is produced (zygote) that has the normal number of pairs of chromosomes of the organism's body cells. What would happen in sexual reproduction if two cells with 23 pairs of chromosomes combined? The offspring would have twice as many chromosomes as the parents! This is where the process of meiosis comes in. Meiosis produces sex cells with half the number of chromosomes than a body cell; one of each pair of chromosomes.

During meiosis, two divisions of the nucleus occur. These divisions are called meiosis I and II. The steps of each division are similar to those in mitosis.

To make it simpler, this diagram shows the process of meiosis in an organism with only two pairs of chromosomes.

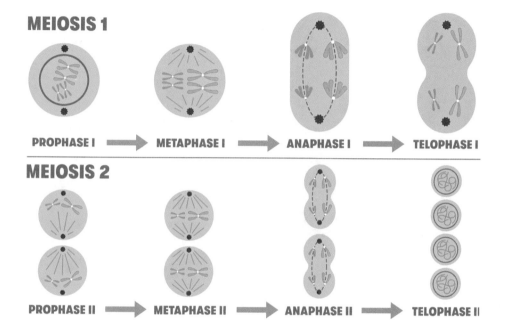

MEIOSIS 1

PROPHASE I → METAPHASE I → ANAPHASE I → TELOPHASE I

MEIOSIS 2

PROPHASE II → METAPHASE II → ANAPHASE II → TELOPHASE II

Let's summarize the key similarities and differences between the two types of cell division. Try to complete the table below.

	MITOSIS	MEIOSIS
Number of new cells produced		4
Type of cells produced	Identical	
Names of phases		
Number of times cytokinesis occurs	1	
What is the purpose?		To produce gametes with half the number of chromosomes

Does this new knowledge about how cells reproduce help you answer the question from the beginning of the chapter? How do all the different types of cells in your body help that cut on your leg heal?

_____

_____

_____

_____

THE BODY'S SYSTEMS

Cells within your body are constantly reproducing to replace damaged or dead cells. In fact, the average adult human body has between 30 and 40 *trillion* (30,000,000,000,000–40,000,000,000,000) cells. Let's take a closer to look to see how all of those cells are organized within your body.

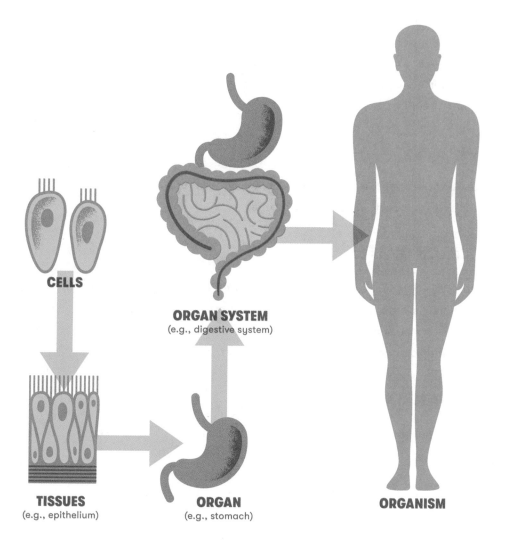

CELLS

TISSUES
(e.g., epithelium)

ORGAN
(e.g., stomach)

ORGAN SYSTEM
(e.g., digestive system)

ORGANISM

BODY CELLS

Cells in multicellular organisms do not work alone. They carry out their own functions but depend in some ways on other cells in the organism.

TISSUES

Cells that work together in the body to perform a specific function form a tissue. For example, muscle tissue consists of muscle cells that contract and relax together, moving some part of your body. A tissue can consist of many cells of the same type or can be a mixture of a few different types of cells. For example, your blood is a tissue that contains different types of cells: red blood cells, white blood cells, and platelets. Each of these cells has its own separate job, and together, they perform the function of blood: transporting oxygen and nutrients to every part of your body and fighting off infections.

ORGANS

Several different types of tissues come together to make up an organ, such as the heart, lungs, brain, or eye.

ORGAN SYSTEMS

An organ system consists of several organs with related functions that all work together to accomplish a larger goal. For example, your digestive system consists of the stomach, liver, intestine, and other organs that work together to extract nutrients from the food you eat.

ORGANISM

Multiple organ systems together make up an organism. For example, your body consists of eleven organ systems.

BODY SYSTEMS WORKING TOGETHER

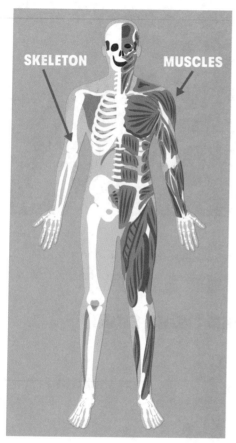

SKELETON   MUSCLES

do this: the skeletal system and the muscular system. The skeleton is like the framework of your body, and your muscles allow you to adjust this rigid framework by moving it. Both organ systems work together to structurally support and protect your internal organs.

THE DIGESTIVE SYSTEM

Other systems work together to help an organism to reproduce, digest food, get rid of wastes, and transport oxygen and nutrients around its body. All of this allows the organism to survive, grow, and pass on its genes to the next generation.

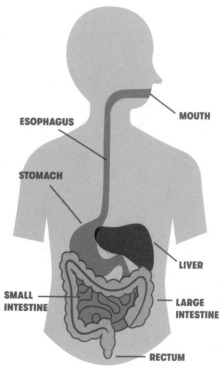

ESOPHAGUS   MOUTH

STOMACH

LIVER

SMALL INTESTINE   LARGE INTESTINE

RECTUM

THE MUSCULOSKELETAL SYSTEM

Several organ systems will band together to accomplish a larger mission. For example, one important task is to support your body structurally, so that you don't become a shapeless blob. Two organ systems work together to

CARDIOVASCULAR SYSTEM

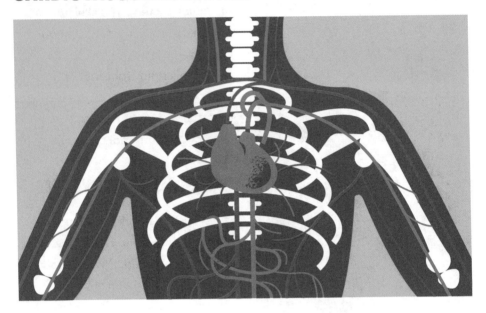

While that is happening, your cardiovascular system—your heart and blood vessels—is busy supplying your entire body with oxygen.

THE INTEGUMENTARY SYSTEM (YOUR SKIN!)

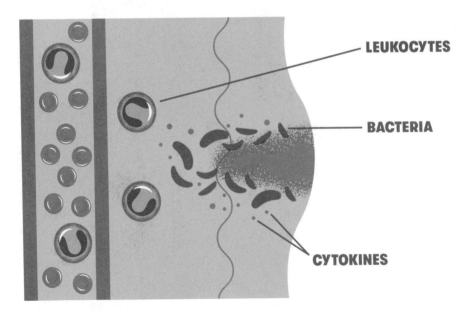

LEUKOCYTES

BACTERIA

CYTOKINES

Organs also defend your body from threats in the external environment, like harsh chemicals, bacteria that cause diseases, or wounds. To accomplish this, your skin, which is, believe it or not, an organ system in itself, works together with your immune system. Different types of cells arrive to assess the situation at a cut site and start cleaning out the dead and damaged skin cells and any bacteria that may have entered through the cut. After the clean-out stage, new cells begin to rebuild the tissue, such as the skin. This is when that thick scab builds up over the cut. It's important to leave the scab where it is to protect the cut beneath it. After the tissue is rebuilt, the new skin and tissue cells are further developed to remove the scab and smooth out newly rebuilt skin.

 Check-in questions:

1. Cells of multicellular organisms are organized into _____, organs, and organ systems.

2. *True/False*: All cells within a tissue are identical.

3. Muscle cells are an example of

    A. cell division

    B. meiosis

    C. a specialized cell

    D. a gamete

THE CONTROL SYSTEM

Your body constantly receives information from body systems and changes in the environment and responds in order to maintain homeostasis. To cope with this enormous task, your body needs a central control center.

Your various sensory receptors, such as light receptors in your eyes, touch receptors in your skin, and sound receptors in your ears, react to new information from the world around you. That new information is called stimuli (singular: stimulus). When sensory receptors detect new stimuli, they send this information along nerves, which are like fast fiber-optic cables, to your brain. Your brain cells then process the information and decide what to do about it. They can issue a command, which travels via nerves to your muscles, causing your muscles to move. This muscle movement is called a response to the stimulus.

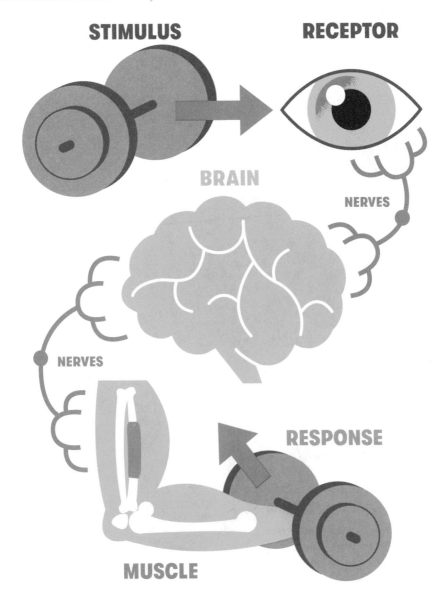

STIMULUS   **RECEPTOR**

BRAIN

NERVES

NERVES

RESPONSE

MUSCLE

Alternatively, your brain can decide to store away the information as a memory and not do anything about it for now.

What are the main body systems that work together to heal a cut on your finger? Circle all that apply.

A. The digestive system

B. The reproductive system

C. The integumentary system

D. The immune system

To sum up, our bodies are amazing machines! First you learned that all living things are made up of cells, which are the smallest units of living matter. Some organisms may be made of just one cell (unicellular), while others may consist of many different numbers and types of cells (multicellular). Cells have special organelles that are responsible for particular functions, for example, the nucleus contains genetic information and ribosomes make proteins. The cell membrane forms the boundary that controls what enters and exits the cell. In multicellular organisms, like us, the body consists of cells, tissues, organs, and organ systems. All of the cells that make up the various parts of the whole system work together and are specialized for particular functions.

Wow, aren't cells amazing? Can you use all of your amazing new knowledge about cells to further develop your understanding of the question from the beginning of this chapter?

How do all the different types of cells in your body help to heal that cut on your leg?

_____

_____

_____

CHAPTER 6 VOCABULARY

active transport: the process in which root cells use up energy in order to move minerals back into the cell across the cell membrane.

anaphase: the process of sister chromatids separating and being pulled apart to opposite poles of the cell. The fourth of five steps during mitosis.

cell: the basic biological unit that makes up an organism.

cell division: the process in which a cell makes a copy of itself.

cell membrane: the outer boundary of a cell.

cell theory: the theory that all living things are made up of one or more cells, cells are the basic unit of life, and all new cells are produced from existing cells.

cell wall: a rigid outer border surrounding the cell membrane in plant cells.

centromere: the location where a pair of sister chromatids are joined together.

centrosomes: organelles that migrate from the nucleus to opposite ends of the cell.

chloroplasts: the organelles in plant cells that contain chlorophyll, which gives the leaves and stems of plants a green color and captures energy from the Sun to make food.

chromosome: a structure in the nucleus of cells that contains the genetic material. The human body, for example, contains 23 pairs of chromosomes (46 in total).

concentration gradient: the changing concentration of particles between an area with high concentration and an area with low concentration.

cytokinesis: the division of one cell into two cells; the final step of meiosis.

cytoplasm: a semi-fluid substance inside of a cell in which the cell's organelles float.

diffusion: the simplest type of membrane transport in which small molecules can pass in between phospholipids.

endoplasmic reticulum: a bunch of tubes that extend from the nucleus of a cell to the cell membrane that process and move materials.

gametes: an organism's reproductive, or sex, cells. In humans, those are sperm and egg cells.

Golgi apparatus: the portion of the cell that sorts, packages, and delivers proteins and other cellular substances to other areas inside the cell.

homeostasis: the ability for a cell to maintain basic stable conditions to remain healthy and survive.

interphase: the process in which the cell grows and prepares for mitosis. The first of five steps in mitosis.

lysosome: the part of the animal cell that breaks down or digests parts of the cell that no longer work.

metaphase: the process in which sister chromatids line up along the center of the cell, exactly midway between the two poles of the spindle apparatus. The third of five steps of mitosis.

metaphase plate: the imaginary line equally separating a cell between the two poles.

microscope: a scientific tool that allows people to see very tiny objects as enlarged images.

meiosis: the process of cell division in which a cell divides twice to form four gametes.

mitochondria: organelles that release energy from the breakdown of food.

mitosis: the process in which one cell divides into two identical cells.

multicellular organism: an organism made up of many cells.

nucleus: the control center of a cell, which contains instructions for everything the cell does.

organ: a structure made of cells and tissue for a specific function, such as the brain and lungs.

organ system: a system that consists of several organs with related functions that all work together to accomplish a larger goal.

organelles: structures within cells that perform different important functions inside the cell.

osmosis: the diffusion of water through a cell membrane.

phospholipid molecules: molecules in which the head is attracted to liquids such as water while the tail avoids the same liquids.

prophase: the process in which the cell prepares to split up its duplicated genetic material equally. The second of five steps of mitosis.

response: the reaction of a cell to external stimuli.

ribosomes: organelles within cells that build proteins.

sister chromatids: a pair of identical copies of the same chromosome that are joined together.

specialized cells: cells designed for a specific function.

spindle apparatus: a system consisting of two organelles called centrosomes on opposite sides of the cell and the fibers running between them.

stimulus: new external information that causes a cellular response.

telophase: the process in which the cell dismantles the spindle apparatus. The last of five steps of mitosis.

tissue: cells that work together in the body to perform a specific function.

unicellular or: an organism made of just one cell.

vacuole: the part of a plant cell that maintains internal water balance and pressure.

CHAPTER 6 ANSWER KEY

PAGE 200

True: Some living creatures are made up of a single cell.

False: All cells are NOT basically identical in size and shape.

True: Microscopes are made out of lenses.

False: Virchow DID NOT determine that cells contain DNA.

PAGES 202–203

ITEM	UNICELLULAR ORGANISMS	MULTICELLULAR ORGANISMS (MISSING ORGANISMS)
Can be seen with the naked eye		X
An amoeba (a tiny creature that lives in pond water)	X	
A sunflower		X
One cell performs all the functions that are necessary for life	X	
A fish		X
Can only be seen with the aid of a microscope	X	
Streptococcus pneumonia (a type of bacteria that can cause the illness pneumonia)	X	
Different cells perform different functions that are necessary for life		X

PAGE 207

Refer to the illustration on page 208 for the correct names of the cell parts, shown here as well.

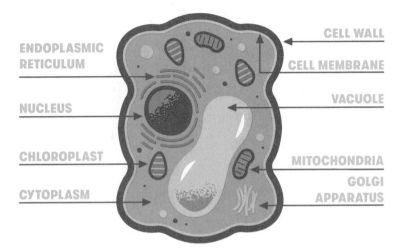

ENDOPLASMIC RETICULUM

NUCLEUS

CHLOROPLAST

CYTOPLASM

CELL WALL

CELL MEMBRANE

VACUOLE

MITOCHONDRIA

GOLGI APPARATUS

PAGES 208–209

Label: **Animal cells**

Label: **Animal cells**

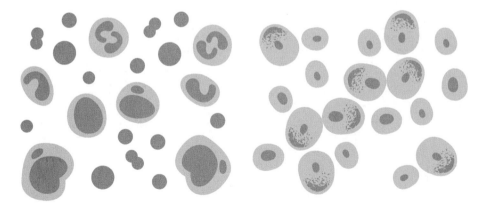

Label: **Plant cells**   Label: **Plant cells**

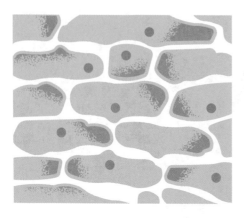   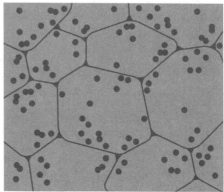

The onion cells do not contain chloroplasts because onions grow underground and are not able to capture the Sun's energy that is used to make food for the plant.

PAGE 210

Chloroplasts, **choice C**, are NOT found in both animal and plant cells.

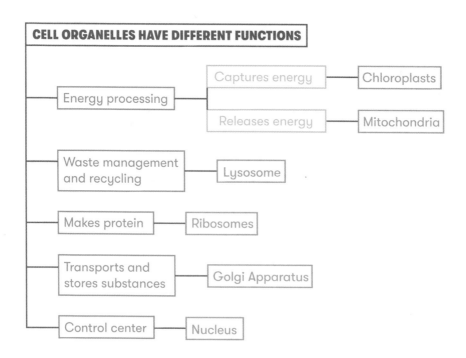

PAGES 214

If an animal cell is placed in pure water, it would swell and burst, **choice A**.

After a plant has been watered, plant cells take in water through osmosis but don't burst because of their cell walls.

When cells use energy to move molecules, it is called active transport, **choice C**.

PAGE 217

Each of the different types of cells, such as skin cells, red blood cells, and muscle cells, that are found in your leg surrounding the cut have their own specific jobs to do as far as what parts of the cut need to be healed and how to do it.

PAGE 218

It is important for a cell to copy its hereditary information before dividing because the nucleus divides in half and each needs its own copy of the hereditary information.

PAGE 220

There are lots of options, here is another example: I peeled my apple today.

PAGE 223

True/False: Each cell produced by mitosis and cell division has the same number and type of chromosomes as the original cell.

Chromosomes duplicate during a cell's life cycle in the interphase, **choice B**.

Chromatids separate during mitosis in prophase, **choice D**.

PAGE 226

	MITOSIS	MEIOSIS
Number of new cells produced	2	4
Type of cells produced	Identical	Non-identical
Names of phases	Interphase, Prophase, Metaphase, Anaphase, Telophase	Meiosis I: Prophase I, Metaphase I, Anaphase I, Telophase I Meiosis II: Prophase II, Metaphase II, Anaphase II, Telophase II
Number of times cytokinesis occurs	1	2
What is the purpose?	To produce gametes with identical chromosomes	To produce gametes with half the number of chromosomes

After cells surround the cut on your leg, they are able to replicate themselves to patch up the damage. For example, skin cells are able to create identical replications of themselves to patch up the skin that was cut.

PAGE 231

1. Cells of multicellular organisms are organized into *tissues*, organs, and organ systems.

2. *True/False:* All cells within a tissue are identical.

3. Muscle cells are an example of a specialized cell, **choice C**.

PAGE 233

The integumentary system, **choice C**, and the immune system, **choice D**, work together to heal a cut on your finger.

Organs will work together to send messages throughout the body to alert specific cells to help heal a cut. Some cells will clean out the dead cells and any invaders, such as bacteria, while other cells begin replicating and carrying needed nutrients and fluids to the site to begin rebuilding the cut skin and tissue.

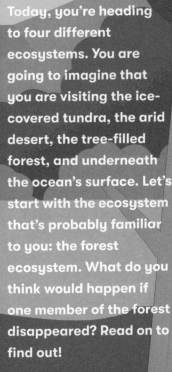

7 ECOSYSTEMS: INTERACTIONS, ENERGY, AND DYNAMICS

Today, you're heading to four different ecosystems. You are going to imagine that you are visiting the ice-covered tundra, the arid desert, the tree-filled forest, and underneath the ocean's surface. Let's start with the ecosystem that's probably familiar to you: the forest ecosystem. What do you think would happen if one member of the forest disappeared? Read on to find out!

What do you think would happen if one important member of your forest ecosystem/habitat, such as the coyotes, one day completely disappeared?

WHAT IS AN ECOSYSTEM?

Ecosystems are everywhere, all around us. And you are part of one (or more) too! But what exactly is an ecosystem? An ecosystem is a group of living things interacting with each other and their environment.

Let's take a closer look. There are living things and nonliving things in an ecosystem. Pause and look up from this book.

Where are you?

_____

What are the living things around you? Don't forget to include yourself!

_____

_____

What are the nonliving things around you? For example, are you sitting on a chair or against a wall?

_____

_____

What you just described is a type of ecosystem. For example, if you are sitting on the floor with your back against the wall, you and the location you are in are an ecosystem. You are a living creature interacting with your nonliving environment—the floor and the wall.

BIOTIC AND ABIOTIC FACTORS

The living things in an ecosystem are called the biotic factors. These include all the animals and plants—everything from the tiniest little bugs to the tallest trees. The nonliving things in an ecosystem are called the abiotic factors. These include everything from the tiniest grain of sand to the tallest mountain, and it includes water, sunlight, and the atmosphere.

 Let's take a look at the tundra, desert, and marine (underneath the ocean) ecosystems. What are the biotic and abiotic factors in each? Use the example of the forest ecosystem above if you need some clues.

Biotic factors: _____

Abiotic factors: _____

Biotic factors: _____

Abiotic factors: _____

Biotic factors: _____

Abiotic factors: _____

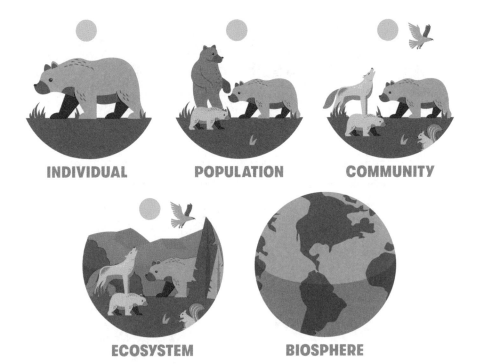

INDIVIDUAL   POPULATION   COMMUNITY

ECOSYSTEM   BIOSPHERE

UNDERSTANDING THE BIOSPHERE

Now let's look further into how the biotic parts of the ecosystem are organized. One animal, such as a bear in the forest, is called an individual. That individual bear makes up one of many bears in the forest. The group of bears as a whole is called a population. The bears, along with all the other creatures that live in the forest are part of a community. That community is part of an ecosystem, the forest, which is in turn part of the biosphere. Remember, the biosphere contains all living things on Earth.

While the bear is perfectly at home in the forest, it probably wouldn't fare well in other ecosystems. Can you imagine a bear living in a marine or desert ecosystem? You might be able to in your imagination, but it wouldn't really happen in reality. The bear calls the forest its home—the natural habitat where bears live.

A lot of different animals call the forest their natural habitat. For example, many forests are also home to deer, coyotes, birds, rabbits, and maybe even large cats. But don't some of these animals eat some of the other animals? Yes they do, but there is a balance between everything in the ecosystem.

POPULATION-LIMITING FACTORS

Within every ecosystem, there are a variety of resources—the necessities that all things need to survive. This includes food, water, space, and shelter. The balance of different plant and animal species within an ecosystem keeps the number of each population in check. This is called the carrying capacity. This is the total number of creatures an ecosystem can sustain.

FOUR FACTORS OF CARRYING CAPACITY

There are four primary categories that determine what the carrying capacity of an ecosystem is: the food and water supply, the amount of space available, the types of shelters available, and extreme natural hazards. These are known as limiting factors, because they limit how much each population can grow.

How do you think each of these would affect the carrying capacity of the ecosystem? Write down your thoughts below.

LIMITING FACTOR	HOW IT AFFECTS THE CARRYING CAPACITY
Food and water supply	
Amount of space	
Shelters	
Extreme natural hazards	

What did you write down for each of the limiting factors? If you had something along the lines of if one goes up, then the population will go up, with the exception of natural hazards, you are on the right track. Let's start with the food and water supply. And before getting into why it is a limiting factor, let's quickly review the food chain.

SECONDARY CONSUMERS (CARNIVORES)

PRIMARY CONSUMERS (HERBIVORES)

PRODUCERS

The bottom of the chain includes producers—all of the plants that can make their own food. But of course, even those plants need water and sunlight to do that. Next in the chain comes primary consumers, or herbivores, that eat plants. Finally, you have secondary consumers, or the carnivores, that eat the herbivores. Remember, this is an overly simplified version of the food chain. But it is enough to make our point here.

So now let's say that one year, there was a good rainfall so the plants grew more than normal. What would happen? Well, because the plants are producers and there are more of them, then the population of primary consumers would increase because they have more to eat. In turn, secondary consumers would also increase because they would also have more to eat.

But let's say that the following year, there wasn't enough rainfall. If a food source were to decrease, the population that relied on that food source would also decrease. And if a food source were to increase, the population that relied on that food source would also increase. All living things need food and water to survive and thrive. The population of a species will grow until it reaches the right size that the resources can support.

The same idea applies to the amount of space and shelter—if the amount of space an ecosystem takes up increases, there would be an increase in shelter and an increase in population size. Extreme natural hazards can include extended droughts, hurricanes, and fires. In those cases, entire communities can be severely limited by the destruction of food sources and shelters, which can cause creatures to move or to shelter in smaller spaces.

And when species are able to have enough resources, they are able to keep their species thriving by reproducing.

What do you think happens to reproduction rates when the ecosystem becomes unbalanced? Circle the correct word to complete the sentences.

If the number of producers increases, the reproduction rates of primary consumers will initially *increase/decrease*. Therefore, the reproduction rates of secondary consumers will also *increase/decrease*. When the number of primary consumers gets too large, the reproduction rate of the producers will *increase/decrease*, and the reproduction rate of secondary consumers will *increase/decrease*.

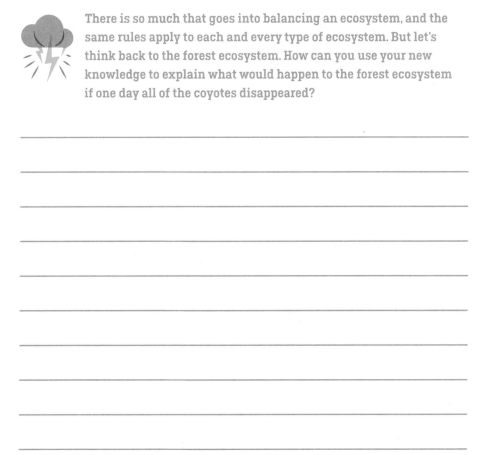

There is so much that goes into balancing an ecosystem, and the same rules apply to each and every type of ecosystem. But let's think back to the forest ecosystem. How can you use your new knowledge to explain what would happen to the forest ecosystem if one day all of the coyotes disappeared?

_____

_____

_____

_____

_____

_____

_____

_____

_____

THE CYCLES OF ENERGY AND MATTER

 In all ecosystems, there is a balance between populations and their environment. Plants feed the herbivores, which in turn feed the carnivores. Eventually carnivores die and their bodies feed the plants.

 If you think about it, this sounds like a cycle, similar to the rock cycle, the water cycle, and the carbon cycle that you read about in previous chapters.

Not only is the matter (the animals, plants, rocks, water, carbon, etc.) conserved, but so is the energy. Let's take a look. If you have a piece of scratch paper and something to sketch with, go ahead and grab them now. If not, follow along in your imagination.

Let's stick with the forest ecosystem here. If you want to sketch the tundra, desert, or marine ecosystem, you can do that instead. Make a quick sketch of where you want to set your scene. Make sure to include some type of producer in your ecosystem.

 What type of ecosystem did you sketch?

_____

What are the biotic and abiotic factors in your scene? Circle the biotic factors that are producers.

Biotic factors: _____

Abiotic factors: _____

Producers are receiving energy to make their own food. Where is that energy coming from?

 Do you remember how photosynthesis works? Circle back to page 159 if you need a refresher.

_____

PRIMARY CONSUMERS

That's right! Primary producers, all of those plants in your ecosystem, collect the energy from the Sun. The plants then turn the sunlight into food, along with water and minerals from the soil. Go ahead and add some arrows to your sketch. While you are at it, draw some primary consumers and some more arrows that show how energy transfers from producers to primary consumers.

ENERGY FROM SUN TO PRODUCERS
ENERGY FROM PRODUCERS TO CONSUMERS

 What are the primary consumers in your ecosystem?

_____

_____

How has the energy moved so far in your ecosystem?

_____

_____

SECONDARY CONSUMERS

You probably already guessed what you are going to add next! That's right, add some secondary consumers. Think about the types of secondary consumers that live in the ecosystem you selected.

ENERGY FROM PRIMARY CONSUMERS TO SECONDARY CONSUMERS
ENERGY FROM SUN TO PRODUCERS
ENERGY FROM PRODUCERS TO CONSUMERS

 What are the secondary consumers in your ecosystem?

_____

_____

How has the energy moved so far in your ecosystem?

_____

_____

But then where does the energy go?

 As you'll learn later on, energy cannot be created or destroyed
(we'll explore this more in Chapter 12). Energy continually
cycles through the ecosystem.

DON'T FORGET THE DECOMPOSERS!

So far, you have traced how the producers use energy from sunlight, which is then transferred to primary consumers and then transferred again to secondary consumers. Animals give off heat while alive, which is another form of energy. So some energy from animals changes into heat and reenters the environment. When animals die, decomposers (see Chapter 5) such as bacteria, earthworms, and even fungi (like mushrooms) break down the animal's body. Energy is then transferred to the decomposers. Eventually, that energy cycles back to producers, primary consumers, and secondary consumers.

THE NITROGEN CYCLE

Energy is not the only thing being reused and recycled in an ecosystem. Matter, or stuff, also cycles through the living and nonliving parts of an ecosystem. And an important chemical component of living things is nitrogen. Let's take a look at how nitrogen, too, is reused and recycled in ecosystems.

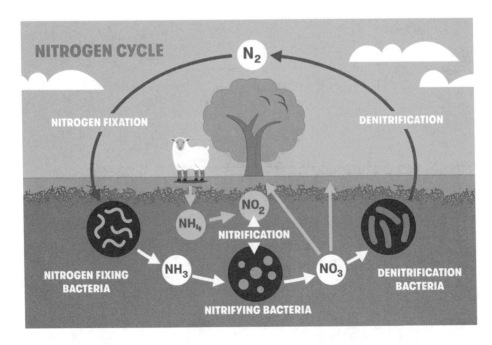

Nitrogen is a critical building block of proteins and DNA (the molecules containing genes). There is a lot of nitrogen in the atmosphere, but animals have no way of getting at it. We humans, for example, can't inhale nitrogen from the air into our bodies the same way we inhale oxygen. That's where bacteria—believe it or not!—help us out.

HELPFUL BACTERIA AND NITRIFICATION

Bacteria living in soil and plant roots help us out by performing nitrogen fixation, which means capturing nitrogen from the air and using it to make ammonia. Ammonia is a smelly, colorless gas that is toxic to a lot of organisms. Fortunately, there are other helpful bacteria in the soil that turn the ammonia into chemicals called nitrates. This process is called nitrification. Nitrates are useful because plants can absorb them from the soil in a process called assimilation. Plants use the nitrates as a building block for making proteins and DNA.

AMMONIFICATION

Animals eat the plants in order to build their own supply of nitrogen for the same reason. And when plants and animals die, all their nitrogen enters the environment again. Decomposers, the same decomposers as in the energy cycle, turn the proteins from dead organisms into ammonia. This is called ammonification. You already know what happens to ammonia once it's in the soil.

Eventually, nitrogen reenters the atmosphere through the process of denitrification. Some of the decomposers break down the nitrates and release nitrogen gas back into the atmosphere. Just like with all of the other cycles you have looked at so far, nitrogen is constantly cycled through the ecosystem and is never created nor destroyed.

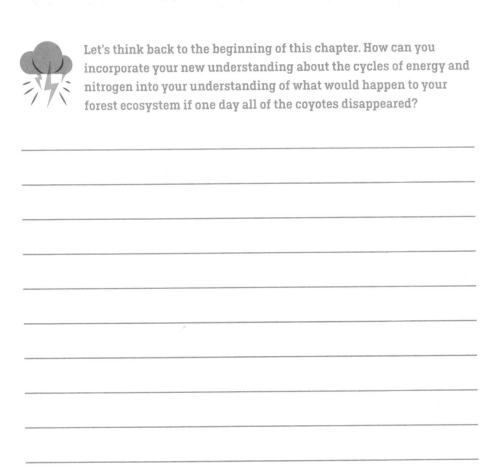

Let's think back to the beginning of this chapter. How can you incorporate your new understanding about the cycles of energy and nitrogen into your understanding of what would happen to your forest ecosystem if one day all of the coyotes disappeared?

BALANCING BIODIVERSITY

Remember, there are many different populations that live in an ecosystem, both plant and animal. The variety of all of the organisms that can be found in an ecosystem is known as biodiversity.

You have already seen that the biodiversity of an ecosystem has a delicate balance. Removing any of the elements or adding new ones can upset the whole system. Sometimes, an ecosystem may be able to catch itself and regain its balance. This ability of an ecosystem to adjust to a disturbance and recover is called ecological resilience.

What kind of disturbance are we talking about? Let's say a new species was introduced—a primary consumer.

How do you think the introduction of a new primary consumer would impact the ecosystem? Circle all that apply.

A. It would blend in easily with the other populations.

B. It would compete with the primary consumers for producers.

C. It would reproduce with the nearest relative population.

D. It would cause an increase in population of secondary producers.

A newly introduced primary consumer would compete with those already existing in the ecosystem for their share of the producers. For example, a rabbit introduced into a new forest ecosystem will compete with the native squirrels for seeds to munch on. This will cause the squirrels to have less food, and their population will decline as the rabbit population grows. As the rabbit population grows, secondary consumers, wolves for example, will also grow because they have an increase in their food source.

But as the wolf population grows, there will be more competition for food (the rabbits). This will further send the ecosystem into an unbalanced state. As the wolf population grows, the rabbit population will quickly decline as the wolves eat them. This will cause the wolf population to then decline as their food source shrinks. This up-and-down size of the two populations may continue and become more drastic, or it may continue and eventually find a balance of the number of rabbits and the number of wolves. But only time will tell for sure.

Disturbances to an ecosystem's biodiversity can also be caused by abiotic factors. For example, the space available for a particular ecosystem may shrink, which would decrease the biodiversity. A wildfire can destroy all of the producers and shelter in another ecosystem, leaving animals homeless and starving.

THREATS TO BIODIVERSITY

Let's take a look at some of the most important threats to biodiversity:

POLLUTION   **HABITAT LOSS**   **CLIMATE CHANGE**

FIRES   THREATS TO BIODIVERSITY   **DISEASES**

NATURAL DISASTERS   **INVASIVE SPECIES**

Many of these threats can be traced back to humans.

For example, pollution, climate change, and the loss of many species' habitat over the past century have primarily been caused by human activity (see Chapter 5 for more details).

However, drastic reductions in biodiversity have also happened before in the Earth's history. The five known mass extinctions occurred before there were any humans to take the blame. The culprits have been glaciations (when large portions of the Earth's surface were iced over), volcanic eruptions, and asteroid impacts. In fact, scientists estimate that of all the species that have ever existed on Earth, 99% are extinct today!

EARTH'S "MASS EXTINCTIONS"

1	2	3	4	5
445 MILLION YEARS AGO	**357–360 MILLION YEARS AGO**	**252 MILLION YEARS AGO**	**200 MILLION YEARS AGO**	**66 MILLION YEARS AGO**
60/70%	**75%**	**95%**	**70/80%**	**75%**
of species became extinct	of species became extinct	of species became extinct	of species became extinct	of species became extinct
Intense Ice Age	Drastic drop in oxygen levels	Asteroid impacts, intensive volcanic activity	In debate: massive volcanic eruptions, asteroids	Asteroid impact

So what's the big deal about biodiversity, anyway? Extinctions have happened before, so is it okay if they happen again? You can think about this in two ways: what a loss of biodiversity would mean for us humans and what it would mean for the Earth's ecosystems in general.

BIODIVERSITY AND YOU

Other organisms provide humans with a lot of resources. Which of the following products are made from resources we get from other species?

 Circle all that apply.

wood furniture

cotton clothing

paper

herbal medicine

wool

fur

vegetarian food

seafood

wood construction materials

meat

How many of the resources from the list did you circle? If you circled all of them, you are correct! All of these, plus countless others, are vital to our everyday lives.

 For example, you learned that plants make oxygen, which humans need to survive. Some types of fungi and bacteria filter waste and pollution out of water, leaving clean water behind. Plants hold soil together with their root systems, allowing us to build on stable ground without worrying that it will crumble away under our feet. You could say that many species perform "services" that humans use.

 All of these resources and services are not just nice to have—they are vital. Many people rely on these resources to earn a living. For example, some people rely on lumber from trees for others to build structures with. Others rely on catching fish to sell to stores and restaurants. Others rely on growing vegetables to sell at their local farmer's market. If these species suddenly went missing, a lot of people would not be able to make a living. In other words, biodiversity has *economic* value for humans. But remember, if one species were to suddenly go missing, the entire ecosystem would be affected.

BIODIVERSITY AND THE PLANET

As you have seen, an ecosystem is a delicate network of elements that depend on and affect each other. Take away some of the elements, and others will follow.

Sometimes, one species is critical to holding the entire ecosystem together. They are known as the keystone species. The population size of the keystone species may be small, but they make a big difference. Sometimes, that species is a plant that provides shelter and food to multiple organisms. Other times, it's a predator that keeps the populations of its prey animals from getting out of control and eating all the producers. When biodiversity decreases, the keystone species may go extinct, bringing down entire ecosystems with them. In other words, biodiversity has *ecological* value for the Earth.

CONSERVING WHAT WE HAVE

THE NUMBER OF ENDANGERED SPECIES IS RISING

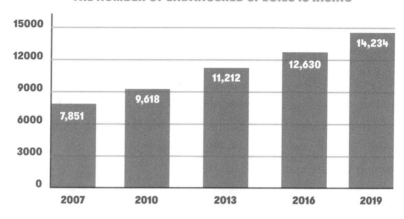

Conservation is incredibly important. And there are many ways that humans can come together to help protect the species we share Earth with.

Pollution, deforestation, and climate change are only some of the processes that can affect all ecosystems around the world. For example, coral reefs, which can be home to thousands of marine species, become bleached and can die when ocean temperatures increase too much. This will severely affect not only the coral reef ecosystem, but also the ocean as a whole. This is because at least 25% of all marine species rely on these reefs at some point in their lives.

That same warming melts the ice in places like the Arctic, which is home to many animals, such as polar bears. When the ice melts, polar bears lose space and shelter in their habitats. This means that more polar bears will be competing for less space and less food.

There are many species that are critically endangered and on the brink of extinction. The Amur leopard, for example, is one of the most endangered large cats. There are fewer than 100 known in the wild. They are affected by many factors, including illegal hunting and trade, habitat loss, and deforestation. Amur leopards are a primary predator and help keep the entire ecosystem in balance. Efforts both in zoos and in the wild are trying to help Amur leopards regrow their population.

Hook Island tortoises were also on the brink of extinction, with only fifteen individuals left. Repopulation efforts over the course of a 44-year program saved the species. Today, there are about 2,000 tortoises back in the ecosystem. You will read more about this particular story in Chapter 9.

These are just some of the many, many ways that humans are helping ecosystems remain balanced and healthy. There are countless ways you can help, from your own backyard to programs around the world. Talk to people in your community or even do a quick Internet search to find how you can help.

Let's think back to the beginning of this chapter. How can you take all that you have learned and apply it to the original question—what would happen to the forest ecosystem if one day all the coyotes disappeared?

CHAPTER 7 VOCABULARY

abiotic: all of the nonliving things in an ecosystem.

ammonification: the process in which decomposers turn proteins from dead organisms into ammonia.

assimilation: the process in which plants absorb nitrates from soil.

biodiversity: the variety of all organisms in an ecosystem.

biotic: all of the living things in an ecosystem.

carrying capacity: the balance of all plant and animal species that an ecosystem can support and sustain.

community: all of the combined populations in a specific habitat.

conservation: the protection and preservation of plants and animals and the entire ecosystems in which they live.

denitrification: the process of nitrogen reentering the atmosphere after decomposers break down nitrates in dead organisms.

ecological resilience: the ability of an ecosystem to adjust to a disturbance and recover.

ecosystem: a group of living things interacting with each other and their environment.

habitat: the natural home where a plant or animal lives.

individual: a single organism that is part of the larger population.

keystone species: a species that is critical to holding the entire ecosystem together.

limiting factors: factors in an ecosystem that determine the carrying capacity, such as food supply, physical space, and water.

matter: any physical substance that has mass and volume.

nitrates: chemicals containing nitrogen and that are used by plants to make proteins and DNA.

nitrification: the process of turning ammonia into nitrates.

nitrogen: an important chemical component of living things.

nitrogen fixation: the process of capturing nitrogen from the air to make ammonia.

population: an entire group of a species in an ecosystem.

primary consumers: the members of an ecosystem that eat plants, such as deer and rabbits.

producers: the members of an ecosystem that can make their own food, such as plants.

resources: the necessities all things need to survive.

secondary consumers: the members of an ecosystem that eat primary consumers.

CHAPTER 7
ANSWER KEY

PAGE 246

- Any answer works here. You could be sitting outside next to a tree, on a seat of a bus, sprawled out on your bed, or anywhere in between.

- Again, your answer will be dependent on what's around you. You are one of the living organisms, maybe the only living organism at the moment. Maybe you have a pet, a sibling, or maybe someone else is on the bus with you. Don't forget that it could also be the tree you are leaning against or the plant in the corner of the room.

- Again, your answer will be dependent on what's around you. You could be sitting on a rock outside or a chair inside, lying on the bed. It could be that bus you may be sitting on or the bed you may be lying on.

PAGES 247–248

Biotic factors: the animals on land, animals and fish in the water, the birds, and the plants in the water.

Abiotic factors: the water, ice, sunlight, cloud, and atmosphere.

Biotic factors: cacti, animals, birds, and plants.

Abiotic factors: sand, rocks, sunlight, mountains, and atmosphere.

Biotic factors: fish, turtles, coral, and plants.

Abiotic factors: the water, sand, and rocks.

PAGE 250

LIMITING FACTOR	HOW IT AFFECTS THE CARRYING CAPACITY
Food and water supply	There is only enough food and water to support a limited number of species.
Amount of space	The more space an ecosystem has, the more species can live there.
Shelters	The more options for shelter an ecosystem has, the more types of species can live there.
Extreme natural hazards	Extreme natural hazards can affect the food and water supply, amount of space, and shelters available for species.

PAGE 253

If the number of producers increases, the reproduction rates of primary consumers will initially increase/decrease. Therefore, the reproduction rates of secondary consumers will also increase/decrease. When the number of primary consumers gets too large, the reproduction rate of producers will increase/decrease, and the reproduction rate of secondary consumers will increase/decrease.

If all of the coyotes were to disappear one day, the population size of the primary consumers would increase because there would be fewer predators hunting them. When the population of the primary consumers grows, there will be more competition for food, space, and shelter. Therefore, the population of producers will also drop.

PAGE 255

- You can select any ecosystem, including the forest, tundra, desert, or marine environment that we have discussed so far.

- Your answer will depend on which ecosystem you selected. The biotic factors will include all of the plant and animal life.

- Your answer will depend on which ecosystem you selected. The abiotic factors will include water, rocks, land, the atmosphere, and sunlight.

- The energy is coming from the Sun.

PAGE 256

- This will depend on which ecosystem you selected. For the forest ecosystem, primary consumers can include deer, rabbits, squirrels, fish, etc.

- Energy has moved from the Sun to the plants, where the plants make their own food. The plants then get eaten by the primary consumers, transferring energy from the plants to primary consumers.

PAGE 257

- This will depend on which ecosystem you selected. For the forest ecosystem, secondary consumers can include bears, wolves, owls, hawks, mountain lions, bobcats, etc.

- Energy has now traveled from the Sun to the plants, then to primary consumers, and then it travels to secondary consumers as they eat primary consumers.

PAGE 260

Ecosystems are delicately balanced and rely on the cycling of energy and matter. If coyotes were to one day disappear, the cycling of energy and matter would be thrown off balance. This will affect the rest of the ecosystem.

PAGE 261

The answers are **choice B** (it would compete with the primary consumers for producers) and **choice D** (it would cause an increase in population of secondary producers).

PAGE 263

wood furniture

cotton clothing

paper

herbal medicine

wool

fur

vegetarian food

seafood

wood construction materials

meat

Yes, all of the words should be circled!

PAGE 267

If all of the coyotes were to one day disappear, their ecosystem would be thrown off balance. As a secondary consumer, the population sizes of primary consumers and producers would be affected by one less population of predators. If one part of an ecosystem changes, the entire ecosystem could be affected, often negatively. If one ecosystem is affected, neighboring ecosystems can also be affected, and so on. With so many species becoming endangered and extinct, the disappearance of the coyotes may one day be a reality. It is very important that we all work together to try to prevent further extinctions, such as the coyotes.

NOTES

8
HEREDITY: INHERITANCE AND VARIATION OF TRAITS

Ever wonder why your eyes are the color they are? Or why the wildflowers in a field are so many different colors? This chapter is all about the science of heredity—the way in which plants and animals pass on their traits to their offspring. Lets take a stroll through the Forest of Heredity to learn more!

A JOURNEY INTO THE FOREST OF HEREDITY

Today, you are going on a walk through the Forest of Heredity, a name known only to those admitted into the super-secret Society of Genetic Scientists.

As a new member of this society, you will learn to predict the characteristics of animals and plants before they even come into existence.

ASEXUAL AND SEXUAL REPRODUCTION

The trail is muddy after yesterday's rain. Unfortunately, you've only just started out on the path when your walking stick spears a worm, splitting it in two. Oh no! To protect the worm from being hurt more, you scoop it into a paper bag and take it home.

At home, you place the worm in a fish tank filled with damp soil and a mushy apple. Over time, you notice something pretty cool.

WEEK	OBSERVATIONS	MODEL
1	Small stubs form on both pieces of the original worm.	
2	Each stub grows larger.	
3	Stubs continue to grow in size.	
4	Now you have two worms!	

REPRODUCTION BY FRAGMENTATION

Two worms! That's the coolest thing ever, but how did that happen? Well, the part with the head grew a new tail, and the tail piece grew a new head. This is called reproduction by fragmentation.

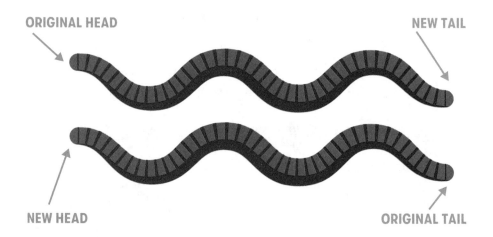

ORIGINAL HEAD

NEW TAIL

NEW HEAD

ORIGINAL TAIL

Reproduction by fragmentation is an example of asexual reproduction. Asexual reproduction is a type of reproduction that only requires one individual. This is because it does not involve the fusion of gametes (like a sperm and egg) or a change in the number of chromosomes. The offspring that form by asexual reproduction from a single cell, or from a multicellular organism, inherit the genes of that single parent only. This means any offspring will be identical to its parent. Think army of clone troopers from *Star Wars*.

Bacteria, tiny germs that can cause diseases like strep throat, also reproduce asexually. Once harmful bacteria get into your body, they quickly use asexual reproduction to multiply, and before you know it, your body is home to a ton of identical bacteria. It's a good thing you can take antibiotics to kill bacteria in short order.

AN EXPERIMENT WITH RASPBERRIES

Keep on walking. Oh, look, a whole thicket of wild raspberry bushes!

 Take a good look at these wild raspberry plants. If you had to take a guess whether they reproduce sexually or asexually, what would your guess be, and why?

_____

_____

_____

Let's dig up one of those raspberry plants and see if you are correct. At home, we'll plant the main raspberry plant in one large pot. We will also take a couple of the lower side branches, cut them off using garden shears, and place each cutting in a smaller pot with some soil.

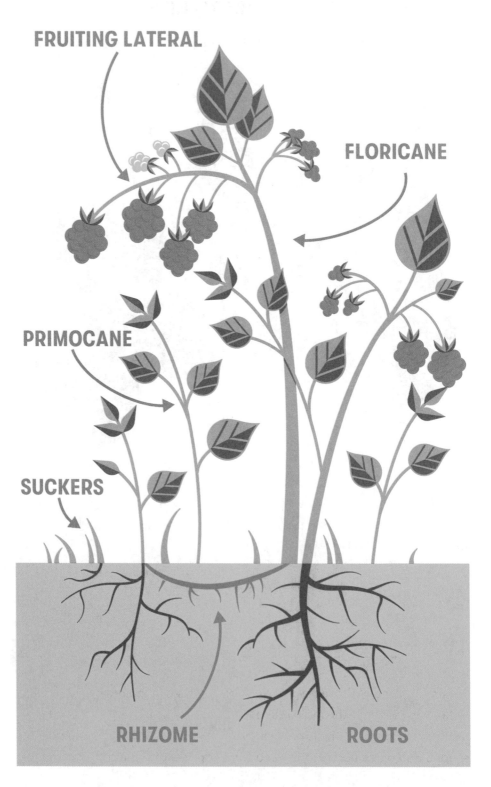

FRUITING LATERAL

FLORICANE

PRIMOCANE

SUCKERS

RHIZOME

ROOTS

We will water each pot every few days and wait several months—sort of a cross between gardening and a science experiment. Keep a weekly log of of your plants' development in the space below.

_____

_____

_____

_____

_____

_____

_____

_____

_____

floricane: a flowering or fruiting stem of a bramble plant such as raspberry.

fruiting lateral: relatively short, fruit-bearing branches that grow from buds at the base of a leaf.

primocane: a new branch or stem on a bramble fruit (such as a raspberry) that will flower and fruit the following year (as a floricane).

suckers: small offshoot plants that come from the roots of the mother plant.

rhizome: a horizontal underground stem that puts out lateral shoots and roots.

roots: the plant organ that anchors the plant in the soil and brings water and nutrients into the body of the plant.

Let's see how the raspberry plant grows each month.

MONTH	OBSERVATIONS	MODEL
1	The small raspberry cuttings are beginning to grow roots.	
3	Each cutting has grown a large root system and is beginning to look like its own raspberry plant.	
12	Each cutting has become its own plant, with raspberries beginning to ripen.	

Now that you have made your initial observations and reviewed the observations of the plant over time, show what you have learned!

Use the words *identical* and *asexual* to complete the statement.

The raspberries at the end of my experiment look _____ to the initial raspberries I observed. So, raspberries must reproduce by _____ reproduction.

 It's easy to assume that all plants must reproduce the same way as raspberry plants, but that's actually not the case. Many plants can reproduce both asexually and sexually. For example, banana trees can either be grown from stem structures underneath the ground (asexual) or from seeds (sexual).

Think back to the field of flowers from the beginning of the chapter. How does this information help explain why there are so many different colors of flowers?

_____

_____

_____

IT STARTED WITH A CURIOUS MONK

Before we take a closer look at sexual reproduction, let's talk about the scientist who started the modern study of genetics, Gregor Mendel (1822–1884). Mendel was a monk, who, like many monks of the time, had to pitch in at the monastery and help to grow food for all the monks to eat. He took the opportunity to conduct some gardening experiments at the same time. His observations with pea plants allowed him to figure out the rules of heredity, which is how Mendel earned his nickname, "the father of modern genetics."

DOMINANT AND RECESSIVE TRAITS

PARENTS

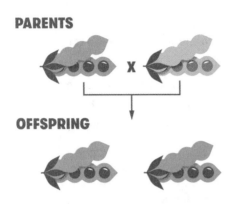

OFFSPRING

Back out on another walk, you notice two people horseback riding! You stop and talk to the riders and learn that the horses are a mother and her foal. But how? They look completely different. The answer can be found in Gregor Mendel's gardening experiments. Let's take a closer look at his pea plants.

Mendel noticed that the pea plants he was growing had some characteristics, or traits, that came in two possible versions. For example, the pea plants could either be short or tall, their flowers could be purple or white, and the pea pods themselves could be either green or yellow. Mendel wanted to understand how these traits were passed down from parent plants to their offspring.

For example, if the first parent plant had green pea pods, and the second parent plant had yellow pea pods, would the offspring plants have pea pods of both colors? When Mendel performed this experiment, he was surprised to find that all the offspring plants ended up with green pea pods.

As it turns out, not all traits are equal. Some traits are what we call dominant, and some are recessive. For example, the green pod color in the pea plants is dominant, while the yellow pod color is recessive. When an individual inherits two different traits from its parents—a dominant one and a recessive one—the dominant trait will "win." In the case of the pea pods, the green color will trump the yellow color, so the offspring plants will all have green pea pods.

Take this information and apply it to the horses you saw on your walk. Since Mom has a black coat and her foal has a chestnut coat, what type of coat do you think Dad has?

It makes sense to think that Dad must have a chestnut coat. What would you say if I told you Dad has a black coat? Wait a second. How can two horses that have black coats produce a foal with a chestnut coat? I bet Gregor Mendel and his pea experiments could help get to the bottom of this.

THE SCIENCE BEHIND MENDEL'S EXPERIMENTS

 Remember how in Chapter 6 you learned that multicellular organisms have cells containing a nucleus with genetic material? Well, this genetic material is found in tightly coiled molecules called chromosomes. The number of chromosomes depends on the species. For example, horses have 64 chromosomes. The chromosomes come in matched pairs—you will see why in a minute.

 Each chromosome contains hundreds or even thousands of different genes. Each gene typically codes for a protein, a building block for something in the horse's body. Saying that a gene "codes" for a protein means that the gene contains instructions which that cell can follow to make the protein in the horse's body. Some genes code for proteins that give a horse its coat color. Other genes code for proteins that make up her muscles. Still others code for the proteins in a horse's beautiful mane. Every tiny protein has some important role in a horse's body. These proteins result in the horse having certain traits, or characteristics—things like height, the color of its fur coat, and the shape of its eyes.

 Take a look at the male horse first. He has 64 chromosomes to choose from, but he will only pass half of them on to his offspring. Remember, they come in matched pairs, or sets. So each set is broken apart with only one of the two chromosomes from the set going to the offspring. The same process occurs when the female horse passes on half of her chromosomes.

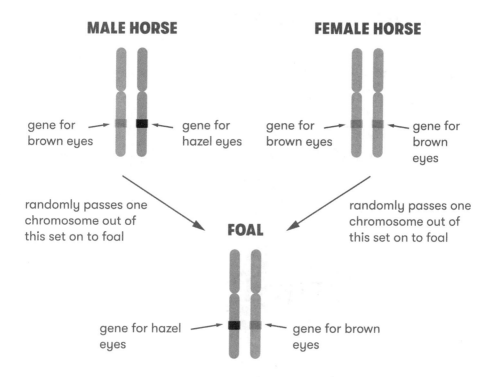

MALE HORSE

gene for brown eyes

gene for hazel eyes

FEMALE HORSE

gene for brown eyes

gene for brown eyes

randomly passes one chromosome out of this set on to foal

FOAL

randomly passes one chromosome out of this set on to foal

gene for hazel eyes

gene for brown eyes

The result is a foal that is a unique combination of half of the female's genetic material and half of the male's. This means that each offspring is unique and different from the others, all thanks to sexual reproduction.

 You may remember that for asexual reproduction, only one mature individual is needed, while for sexual reproduction, two parents are required. You may also remember that asexual reproduction results in offspring that look the same, whereas sexual reproduction results in different, unique offspring.

CHECK YOUR UNDERSTANDING

Use your understanding of asexual and sexual reproduction to complete the chart below. Place an X next to the reproduction type that best fits each description.

DESCRIPTION	IMAGE	ASEXUAL REPRODUCTION	SEXUAL REPRODUCTION
2 parents			
1 parent			
Identical offspring			
Unique offspring			

DESCRIPTION	IMAGE	ASEXUAL REPRODUCTION	SEXUAL REPRODUCTION
A starfish breaks apart, and the two broken pieces regrow to become two complete starfish.			
A cat has a litter of kittens.			

Think back to the field of flowers from the beginning of the chapter. How does this information help you explain why there are so many different colors of flowers?

_____

_____

_____

_____

IT'S ALL ABOUT THE GENES

 As you know, genes determine traits. For some genes, there might only be one possible version that pretty much all horses share. For example, horses, like all mammals, have four limbs. You're not likely to find a horse walking around on eight or ten legs. If you were to look at the genes that control limb development, you would find identical versions of these genes across thousands of different mammals.

ALLELES: VARIETY IS THE SPICE OF LIFE

But for many genes, multiple versions are possible.

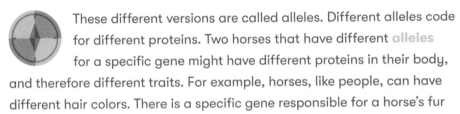 These different versions are called alleles. Different alleles code for different proteins. Two horses that have different alleles for a specific gene might have different proteins in their body, and therefore different traits. For example, horses, like people, can have different hair colors. There is a specific gene responsible for a horse's fur coat color.

 Now, remember, every horse gets half of its genetic material from its mother and half from its father. Both parents give their foal one copy of every gene. Therefore, the foal receives two copies of the fur coat color gene. These two copies might be the same allele, or they might be different alleles. If they are the same, you would say that the foal is homozygous for that trait. If the two alleles are different, the foal is heterozygous for that trait.

Can you figure out whether the last pair of chromosomes in the picture below is homozygous or heterozygous?

HOMOZYGOUS   HETEROZYGOUS   _____

ALLELE A   ALLELE *a*

Tip: "Homo" means "same" in Greek, while "hetero" means "different." If you can memorize that, the terms *homozygous* and *heterozygous* will be easier to remember.

A HANDY NOTATION FOR DOMINANT AND RECESSIVE TRAITS

To make it easier to remember which alleles are dominant and which are recessive, geneticists use a simple system. For example, in the case of horse coat color, the dominant allele codes for a black coat. Scientists might call the black color allele *B*, because the word "black" starts with the letter "*B*." They would also make the letter uppercase to show that the black color is *dominant*. The other possible allele codes for a chestnut coat, but scientists don't call it *C*. Instead, they write it as *b*. That means it's *recessive* (that's why it's a lowercase letter), and it's also a reminder that the dominant trait is still black.

Now, suppose a black stallion and a chestnut mare have offspring together. Imagine that the stallion has two dominant *B* alleles. In other words, he is homozygous dominant. The mare, on the other hand, has two recessive *b* alleles, so you would call her homozygous recessive.

Use your probability skills to figure out all the possible allele combinations that the offspring of this pair of horses might inherit.

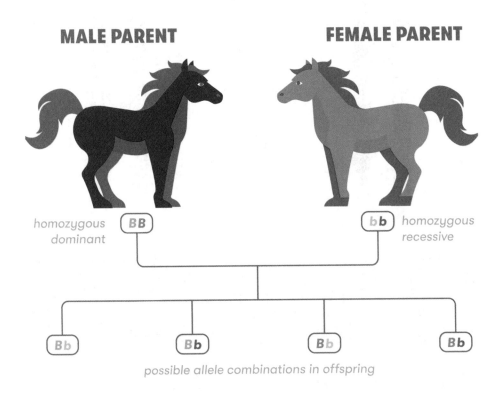

MALE PARENT

FEMALE PARENT

homozygous dominant **B B**

b b homozygous recessive

B b   **B b**   **B b**   **B b**

possible allele combinations in offspring

GENOTYPES AND PHENOTYPES

The alleles an individual possesses are also called one's genotype. In other words, you could say the female horse in the example has the genotype *bb*. Her phenotype, on the other hand, is the appearance or behavior that results from the alleles she possesses. In this case, her phenotype is the chestnut coat color. When you look at an organism, you can see its phenotype but not its genotype. Another way to remember this is that *genotype* is about the *genes* an individual has, while *phenotype* is about a *phenomenon* (something that you can observe).

GENOTYPE VS. PHENOTYPE

PHENOTYPE	Black coat Swatch of black	Chestnut coat Swatch of chestnut or approximation
GENOTYPE	*BB* or *Bb*	*bb*

 Try to complete the following sentence with the terms *genotype* and *phenotype*:

The male horse's _____ is a black coat, and his _____ is *BB*.

THE PUNNETT SQUARE

Instead of always drawing out family trees like in the example above, you can use a handy scientific tool called a Punnett square to predict which alleles parents can pass on to their offspring. You set it up like this:

		MALE PARENT	
		B	*B*
FEMALE PARENT	*b*		
	b		

Key

B = black coat allele

b = chestnut coat allele

There are four empty cells left. Each of these cells represents a possible combination of alleles that the offspring might receive from these two parents.

Let's fill in those cells and reveal the possible fur coats for their offspring. For each empty cell, look up along the column to find the first allele (from their male parent), then look left along the row to find the second allele (from their female parent).

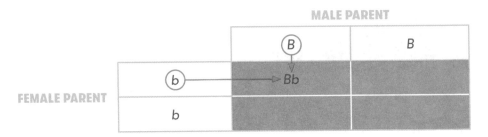

Key

B = black coat allele

b = chestnut coat allele

The male parent could give the offspring the *B* allele, and the female parent could give the offspring the *b* allele, so that the offspring ends up with the allele combination *Bb*. Scientists write any dominant alleles first, so you would write *Bb*, not *bB*. Since this foal inherits two different alleles, its genotype is heterozygous. Remember, the dominant allele always trumps the recessive allele, which means the dominant allele will instruct the body to make its protein and not the recessive allele's protein. In this case, the dominant allele codes for the black coat color protein, so the foal's phenotype will be a black coat.

Ready to see the other possible allele combinations? Let's continue filling in the rest of the empty cells.

MALE PARENT

	(B)	B
(b)	Bb	Bb
b		

FEMALE PARENT

Complete the sentence on the following page by choosing one of the following terms: *homozygous recessive, heterozygous,* or *homozygous dominant.*

A foal who inherits this second allele combination will have a
_____ genotype.

		B	B
	b	Bb	Bb
FEMALE PARENT	b	Bb	

Color the horse below to show the coat color that will result from the third possible allele combination.

One last possible combination left!

		B	B
	b	Bb	Bb
FEMALE PARENT	b	Bb	Bb

You can see from this Punnett square that every possible combination of the two parent coat alleles gives the same result for the offspring: *Bb*. In other words, you would say the chances of this pair of horses having offspring that are heterozygous for coat color are 100%—no crystal ball required! Not only that, you can bet that the foals' phenotype will be black coats.

Think back to the chestnut foal you met on your walk. How can a foal have a chestnut coat if both parents have black coats?

_____

_____

_____

Take a closer look at how this can happen. To figure out what the offspring of these two horses might look like, just draw a Punnett square.

		MALE PARENT	
		B	b
FEMALE PARENT	B	BB	Bb
	b	Bb	bb

Key

B = black coat allele

b = chestnut coat allele

Try your hand at interpreting this square by answering the questions below.

1. What is the female parent's coat color? _____

2. What is the male parent's coat color? _____

3. How many of the possible allele combinations result in a homozygous dominant genotype? _____

4. How many of the possible allele combinations result in a black foal? _____

Out of four cells in our table, only one results in a chestnut coat, so we would say the odds of these parents having a chestnut foal are ¼, or 25%. The rest of the combinations: *BB*, *Bb*, and the other *Bb*, all yield horses with black coats, so the odds of this type of offspring are ¾, or 75%.

A common mistake is to assume that if these two parent horses have four offspring, they will have exactly three offspring with black coats and one with a chestnut coat. However, that is not the case, because each offspring's genes are determined independently—even in species that have many offspring at the same time. In other words, every single offspring of this couple has a 75% chance of inheriting a black coat and a 25% chance of inheriting a chestnut coat. Therefore, it is actually possible, though highly unlikely, that they could have 100 offspring and all of those offspring could, by chance, inherit chestnut coats.

CHECK YOUR UNDERSTANDING

Ready for a challenge? This time, take a look at the offspring and predict what the parents might look like.

Offspring allele combination: *bb*

Circle the words that make the statement true.

Since the foal has *dominant/recessive* alleles, it will have *black/chestnut* colored hair.

List all the possible allele combinations for the parent generation. Use a Punnett square to provide evidence for your answer.

FEMALE PARENT

Possible allele combinations for the parents:

- _____ and _____

- _____ and _____

- _____ and _____

INHERITANCE OF TRAITS OVER GENERATIONS

The curious thing about the case of the black mare and its chestnut foal is that it shows how an individual can sometimes end up looking different from either of its parents. Let's take a closer look at how traits get passed down over multiple generations. Mendel performed these types of experiments with pea plants, but this can also be demonstrated with another convenient model organism: the fruit fly.

You know those tiny little annoying flies that seem to appear out of nowhere when you accidentally forget a banana in your locker? Genetic scientists love them, and no wonder: since an American scientist named Thomas Hunt Morgan (1866–1945) first began to study them in the early twentieth century, eight Nobel Prizes have been given out for fruit fly research.

The fruit fly is fun to study because it's pretty easy to keep in the lab. Its life cycle is short, which means it quickly becomes an adult and has offspring—a lot of them—making it easy to track how different traits get passed down from one generation to the next. Also, the fruit fly has only four pairs of chromosomes, and scientists have now examined all the genes that are on them.

Flies, like people, can have different eye colors. Most fruit flies have red eyes because their bodies make a specific red-colored protein called drosopterin. There is a specific allele that tells the fly's body to make this red protein: let's call it *R* because it is the dominant allele. However, some flies have a different allele that tells the body to produce a greenish pigment instead of the red one. Let's call this allele *r* because it's recessive.

Now, pretend that the two Punnett squares below represent two generations in the same fly family.

First generation: *RR* x *rr*

		MALE PARENT	
		R	R
FEMALE PARENT	r	Rr red eyes	Rr red eyes
	r	Rr red eyes	Rr red eyes

Second generation: *Rr* x *Rr*

		MALE PARENT	
		R	r
FEMALE PARENT	R	RR red eyes	Rr red eyes
	r	Rr red eyes	rr green eyes

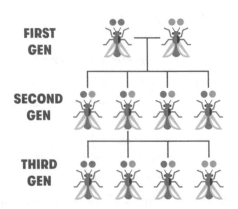

FIRST GEN

SECOND GEN

THIRD GEN

You can see in that in the first generation, a red-eyed fly and a green-eyed fly have red-eyed offspring. When those red-eyed offspring grow up, these second-generation flies have a 75% chance of having red-eyed offspring and a 25% chance of having green-eyed offspring.

WHERE DID THAT TRAIT COME FROM?

 In this example, some might say that the green eye color "skipped generations": it was there in the first generation, "disappeared" in the second generation, and then returned in the third generation. It might seem like the green eye color in the third generation came out of nowhere. However, members of the secret Society of Genetic Scientists know that the recessive green-eye allele was there all along, even in the second-generation flies. It wasn't visible, because the dominant red-eye allele trumped the recessive green-eye allele. So all those second-generation flies displayed the dominant red eyes but still carried the recessive trait, which was then passed on to their offspring.

Now let's imagine that two flies from this third generation also start to reproduce. Specifically, suppose that flies with these allele combinations are the new parents: *Rr* and *rr*.

Try to complete the Punnett square for this pairing.

Third generation: *Rr* x *rr*

		MALE PARENT	
		R	r
FEMALE PARENT	r		
	r		

If these third-generation flies came to you as they were about to reproduce and asked you what their chances were of having green-eyed offspring, what would you tell them?

Fill in the blank: These two parents have a _____% chance of having green-eyed offspring.

MUTATIONS

On your walk, you met a black and a chestnut horse, but you have probably also seen white horses. The white color can occur as a result of a mutation—a random change in the gene that codes for the pigment in the horse's fur coat. Instead of giving cells the proper instructions for making the pigment protein, the gene is "broken," so that horses with this mutation cannot produce the pigment and have a snowy white coat instead.

Some mutations change a gene in a tiny way that makes no difference. The gene still codes for the correct protein, giving the organism's cells clear instructions for making that protein. At the other extreme, some mutations change the gene so much that it no longer codes for any protein. Finally, some mutations change the gene in such a way that it still codes for a protein, but not the right one. The new protein might be helpful to the organism, but it could also be useless, or possibly even harmful.

SICKLE CELL ANEMIA

One mutation that people can inherit causes the disease sickle cell anemia. This mutation affects blood cells. All humans have red blood cells in our blood, which look like tiny red frisbees. Red blood cells have a very important job, carrying oxygen to different parts of the body. They are able to do this because they contain a protein called hemoglobin that can "grab" oxygen. Therefore, the gene that codes for hemoglobin is extremely important for your health.

A mutation in this gene can cause a person to have a broken hemoglobin protein. Red blood cells that contain this type of broken hemoglobin will have a distorted shape.

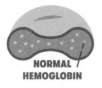

**NORMAL
RED BLOOD CELL**

**NORMAL
HEMOGLOBIN**

SICKLE CELL

**ABNORMAL
HEMOGLOBIN**

These distorted "sickled" blood cells can get stuck in a person's arteries, meaning the blood cells can't do their job of delivering oxygen to the organs that need them. These oxygen-starved organs then start to malfunction, causing intense pain.

Take a look at a family where the mother has two copies of the normal hemoglobin gene, and the father has two copies of the mutant sickle cell gene—in other words, he suffers from sickle cell anemia. Do you think the children of this couple are going to end up with sickle cell anemia?

_____

_____

_____

_____

_____

Fortunately, you don't need to guess—you are going to predict the future using a Punnett square. Use the following notation: _H_ for the normal hemoglobin gene and _h_ for the mutant gene.

Quick question: Based on this notation, do you think the mutant gene is _dominant_ or _recessive_? Circle one.

Okay, now you are ready to complete your square, assuming that the mother in this family has two *H* alleles and the father has two *h* alleles.

MALE PARENT

FEMALE PARENT

 Based on your Punnett square, what is the probability of a child inheriting each of the following allele combinations?

HH: _____%

Hh: _____%

hh: _____%

From the Punnett square, you can see that all four offspring should contain the same allele combination: *Hh*.

 Based on what you know about how dominant and recessive alleles work, would you expect that a child with this allele combination would suffer from sickle cell anemia? Explain your reasoning.

_____

_____

It's starting to get dark. We'd better say goodbye to the Forest of Heredity and head back.

 Before you go, think back one more time to the field of flowers from the beginning of the chapter. How does your new knowledge about mutations help explain why there are so many different colors of flowers?

_____

_____

CHAPTER 8 VOCABULARY

allele: one of many different versions of a gene found in the same place on a chromosome, such as the gene that controls limb development.

asexual reproduction: reproduction that only requires one individual, such as reproduction by fragmentation.

dominant trait: traits that always overtake recessive traits when both are inherited.

gene: the building blocks that determine an organism's traits.

genotype: the alleles an individual possesses.

heterozygous: an organism that receives two different alleles from their parents.

homozygous: an organism that receives two of the same alleles from their parents.

homozygous dominant: an organism that has two of the same dominant alleles.

homozygous recessive: an organism that has two of the same recessive alleles.

mutation: a random change in a gene that alters the genetic code carried by the gene.

phenotype: the appearance or behavior that results from the alleles an organism possesses.

protein: the building blocks of all organisms, including genetic traits.

recessive trait: traits that are overtaken when dominant traits are inherited.

reproduction by fragmentation: a type of asexual reproduction where an organism splits into two pieces, each half becoming their own organism.

sexual reproduction: a type of reproduction that requires two individual organisms.

trait: a distinguishing characteristic of an organism.

CHAPTER 8 ANSWER KEY

PAGE 281

All the wild raspberry plants look pretty much the same: they all have berries at different stages of ripening and leaves arranged in groups of five. Therefore, you might guess that they reproduce asexually, resulting in genetically identical offspring.

PAGE 283

Initial observations include: the raspberry plant has berries at different stages of ripening, leaves arranged in groups of five, and several branches are pinned to the ground with soil underneath.

PAGE 285

The raspberries at the end of the experiment look identical to the initial raspberries we observed. So, raspberries must reproduce by asexual reproduction.

The flowers are different colors. Because they are not the same, or identical, then they must not reproduce asexually.

PAGES 290–291

DESCRIPTION	IMAGE	ASEXUAL REPRODUCTION	SEXUAL REPRODUCTION
2 parents			X

DESCRIPTION	IMAGE	ASEXUAL REPRODUCTION	SEXUAL REPRODUCTION
1 parent		X	
Identical offspring		X	
Unique offspring			X
A starfish breaks apart, and the two broken pieces regrow to become two complete starfish.		X	
A cat has a litter of kittens.			X

PAGE 291

Since the flowers are all unique (different colors), they must reproduce sexually.

PAGE 293

The last pair of chromosomes are homozygous.

PAGE 295

The male horse's phenotype is a black coat, and his genotype is *BB*.

PAGES 296–297

A foal who inherits this second allele combination will have a heterozygous genotype.

PAGE 298

Both parents must have a recessive allele that they pass on to the foal.

1. Black
2. Black
3. 1
4. 3

PAGES 299–300

Since the foal has recessive alleles, it will have chestnut colored hair.

- *Bb* and *bb*
- *bb* and *bb*
- *Bb* and *Bb*

PAGE 303

	MALE PARENT	
	R	r
r	Rr red eyes	rr green eyes
r	Rr red eyes	rr green eyes

FEMALE PARENT (left label for rows)

These two parents have a 50% chance of having green-eyed offspring.

PAGE 305

Any prediction is reasonable based on the information available so far.

The mutant gene is recessive.

PAGE 306

	MALE PARENT	
	h	h
H	Hh	Hh
H	Hh	Hh

FEMALE PARENT (left label for rows)

HH: 0%

Hh: 100%

hh: 0%

- No, the child will not suffer from sickle cell anemia, because the normal hemoglobin allele, *H*, is dominant.

- Mutations may be why some flowers have different colors. A mutation in the gene that codes for flower color can cause the flower not to produce the correct pigment.

NOTES

9
BIOLOGICAL EVOLUTION: UNITY AND DIVERSITY

You probably already know that plants and animals (including humans) adapt and evolve over long periods of time. Maybe you read somewhere that the dogs we know and love as pets have descended from wolves. But dinosaurs—the ancient extinct creatures—descended from birds? How and why do living things evolve? Let's dig in and find out more!

Why do scientists believe birds and dinosaurs are related?

EVOLUTIONARY DETECTIVES: THE FOSSIL RECORD

Ah, those beautiful strata of cliff walls ... remember the illustrations of rock layers containing fossils from Chapter 2? Let's see if you can remember how to date them. Circle the correct answer.

THE ROCK LAYERS CAN BE RELATIVELY DATED BY COMPARING THE:	THE ROCK LAYERS CAN BE ABSOLUTELY DATED BY COMPARING THE:
A. layers on top and the layers on the bottom	A. layers on top and the layers on the bottom
B. igneous, sedimentary, and metamorphic rocks	B. igneous, sedimentary, and metamorphic rocks
C. radioactive dating of fossils	C. radioactive dating of fossils

Here's a hint: remember that rock layers form from the bottom up. This means that the layers at the bottom are older than the ones on top. And that fossils can get stuck in the rock layers as they form.

You know fossils are used for dating rock layers. But what else can you use fossils for? Fossils are what's left of creatures that lived during different periods in Earth's history. Fossils show what types of animals and plants lived on Earth during those times. There were no historians around to record important events like the extinction of some animals or the appearance of new ones. Fortunately, the fossils in the rock layers give clues to help determine when certain creatures appeared, changed, or disappeared. That's why scientists call it the fossil record—it's a record of events that happened before there were any people to witness them. Let's check out some fossils!

DIGGING FOR SKELETONS (AND CLUES)

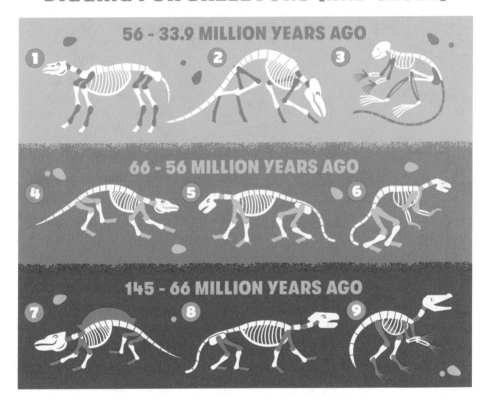

Now, let's be paleontologists—scientists who study fossils. You can see that the animals in the bottom layer look different from the animals in the other two layers. In other words, they have differences in their anatomy, or structure. However, they also share some anatomical similarities.

 List two anatomical features that all the animals in the top layer have in common with the animals in the middle layer:

1. _____

2. _____

SPECIES CHANGED OVER TIME

You can see that over millions of years, species changed. For example, Animal 1 in the top layer is actually a descendant of Animal 4 in the middle layer. This means that, over thousands of generations, animals that looked like Animal 4 changed through natural selection to look like Animal 1.

 List two anatomical features that differ between Animal 1 and Animal 4:

1. _____

2. _____

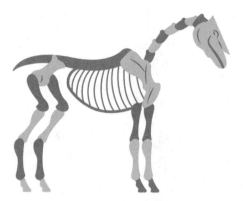

Paleontologists compare the anatomy of the different species to figure out how older species may be related to younger species. Let's look at an example.

 Take a good look at this skeleton of a modern-day horse. Which animal from the top (most superficial) layer of the dig looks most similar to the horse?

_____

_____

_____

In fact, scientists believe that Animal 1 in the top rock layer is a very distant ancestor of today's horses. Quite a few things changed between then and now: for example, the bony part of the horse's tail is much shorter compared to its ancestor's. Another new feature is the hoof, which took the place of the ancestor's toes.

FROM HYRACOTHERIUM TO HORSE: A 50-MILLION YEAR EVOLUTION

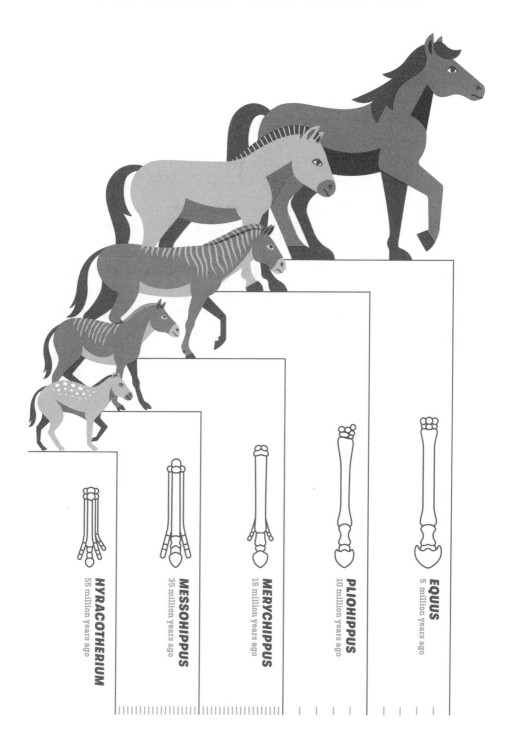

HYRACOTHERIUM
55 million years ago

MESSOHIPPUS
35 million years ago

MERYCHIPPUS
15 million years ago

PLIOHIPPUS
10 million years ago

EQUUS
5 million years ago

Take a look at the hoof of today's horse. How does it compare to the previous relatives of today's horses?

_____

_____

_____

Comparing today's species to fossils is one way that scientists can trace back the origins of modern life forms. By noticing that multiple species share certain anatomical features, scientists can determine that the animals may have evolved from a common ancestor. In other words, all the animals who share these features may be descendants of the same species who lived in the distant past. So how can you tell for sure that these animals were once related? By studying the embryological development—how animals look before they are born (for species that give birth) or before they hatch (for species that lay eggs).

EMBRYOLOGICAL DEVELOPMENT

When an animal is developing in its egg or in its mother's womb, it follows a program laid out by its genes. Many of these genes have been passed down from one generation to another for millions of years, even as species change and evolve. That's why looking at the stages of development that an animal goes through can give you clues to understanding its evolutionary history. Animals that have shared ancestors, even if they look quite different as adults, might look more similar in the early stages of development.

EARLY EMBRYO

MID-STAGE EMBRYO

MATURE EMBRYO (FETUS)

FISH   CHICK   CALF   RABBIT   HUMAN

For example, take a look at the images above, which show snapshots of three stages in the development of different species of animals. Remarkably, all these different animals look quite similar in the early stages of development, which is further evidence that they all evolved from a common ancestor long, long ago.

Now let's examine the development of another species (below). Based on what this animal looks like at each stage, which of the species above would you expect to be its closest relative?

_____

_____

_____

_____

EARLY EMBRYO	**MID-STAGE EMBRYO**	**MATURE EMBRYO (FETUS)**

In fact, this is a species of tortoise, a reptile that can live in a variety of environments, from the desert to a wet tropical forest. As an adult, it doesn't look very much like any of the other seven types of animals. But if you look at the embryological development of each of these species, you can get an insight into who its evolutionary relatives might be. So how do animals evolve over millions of years?

 Do you think you have part of the puzzle of the dinosaur and the bird now? How can you use what you have learned so far to explain if dinosaurs and birds are related?

_____

_____

_____

NATURAL SELECTION

Over the centuries, many scientists have tried to explain how new species arise on Earth. In studying fossils, they knew that animals of the distant past did not look like those of today. Scientists came up with all kinds of explanations, but none of the theories were able to explain all of the evidence. That is, until Charles Darwin (1808–1892) proposed his **Theory of Evolution by Natural Selection** in the 1800s. As an avid naturalist (a word people used in those days to describe a scientist who studies nature), Darwin spent nearly five years aboard a ship, traveling all over the world, collecting specimens, and making observations to support his ideas. These observations gave Darwin enough information to allow him to write his now-famous book called *On the Origin of Species*.

Let's explore Darwin's theory in action by looking at a case study.

THE CASE OF THE LOPSIDED FISH

The fish on the previous page are native to Lake Tanganyika, which is shared between four countries in eastern Africa.

If you look really closely, you may notice something interesting: one of them has a mouth slanted to the right, and one has a mouth slanted to the left. Most animals are symmetrical—the same on both sides—so this is a little odd.

Can you brainstorm an explanation or two for why the mouths of these fish are angled like this?

_____

_____

_____

_____

_____

Scientists call animals that are all members of the same species and live in the same habitat a population. Suppose you studied 100 fish from this population. Let's count how of them many have right-slanted mouths—let's say there are 60. Now, let's create a data table:

TOTAL NUMBER OF FISH	100
NUMBER OF FISH WITH RIGHT-SLANTED MOUTHS	60

From these numbers, you can calculate the proportion of fish that have right-slanted mouths. All you have to do is divide the number of fish with right-slanted mouths by the total number of fish. 60 divided by 100 is 0.60.

Now suppose you continue to study the population of fish and return here once a year, each time studying 100 fish and counting how many have right-slanted mouths. Imagine you came up with a data table like this:

	THIS YEAR	1 YEAR FROM NOW	2 YEARS FROM NOW	3 YEARS FROM NOW	4 YEARS FROM NOW
TOTAL NUMBER OF FISH	100	100	100	100	100
NUMBER OF FISH WITH RIGHT-SLANTED MOUTHS	60	40	57	38	65
PROPORTION OF FISH WITH RIGHT-SLANTED MOUTHS	0.6				

 Complete the bottom row of the table using the formula: proportion of fish with right-slanted mouths = number of fish with right-slanted mouths ÷ total number of fish

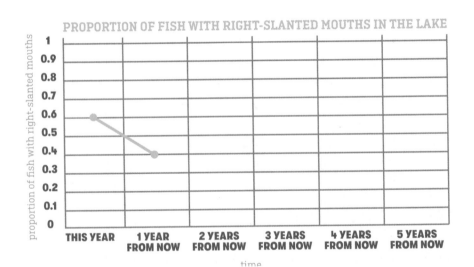

PROPORTION OF FISH WITH RIGHT-SLANTED MOUTHS IN THE LAKE

proportion of fish with right-slanted mouths

THIS YEAR / 1 YEAR FROM NOW / 2 YEARS FROM NOW / 3 YEARS FROM NOW / 4 YEARS FROM NOW / 5 YEARS FROM NOW

time

On the graph above, add the last three points of data to complete the plot. Do you notice any patterns? Try to predict what the proportion of fish with right-slanted mouths might be 5 years from now. Pencil in an additional point; don't worry about the exact number; just try to determine approximately where the next point might be.

Hopefully, you've noticed a trend: one year, more than half of the fish have right-slanted mouths, but the next year, the reverse is true, and the year after that, more than half have right-slanted mouths again. What can you possibly make of this?

A CLUE FROM THEIR EATING HABITS

Well, it turns out these little fish are parasites, like fleas and head lice. They survive by eating the scales of larger fish in the lake. Naturally, the larger fish don't like this, so the scale-eaters have to sneak up from behind, charging suddenly and snatching a quick bite out of their prey's side.

 Knowing this information, can you take a guess why the little fish have slanted mouths rather than straight, symmetrical ones?

_____

_____

_____

Scientists have determined that the direction of the slant in the mouths of these fish is inherited. This means that the parent fish passed this trait on to their offspring. Now, based on our measurements, this year, more than half of the fish in the lake have mouths slanted to the right. For these "righties," it's going to be more convenient to attack their prey's left side.

A LEARNING CURVE

After a while, the larger fish will learn from experience that they need to look out for small fish approaching from the left side. So, you might expect that over time, the prey will get better at detecting the "righties" fish. This will allow them to escape and leave the parasites hungry. But the "lefties," which are less common, might have more success sneaking up from the right and grabbing their dinner.

The fish that miss their dinner too often might not survive. And those who don't survive won't have a chance to pass their genes on to their offspring.

 Knowing that the right-mouthed fish are more common this year, how would you complete the statement below?

This year, the chances of surviving and reproducing for right-mouthed fish are:

    A. the same as for left-mouthed fish.

    B. higher than for left-mouthed fish.

    C. lower than for left-mouthed fish.

What did you choose? If you chose C, you're on to something. The "righties" would have a lower chance of a successful attack on their prey as their prey learns their attack patterns. This means that they will be less likely to survive and reproduce. By not reproducing, the right-mouthed trait would not be passed on.

 Armed with everything you now know about these parasitic fish, can you explain why the proportion of right-mouthed fish jumps up and down every year?

_____

_____

_____

_____

NATURAL SELECTION IN ACTION

THE THEORY OF NATURAL SELECTION AND THE SCALE-EATING FISH

This case study of the scale-eating fish is a real-life example of natural selection at work. It illustrates the four main points of Darwin's Theory of Evolution by Natural Selection.

GENERAL RULE	HOW IT APPLIES TO THE SCALE-EATING FISH
1. Members of a population have inheritable variations in traits.	Some fish have a right-slanted mouth and others have a left-slanted mouth. These traits are passed on to their offspring.
2. More individuals are born in each generation than can survive on the available resources.	Some scale-eaters will be detected by their prey, so they will fail to obtain enough food to survive.
3. Some individuals have advantageous traits that allow them to better compete for resources. These individuals have a higher chance of surviving and reproducing.	The fish with the less common mouth slant are more likely to succeed at sneaking up on their prey and growing their population. In other words, if right-mouthed fish are more common this year, then the advantageous trait is having a left-slanted mouth. Individuals with a left-slanted mouth are more likely to survive and reproduce compared to the fish with the more common mouth slant. This idea is also known as evolutionary fitness.

GENERAL RULE	HOW IT APPLIES TO THE SCALE-EATING FISH
4. Natural selection results in the next generation having more individuals with the favorable trait.	If the favorable trait this year is a left-slanted mouth, then the next generation should end up with more left-mouthed fish, which is exactly what happens. You would say that the fish's environment has selected for left-slanted mouths.

There is another part to the fourth point of Darwin's theory. Over time, the population becomes more adapted to the environment. Adapting means adjusting to the environment. When a species adapts to the environment, it changes in a way that allows it to survive more easily in the environment.

Take a look at this picture:

NATURAL SELECTION IN ACTION

 How does this image represent natural selection?

_____

_____

_____

DARWIN'S FINCHES

Let's look at another example of adaptation. When Darwin visited the
Galapagos Islands during his travels, he studied a variety of species of
finches, which are now collectively called Darwin's finches. He noticed that
the finches looked a bit different depending on which part of the islands
they were found on. He realized that while they were all finches, they had
adapted to each unique environment on their little corner of the Galapagos.

Let's see if you can match up the finches to what they like to eat based on the shape of their beak, using these clues. Draw a line from each beak shape to its corresponding food source. The thinnest beaks are useful for getting into small, tight places. The short, sharp beaks are meant for crushing. The short, rounded beaks are perfect to hold on to things. The larger the beak, the larger the objects the finch can eat.

FINCHES	BEAK SHAPES	FOODS THEY EAT

fruit

crushing seeds

probing for insects

grabbing for insects

MUTATIONS AND ADAPTATIONS

In the previous chapter, you learned how mutations can give rise to new traits, which can be advantageous or harmful to the individual's survival. Remember, white horses are white because of a mutation—a random change in the gene that codes for the pigment in the horse's fur caused by a "broken" gene.

Can you think of an advantage and disadvantage of being a white horse?

An advantage of being a white horse is

_____

A disadvantage of being a white horse is

_____

 Wow, you just learned a whole lot about natural selection and adaptation! How do these examples help you develop your idea about how dinosaurs and birds might be related?

_____

_____

_____

Sometimes, mutations can be passed down through the generations. If these traits are thought of as beneficial, humans can even help them along.

ARTIFICIAL SELECTION

During natural selection, the natural environment selects for traits that are advantageous for a species' survival. But the evolution of a species by natural selection can be a slow and irregular process that can seem random. So sometimes, humans want to take matters into their own hands.

SELECTIVE BREEDING: WOLVES TO DOGS

For example, humans started domesticating wolves more than 30,000 years ago. Over thousands of years, those wolves were bred to develop specific qualities, like high speed, a keen sense of smell, or cute wrinkles. Rather than leaving evolution to take its course, humans have used artificial selection, also known as selective breeding, to achieve their goals. For example, newfoundland dogs were bred to have partially webbed feet, making them excellent swimmers and often used in water rescues. Bloodhounds were bred for their excellent sense of smell and tracking abilities. Collies and shepherds were bred to herd groups of animals such as sheep and cattle. Greyhounds were bred for their incredible speed. Golden retrievers were bred to retrieve the prey from hunting parties. Today, many species of dogs are bred for companionship.

DIEGO THE GIANT TORTOISE

Now, let's look at another example of selective breeding. Have you ever heard of Diego the giant tortoise?

Diego is a tortoise from the Galapagos Islands. Diego is a member of the Hook Island species of tortoise, one of only a few different species left on the island today. Until recently, people had been killing the giant tortoises for food and settling in their habitat, causing several species of tortoise to become extinct.

In 1976, scientists started a breeding program to save the Hook Island tortoises. Diego was one of only fifteen surviving members of the Hook Island tortoises, three of which, including Diego, were male. When the program ended in early 2020, the population of Hook Island tortoises had grown to about 2,000 members!

SELECTIVELY BREEDING PLANTS

Dogs and tortoises are only two of many examples that have been selectively bred by humans to highlight specific qualities, and to save species from extinction. But humans don't only selectively breed animals.

TEOSINTE   MODERN CORN

Since humans began cultivating crops about 12,000 years ago, they have been artificially selecting specific qualities of plants and food. Do you enjoy corn on the cob during the summer? Do you think it always looked and tasted like that?

Take a look at the two plants. What do you notice? The teosinte is a grass that was selectively bred over thousands of years to grow larger, sweeter, and with softer kernels that are more easily chewed and digested by humans.

And corn isn't the only vegetable to undergo artificial selection. Broccoli, cauliflower, cabbage, and even kale were also selectively bred—and those examples all came from the same original plant!

In addition to increasing the variety of produce at the grocery stores, selectively bred crops have additional benefits. Some crops are bred to be more resistant to drought, making them grow better in drier regions where fresh vegetables and fruit may be hard to come by. Other crops are bred to include more nutrients, to help make sure that malnourishment becomes a problem of the past.

There are a lot of examples of natural and artificial selection all around you. Take a look at the Venn diagram on the next page. Can you use it to come up with your own examples and explanations for something that you see around you? Give it a try!

NATURAL AND ARTIFICIAL SELECTION, COMPARED

NATURAL SELECTION   ARTIFICIAL SELECTION

Occurs mainly in wild populations

Selects for traits that are advantageous for survival in a given environment

Results in slow and irregular change in a population

Allows only individuals with specific traits to reproduce

Can only select for traits that are inherited (passed on through genes)

Leads a population to change over time

Occurs mainly in domestic populations

Selects for traits that are preferred by huamns

Results in rapid and methodical change in a population

Let's start with identifying some processes. Using this diagram, can you figure out whether each of the following examples is a product of natural or artificial selection?

After centuries of hunting at night, bats have very sensitive hearing.

circle one: **Natural selection**   **Artificial selection**

After generations of cultivation, watermelons become sweeter, and their seeds become tiny and soft.

circle one: **Natural selection**   **Artificial selection**

After generations of living in sewers, New York City rats have become more resistant to poison.

circle one: **Natural selection**   **Artificial selection**

Now come up with your own example and state whether it is a product of natural or artificial selection.

_____

_____

_____

Let's think back to the question at the beginning of the chapter. How can you incorporate everything you have learned into understanding how dinosaurs and birds can be related?

_____

_____

_____

CHAPTER 9 VOCABULARY

adapt: to adjust to the environment.

artificial selection: the process of humans breeding other species for particular traits.

anatomy: the bodily structure of an organism.

common ancestor: an ancestor from which several species may have descended.

descendant: an organism related to another organism that lived at an earlier time.

embryological development: how animals look before they are born (for species that give birth) or before they hatch (for species that lay eggs).

evolutionary fitness: how likely an organism is to survive in a given habitat.

fossil record: a record of events that happened before there were any people to witness them.

paleontologist: a scientist who studies fossils.

population: all members of the same species that live in the same habitat.

selective breeding: a form of artificial selection.

Theory of Evolution by Natural Selection: the theory proposed by Charles Darwin that says that animals that are biologically more equipped to survive in their environment will reproduce more, and that over time, animals will develop traits appropriate to their environment.

CHAPTER 9
ANSWER KEY

PAGE 316

THE ROCK LAYERS CAN BE RELATIVELY DATED BY COMPARING THE:	THE ROCK LAYERS CAN BE ABSOLUTELY DATED BY COMPARING THE:
A. layers on top and the layers on the bottom	A. layers on top and the layers on the bottom
B. igneous, sedimentary, and metamorphic rocks	B. igneous, sedimentary, and metamorphic rocks
C. radioactive dating of fossils	C. radioactive dating of fossils

PAGE 317

There are many possible correct answers. All the animals in these two layers have four legs, a tail, a similar hind leg bone structure that creates a "knee," etc.

PAGE 318

There are many possible correct answers. For example, Animal 1 has a different spine curvature and a different number of bones in the feet compared with Animal 4.

Animal 1 or Animal 2 are reasonable answers, but based on posture, Animal 1 looks most similar to the horse.

PAGE 320

The horse's hoof evolved over millions of years from a 4-toed foot to a single hoof.

PAGE 322

This animal appears to be most closely related to the fish.

PAGE 323

Dinosaurs and birds may have had a common ancestor, which can be determined by looking at both of their embryological developments. Maybe in studying the fossils of the dinosaurs, there have been enough changes that allowed the dinosaur to eventually turn into a bird.

PAGE 325

At this point, you don't have much information about these fish, but you can speculate that their mouth shapes have to do with what they eat or how they eat it. Maybe the fish with left-slanted mouths and the fish with the right-slanted mouths eat different kinds of food, or maybe they eat the same kind of food in a different manner.

PAGE 326

	THIS YEAR	1 YEAR FROM NOW	2 YEARS FROM NOW	3 YEARS FROM NOW	4 YEARS FROM NOW
TOTAL NUMBER OF FISH	100	100	100	100	100
NUMBER OF FISH WITH RIGHT-SLANTED MOUTHS	60	40	57	38	65
PROPORTION OF FISH WITH RIGHT-SLANTED MOUTHS	0.6	0.4	0.57	0.38	0.65

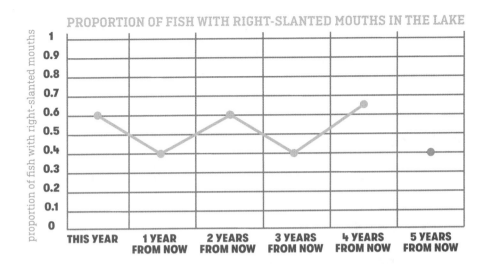

PROPORTION OF FISH WITH RIGHT-SLANTED MOUTHS IN THE LAKE

proportion of fish with right-slanted mouths

THIS YEAR | 1 YEAR FROM NOW | 2 YEARS FROM NOW | 3 YEARS FROM NOW | 4 YEARS FROM NOW | 5 YEARS FROM NOW

PAGE 327

The slant of the mouth makes it easier for the small fish to attack the sides of larger fish.

PAGE 328

The answer is **choice C**, lower than for left-mouthed fish.

When more than half of the fish are right-mouthed (proportion is greater than 0.5), prey fish learn to expect their attacks. Therefore, these right-mouthed fish have less success at obtaining food and lower chances of surviving and reproducing. Because mouth slant is hereditary, this means that in the next generation, there will be fewer right-mouthed fish. Then, there will be more left-mouthed fish, and the same thing will happen. This see-saw pattern will continue, with the proportion of right-mouthed fish rising above 0.5 about every other year.

PAGE 330

Taller giraffes can reach the leaves better than shorter giraffes, so taller giraffes will have more success at getting food, surviving, and reproducing.

PAGE 332

FINCHES	BEAK SHAPES	FOODS THEY EAT

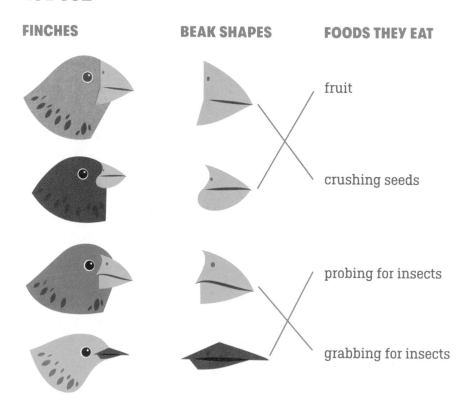

PAGE 333

- An advantage of being a white horse is that they can blend in better with the snow during the winter and be less likely to be attacked by predators.

- A disadvantage of being a white horse is that they won't be able to blend into their surroundings when it isn't snowing and are more likely to be attacked by predators.

PAGE 334

The fossil record may show that dinosaurs and birds may have a common ancestor, and that the dinosaur evolved through natural selection. Eventually, the dinosaur may have adapted the ability to fly. Then, it may have further evolved into a current-day bird.

PAGES 338–339

- Natural selection

- Artificial selection

- Natural selection

There are so many examples you can use here, from pretty much any food that you like to eat to all the animals around you.

PAGE 339

Dinosaurs and birds may have a common ancestor, which can be determined by fossil records and by looking at the embryotic development of both species. Through natural selection and adapting to different environments, dinosaurs slowly evolved into birds. Birds may have gone through periods of artificial selection to increase the number of species based on traits desirable to humans.

10 MATTER AND ITS INTERACTIONS

You and a friend visit the beach one day, and among the seashells and multi-colored pebbles, you find a piece of driftwood with a rusty hunk of metal stuck in it. Pretty cool! You know from experience that metal can rust after it gets wet. But you start to wonder: why does metal rust, but not wood? Let's find out!

CHAPTER CONTENTS

Why do some substances react when combined and others don't?

EXPLORING REACTIONS

When you get home, you want to clean off your beach finds. You remember that your mom cleans the kitchen with vinegar, so you walk into the kitchen, pull out a wide bowl, and put your seashells and rocks in there. You pour some vinegar over the samples and notice that there are bubbles forming. Whoa! Where did those come from?

You look more closely and notice that the bubbles are mainly on the seashells, while the pebbles just look wet. Interesting. Let's stop and think about that for a second.

Why do you think there were bubbles on the shells but not the pebbles?

_____

_____

_____

_____

You tell your mom about what you just saw, and as she listens, she gets out a small bowl, pours some white powdery stuff in it, and places it on the counter in front of you. Then she hands you the bottle of vinegar and asks you to pour some into the bowl. As you pour the vinegar, a thick, bubbly foam comes pouring out of the bowl and spills all over the counter and onto the floor.

You begin to wonder what else has the same reaction when you pour vinegar over it. So you decide to grab some baking ingredients, as well as some other objects from around your home, and try a little experiment of your own.

Take a look at the items in the table on the following page.

Do you think there will be a reaction if you combine each item with vinegar or water? Predict if you think there will be a reaction or not.

EXPERIMENTING WITH REACTIONS

ITEM	VINEGAR	WATER
Baking soda		
Table salt		
Flour		
Sugar		
Milk		
Bath bomb		
Dirty penny		
Dark chocolate		
Banana		
Coffee		
Limestone rock		
Granite rock		
Soap		

Please remember that it is essential to ask an adult for permission before beginning your own experiment or mixing any chemicals together. Also remember to wear safety goggles and gloves!

ACIDS AND BASES

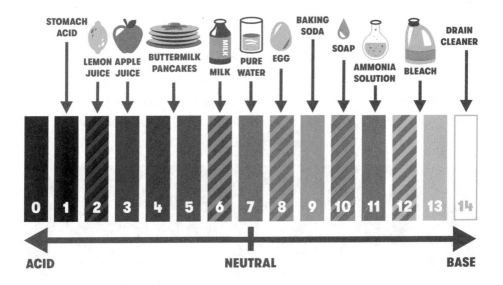

STOMACH ACID

LEMON JUICE | APPLE JUICE | BUTTERMILK PANCAKES | MILK | PURE WATER | EGG | BAKING SODA | SOAP | AMMONIA SOLUTION | BLEACH | DRAIN CLEANER

0 1 2 3 4 5 6 7 8 9 10 11 12 13 14

ACID   **NEUTRAL**   **BASE**

Substances, such as vinegar, milk, and soap, are placed on a scale that indicates how acidic or basic they are. This scale is called the pH scale, also known as the "power of hydrogen," and it is based on how likely the substance is to give up a hydrogen ion (acid) or to take a hydrogen ion (base). Don't worry about the word "ion" yet; we will get to that very soon. Acids range on the scale from 0–7 and bases range from 7–14, with pure water being neutral right at 7. Acids are stronger the closer to 0 they get. Bases are stronger the closer to 14 they get.

In some cases, acids and bases can change the pH of other substances when they are combined. This means that normally when you add an acid to a base or a base to an acid, the substance becomes either less acidic or less basic, respectively.

Adding lemon juice to milk to make sour milk lowers the overall pH of the milk to match the pH of buttermilk, which has a pH of about 4.5. Ready for a stack of buttermilk pancakes? Yum!

In other cases, acids and bases can completely cancel out each other and the properties that come with being an acid or a base. This means that combining an acid and a base can result in a new pH that is very close to 7. And usually, there is some solid stuff left over.

Taking the acid known as hydrochloric acid (pH = 3) and combining it with the base called sodium hydroxide (pH = 12) makes what you know as table salt and water. Yes, the same salt you sprinkle over your dinner. How awesome is it that two dangerous chemicals come together to create those two simple ingredients with neutral pHs that you use so often?

Vinegar and bleach are two substances that are often used for cleaning. But don't ever combine them!

Vinegar is an acid with a pH of 2.5 and bleach is a base with a pH of 12, so won't they cancel each other out? Not in this case! The acid in vinegar is called acetic acid and the base in bleach is called sodium hypochlorite. When you combine those two chemicals, a dangerous gas is created—chlorine gas. Yes, chlorine is what makes pools safe to swim in—in very, very small amounts. But the gas created by combining vinegar and bleach can make you very sick.

Any acids with a pH close to 0 and bases with a pH close to 14 can be dangerous and can cause severe injury if touched or swallowed.

Sometimes, the reactions between acids and bases are as calm as pouring lemon juice into milk. But sometimes, combining acids and bases can lead to explosive results. Even bigger than the bubble flow created when you poured vinegar into baking soda!

Based on what you have learned about the pH scale, predict if the substances you are testing are an acid, a base, or neutral by putting an X in the corresponding column.

ITEM	ACID	BASE	NEUTRAL
Baking soda			
Table salt			
Flour			
Sugar			
Milk			
Bath bomb			
Dirty penny			
Dark chocolate			
Banana			
Coffee			
Limestone rock			
Granite rock			
Soap			

Armed with your new understanding of acids and bases and how they can react with each other, you begin your experiment. You combine small amounts of each substance with vinegar and then repeat with water. The results are shown in the table on the following page.

TESTING HOUSEHOLD SAMPLES

ITEM	VINEGAR	WATER
Baking soda	Reaction	No reaction
Table salt	No reaction	No reaction
Flour	No reaction	No reaction
Sugar	No reaction	No reaction
Milk	No reaction	No reaction
Bath bomb	Reaction	Reaction
Dirty penny	Reaction	No reaction
Dark chocolate	No reaction	No reaction
Banana	No reaction	No reaction
Coffee	No reaction	No reaction
Limestone rock	Reaction	Reaction
Granite rock	No reaction	No reaction
Soap	Reaction	No reaction

SORT THE ITEMS BY THEIR REACTION

VINEGAR	
REACTION	NO REACTION

WATER	
REACTION	**NO REACTION**

ANALYSIS AND CONCLUSION

Now that we are done with our experiment and have determined which items react with vinegar and with water, let's see how the predictions match up against the pH scale.

Circle the word that makes each statement true.

1. The items that reacted to the vinegar are *more/less/neither* acidic than the vinegar. The items that did not react to the vinegar are *more/less/neither* acidic than the vinegar.

2. The acidity of the items that reacted with the water *increased/ decreased/remained the same*. The acidity of the items that did not react with the water *increased/decreased/remained the same*.

Let's go back to the question about reactions from the beginning of the chapter.

Can you use some of your newfound knowledge to help you explain why some substances react when combined and others do not?

_____

_____

_____

ATOMS

To better understand why some of the items and substances reacted with the vinegar and water and others didn't, let's take a much closer look at what each is made up of. Have you ever heard of atoms, tiny particles that make up everything—including you, this book, your favorite snack, the Earth, and everything else in the universe?

What is an **atom**? The idea of an atom has changed a lot since Leucippus and Democritus first described it in about 5 B.C.E. The two natural philosophers, the name for scientists at that time, thought that if you start out with a substance and cut it in half, and then cut the half in half again, and continue the process, you would eventually get down to the smallest possible piece. This tiny piece was considered to be "indivisible." The Greek word for that indivisible piece is "atomos." Atoms were considered the tiny, indivisible, and invisible building blocks of all matter.

PROTONS, NEUTRONS, AND ELECTRONS... OH MY!

THE EVOLUTION OF ATOMIC THEORY

WHEN	THE IDEA	WHAT IT LOOKED LIKE
5 B.C.E.	Democritus's Atomic Model (the earliest known atomic model): The smallest piece of matter that was indivisible.	A round, blank sphere.
1904	Thomson's Atomic Model, aka Plum Pudding: Atoms are made up of a positively charged substance with negatively charged particles moving around in it.	Think of a bowl of vegetable soup—the broth is the positive substance, and the small pieces of vegetables are the negative particles.
1911	Rutherford's Atomic Model: The positive charges are located in the center of the atom called the nucleus and the electrons orbit the nucleus in fixed paths.	Also called the planetary model of the atom—you can probably guess why.
1913	Bohr's Atomic Model: The orbits of electrons are determined by their energy. The electron can change its energy level by absorbing additional or emitting extra energy.	Similar to Rutherford's, but with a series of concentric circles representing increasing energy levels.
1926	Schrödinger's Atomic Model, aka the Quantum Model (the current atomic model): Electrons travel in clouds around the nucleus. The position of the electrons is based on probabilities of where it is most likely to be found in its orbit.	In place of rings or orbits, a hazy cloud of electrons surrounds the nucleus.

The components of an atom continued to change with each scientific discovery. Today, we know that atoms are in fact divisible. The center of the atom, or the nucleus, is made up of protons and neutrons. Protons are positively charged particles. They have a charge of +1. Neutrons have no charge. Electrons zoom around the nucleus in what is called the electron cloud. Electrons have a charge of –1.

COMPONENTS OF THE ELECTRON CLOUD

ELECTRON

NEUTRON

PROTON

The electron cloud is not the same as a cloud that you see in the sky. The electron cloud can be thought of as where the electrons are most likely to be found within the atom.

WHAT MAKES UP AN ATOM?

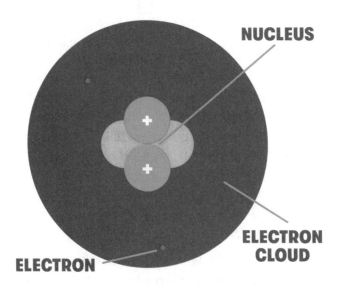

Look at the image of the atom on the previous page and complete the table.

		NUMBER OF PARTICLES	CHARGE OF EACH PARTICLE	TOTAL CHARGE OF PARTICLES
⊖	ELECTRON			
⊕	PROTON			
●	NEUTRON			
	Total charge of the atom:			

These protons, neutrons, and electrons are really important. But what makes them so special? Well, they're special because no two elements have the same combination of protons, neutrons, and electrons. For example, hydrogen has one proton and one electron, while oxygen has eight protons, eight neutrons, and eight electrons.

Even though electrons exist within the electron cloud, they are often depicted in a planetary model to easily see the number of electrons. It is also called the Bohr model, named after Niels Bohr (1885–1962), a Danish physicist who specialized in atomic and quantum physics.

ANALYZING ATOMS

Use the images to complete the table.

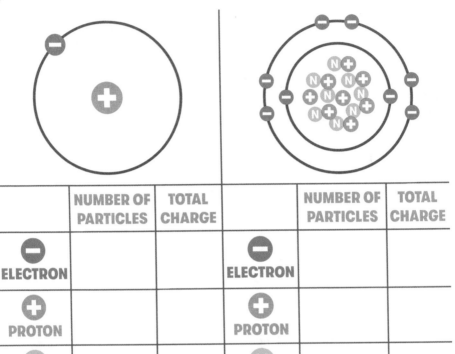

	NUMBER OF PARTICLES	TOTAL CHARGE		NUMBER OF PARTICLES	TOTAL CHARGE
ELECTRON			ELECTRON		
PROTON			PROTON		
NEUTRON			NEUTRON		

Now that you are an expert on what makes up an atom, let's take another jump forward and look at ions.

Remember when you first saw the pH scale and determined that acids were more likely to give up a hydrogen ion and bases were most likely to take the hydrogen ion? Well, an ion is an atom that has an overall positive or negative charge.

FINDING THE OVERALL CHARGE OF AN ATOM

Predict if the following ions would have an overall positive or negative charge.

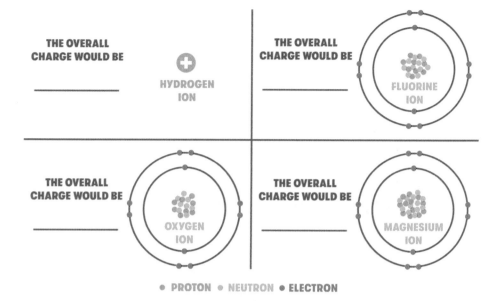

THE OVERALL CHARGE WOULD BE

_____

HYDROGEN ION

THE OVERALL CHARGE WOULD BE

_____

FLUORINE ION

THE OVERALL CHARGE WOULD BE

_____

OXYGEN ION

THE OVERALL CHARGE WOULD BE

_____

MAGNESIUM ION

• PROTON • NEUTRON • ELECTRON

So what makes an atom positive or negative? Is it even important if an atom is positive or negative? Electrons are the outermost particles in an atom. Protons are safe inside the middle of the atom. Because of their location, electrons are more likely than protons to leave an atom or join another.

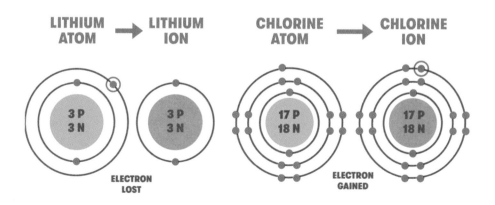

LITHIUM ATOM → LITHIUM ION

3 P
3 N

ELECTRON LOST

CHLORINE ATOM → CHLORINE ION

17 P
18 N

17 P
18 N

ELECTRON GAINED

An atom that loses an electron becomes positive because there are more protons than electrons. An atom that gains an electron becomes negative because there are more electrons than protons. So, an ion is another name for an atom that has a negative or positive charge.

Answer the following question and then draw what would happen on the model of the sodium atom.

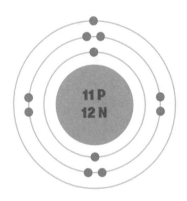

A sodium atom consists of 11 protons, 12 neutrons, and 11 electrons. It can become a positive ion by

A. gaining a proton

B. gaining an electron

C. losing a proton

D. losing an electron

Draw a model of what the sodium model would look like based on your answer to the question above.

Potassium is an example of an element that is usually found as an ion.

When potassium is added to water, it reacts instantly to form a bright purple flame, bubbles, and gas. And if too much potassium is added to water, it could cause a large explosion! (Don't try this at home!)

Let's go back to the question about reactions from the beginning of the chapter. How can you build upon your previous answer? Use your new knowledge to explain why some substances react when combined and others do not?

_____

_____

_____

_____

COMPARING MASS

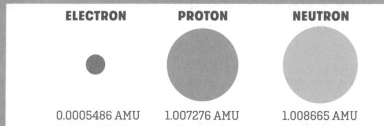

ELECTRON	PROTON	NEUTRON
0.0005486 AMU	1.007276 AMU	1.008665 AMU

The mass of an atom comes almost entirely from the protons and neutrons in the nucleus. Protons and neutrons have very similar mass. Electrons are so tiny that they barely register on the scale next to a proton or a neutron. To make calculations easier, scientists define the mass of a proton and neutron to be very close to one. The units scientists use are called atomic mass units, or amu. It would take more than 1,800 electrons to equal the mass of one proton!

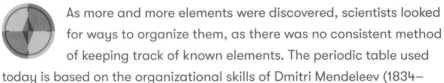

THE PERIODIC TABLE

As more and more elements were discovered, scientists looked for ways to organize them, as there was no consistent method of keeping track of known elements. The periodic table used today is based on the organizational skills of Dmitri Mendeleev (1834–1907), a Russian chemist and teacher. In a rush to get his book published, Mendeleev quickly listed known elements and grouped them based on their atomic weights and known properties. There were about sixty known elements when Mendeleev published the first draft of his table in 1869.

FINDING PATTERNS

While he was listing known elements, Mendeleev noticed that patterns within his table repeated in a very specific way. By following that pattern, he noticed that there were blank spaces scattered across his list. When he sent his table to the publisher, Mendeleev had left blank spaces in the gaps and even predicted the masses and properties of unknown elements. For example, he described an element with characteristics similar to aluminum that perfectly fit directly below it on his table. That element is gallium, which was discovered in 1875 by other scientists who were hunting for Mendeleev's predicted elements. This table came to be known as the periodic table of elements.

As even more new elements were discovered, more so than even Mendeleev predicted, scientists noticed that those elements continued to fit nicely into Mendeleev's table. Some even exactly matched Mendeleev's predictions!

How did Mendeleev predict properties of elements that hadn't even been discovered yet?

_____

_____

_____

Scientists slightly adjusted the periodic table as new elements were discovered and as atomic theories were developed. For example, the same group of scientists discovered argon in 1894 and neon, krypton, and xenon in 1898. They also were able to *isolate* helium, or get it on its own, in 1895 (although it was discovered in 1868).

So, because these new elements all shared similar properties that didn't match any of the other groups on the periodic table, the scientists added a column to the right side of the periodic table. Even with the changes and additions, today's periodic table still closely resembles the foundation laid out by Mendeleev.

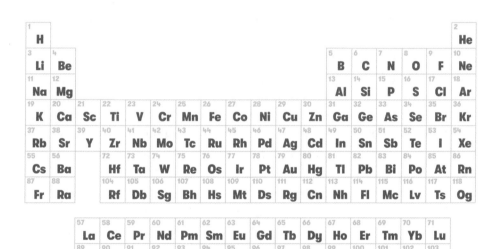

Next, let's talk about some of the groups on the periodic table. Follow along as we color our way through the periodic table!

NOBLE GASES

The elements in the rightmost column on the periodic table that contains helium, neon, argon, and so forth are called the noble gases. Let's go ahead and color that right column containing the noble gases purple. We won't color oganesson (Og) right now; that one's for another time.

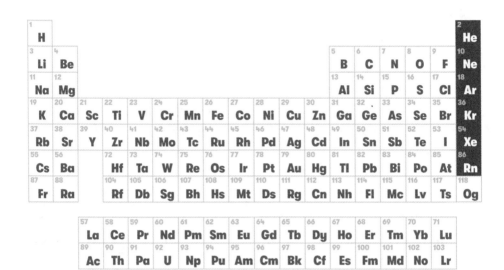

Noble gases almost never react with anything. They are usually found existing happily on their own. And that's about as exciting as these elements get.

ALKALI METALS

Potassium, the element that causes that bright purple flame when you added to water, is a member of the group called alkali metals. The other members in this group are lithium, sodium, rubidium, cesium, and francium. Let's go ahead and color those elements red. Leave hydrogen (H) uncolored for now.

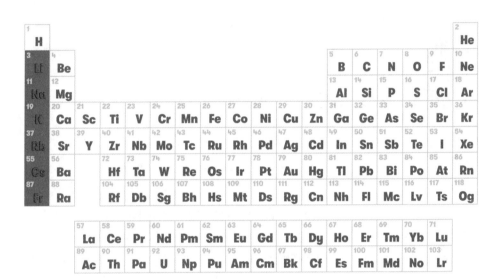

Alkali metals are very reactive, even with water. Cesium is the most reactive of the group, and even just a tiny amount explodes when it comes into contact with water. Alkali metals also tend to lose one electron to make the atoms positive. They are metals, which means they also share properties with all the other metals across the periodic table, such as being shiny, easy to shape, able to be used in electrical applications, and prone to react with nonmetals. Alkali metals are the softest of the metals and can even be cut with a kitchen knife.

ALKALINE EARTH METALS

Now we're going to color the entire column from beryllium to radium orange. These belong to the alkaline earth metal group.

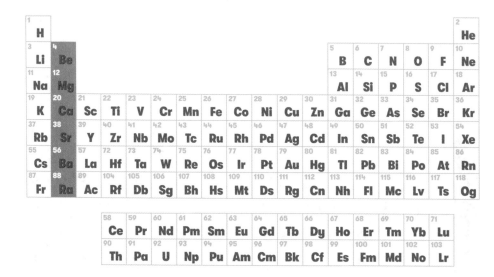

Alkaline earth metals are reactive, just not quite as much as alkali metals. They tend to lose two electrons to give the atoms a +2 charge. They also share the properties of other metals, such as shiny appearances and being easy to shape, although they aren't quite as soft as alkali metals.

POST-TRANSITION METALS

We are going to skip over the middle of the periodic table and head to aluminum. Now, this group, which includes the elements aluminum, gallium, indium, thallium, tin, lead, bismuth, and polonium, gets a bit weird. Let's color them yellow.

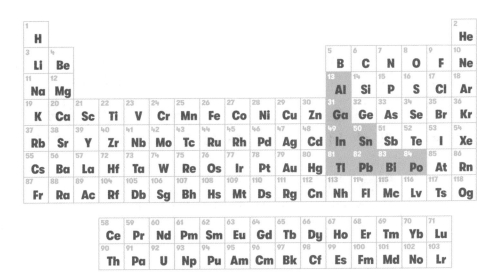

This group of elements has properties that align with a few different groups, but they are also sometimes called the "other metals" because they don't cleanly fit into any one group. This misfit group sometimes even contains other members to the left, right, and below, depending on which properties of those atoms the scientists are interested in.

METALLOIDS

We'll use green to color in boron, silicon, germanium, arsenic, antimony, tellurium, and astatine. These elements are known as the metalloids.

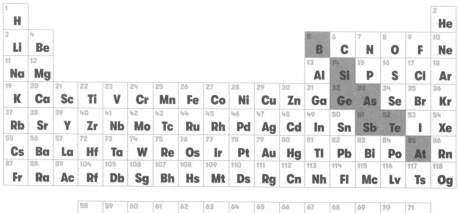

Depending on exactly which column the metalloid falls in, these elements have different properties and in varying degrees. Some metalloids act like metals, while some act like nonmetals. Properties of nonmetals include not being solid at room temperature, being brittle and crumbly, unsuitable for electrical applications, and prone to react with metals.

REACTIVE NONMETALS

Reactive nonmetals are the last group you are going to look at today. Hydrogen joins a handful of other elements in this group. Let's color these ones blue: hydrogen, carbon, nitrogen, oxygen, fluorine, phosphorus, sulfur, chlorine, selenium, bromine, and iodine.

This group of elements shares many properties with alkali earth metals, especially their reactivity with water. In fact, fluorine is the most reactive element in existence. Fluorine must be handled with extreme caution because of how reactive it is. The primary difference between alkali metals and reactive nonmetals is in the name—one is a metal and the other is not. Reactive nonmetals range from solid to liquid to gas and have varying degrees of reactiveness.

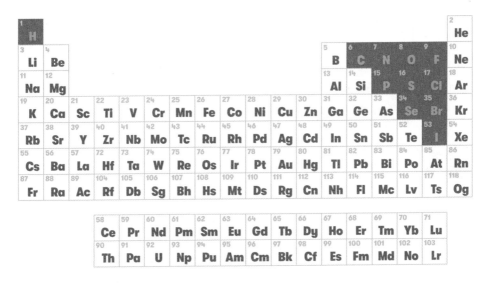

There are other groups and many other properties that exist in the periodic table, but those are for another time.

Now, let's review these groups with a little game. Match the group with a property from that group.

GROUP	PROPERTY
Alkali metals	The misfit group of atoms
Alkaline earth metals	Contains the most reactive known element
Post-transition metals	Metals that can violently react with water
Metalloids	Super chill and peaceful elements
Reactive nonmetals	The atoms tend to have a charge of +2
Noble gases	Crumbly, metal-looking elements

Let's go back to the question about reactions from the beginning of the chapter. You may not have quite enough information to fully answer the question yet, but you should be getting close.

Can you use your new knowledge to explain why some substances react when combined and others do not?

_____

_____

_____

_____

_____

_____

_____

VALENCE ELECTRONS

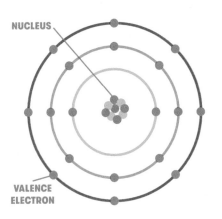

NUCLEUS

VALENCE ELECTRON

While each of the groups that you just learned about has its own characteristics shared across members, there are other patterns on the periodic table that are also important. One very important pattern, which explains the similarities in properties among element groups, is that each element in a column has the same number of valence electrons.

So what makes valence electrons different from regular electrons? Electrons orbit in energy levels around the nucleus, each level containing up to a certain number of electrons. You know that electrons zip around the nucleus in a cloud, but in this case, it is easier to show the energy levels of the electrons using the planetary model:

- The innermost level holds up to two electrons.
- Every other level holds up to eight electrons.
- Valence electrons are the electrons on the outermost level.

NUMBER OF VALENCE ELECTRONS

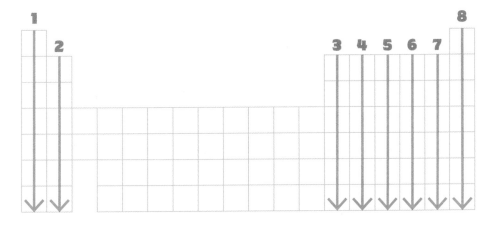

All the elements in the first column of the periodic table have one valence electron. All the elements in column 2 have two valence electrons, and so on across most of the periodic table. Valence electron calculations and patterns get complicated in the middle of the table, so we are going to ignore that area for now.

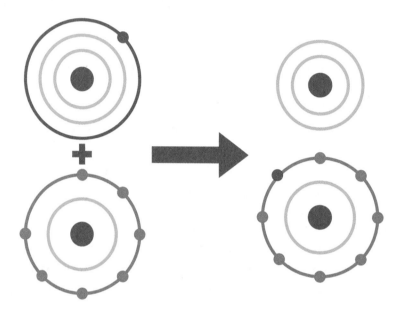

Why are valence electrons important? For starters, the number of electrons at the edge of an atom will determine if an atom is more likely to kick an electron out or to try to nab another atom's electron. Atoms with fewer valence electrons are more likely to kick the electrons out. Atoms with more valence electrons are more likely to gain electrons. Atoms with eight valence electrons are more likely to enjoy being on their own as they are.

 Using the periodic tables on the previous pages for reference, circle the elements that are most likely going to give up an electron. Underline the elements that are most likely going to gain an electron.

Bromine (Br), Calcium (Ca), Radium (Ra), Hydrogen (H), Sodium (Na), Chlorine (Cl),

Oxygen (O), Helium (He), Beryllium (Be), Cesium (Cs), Argon (Ar), Iodine (I)

Sometimes, instead of trading electrons back and forth, atoms come together to share electrons. Water, for example, is made by one oxygen atom coming together with two hydrogen atoms. The shared electrons give both the hydrogen and oxygen atoms full valence shells.

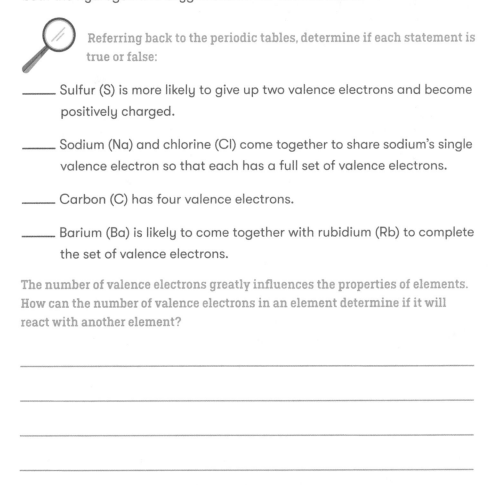 Referring back to the periodic tables, determine if each statement is true or false:

_____ Sulfur (S) is more likely to give up two valence electrons and become positively charged.

_____ Sodium (Na) and chlorine (Cl) come together to share sodium's single valence electron so that each has a full set of valence electrons.

_____ Carbon (C) has four valence electrons.

_____ Barium (Ba) is likely to come together with rubidium (Rb) to complete the set of valence electrons.

The number of valence electrons greatly influences the properties of elements. How can the number of valence electrons in an element determine if it will react with another element?

_____

_____

_____

_____

Due to the number of valence electrons, some elements are more likely to react than others. Elements with full valence shells are the least reactive, while elements without a full valence shell are more reactive. From looking at your periodic table, you may notice that the most reactive elements are those with 1 valence electron or those with 7 valence electrons.

The number of valence electrons also determines what elements are more likely to join with other elements. And most of the elements found on the periodic table are almost always found stuck together with other elements.

BONDS BETWEEN ATOMS

BONDED ATOMS

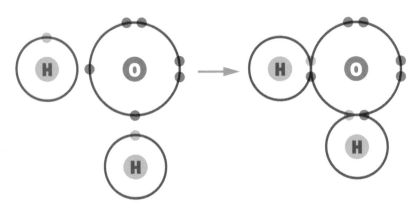

Atoms that are stuck together are called bonded atoms. For example, a bond exists between the oxygen and hydrogen atoms in water to make the three atoms stick together and become a water molecule. A molecule is a collection of atoms bonded together.

Without these bonds, water wouldn't exist—it would just be a sea of individual hydrogen and oxygen atoms. Even worse, chocolate would be a pile of carbon, oxygen, hydrogen, and nitrogen atoms. Nothing would exist without these special bonds between atoms—no humans, no cats, no flowers, no Earth, no Sun . . . no universe as you know it.

Bonds can form between two or more atoms to create different molecules. Sometimes the same atoms can come together in different combinations to form different molecules. The main molecule in vinegar is called acetic acid. Acetic acid is made by eight atoms bonded together: two carbon atoms, two oxygen atoms, and four hydrogen atoms. As you may recall, vinegar reacts with seashells. Shells are made up of a molecule called calcium carbonate—a base. A calcium carbonate molecule contains two carbon atoms, three oxygen atoms, and one calcium atom.

BREAKING DOWN MOLECULES

MOLECULE	ATOMS IN MOLECULE	MODEL
Vinegar (acetic acid)	Acetic acid contains 2 carbon atoms, 2 oxygen atoms, and 4 hydrogen atoms.	
Calcium carbonate (seashells)	Calcium carbonate contains 1 carbon atom, 3 oxygen atoms, and 1 calcium atom.	

EAT THAT MOLECULE!

Do you ever wonder what some of your favorite foods and beverages look like on the atomic scale? Here are a few more examples of molecules!

MOLECULE	ATOMS IN MOLECULE	MODEL
Chocolate	Chocolate contains 7 carbon atoms, 8 hydrogen atoms, 4 nitrogen atoms, and 2 oxygen atoms.	
Sugar	Sugar contains 12 carbon atoms, 11 oxygen atoms, and 22 hydrogen atoms.	
Caffeine	Caffeine contains 8 carbon atoms, 10 hydrogen atoms, 4 nitrogen atoms, and 2 oxygen atoms.	

Which of the above molecules are made up of the same atoms but in different combinations?

_____

_____

_____

_____

COVALENT AND IONIC BONDS

 There are two primary types of bonds that occur between the atoms within a molecule: covalent and ionic.

COVALENT BONDS
electrons shared

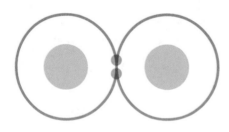

These are the bonds that are responsible for water molecules, and basically all life on Earth. Atoms become close enough to each other to share their valence electrons with one another. This allows the atoms to be happy with a full set of valence electrons.

IONIC BONDS
electrons transferred

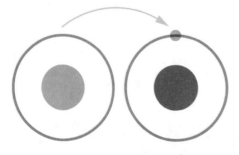

Have you ever heard the term "opposites attract"? Ionic bonds are created when positive ions and negative ions come together. The opposite charges attract the two atoms together and allow them to stick when they get close enough. Usually, ionic bonds are made to give the molecule a neutral charge.

Sometimes, both types of bonds occur within a single molecule. For example, take three oxygen atoms covalently bonded to a carbon atom. That molecule ends up having a charge of −2. Now let's take a look at calcium, which is an alkaline earth metal, so it tends to be found with a charge of +2. So the carbon and oxygen part of the molecule forms an ionic bond with the calcium atom, making calcium carbonate.

Let's go back to the question about reactions from the beginning of the chapter. Think about everything you have learned in this chapter and how you can bring it together to answer the question.

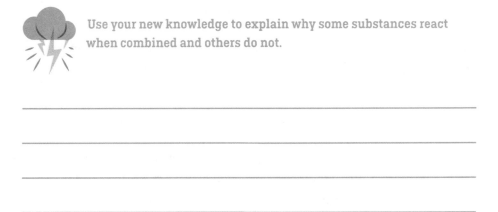 Use your new knowledge to explain why some substances react when combined and others do not.

_____

_____

_____

_____

CHAPTER 10 VOCABULARY

acid: a substance likely to give up a hydrogen ion. A substance that has a pH between 0 (strong acid) and 7 (neutral).

atom: the basic unit of a chemical element. Atoms are made up of protons, neutrons, and electrons.

atomic weight: the mass of a single atom of an element.

base: a substance that is likely to take on a hydrogen ion. A substance that has a pH of between 7 (neutral) and 14 (strong base).

bond: the physical connection between atoms by either sharing valence electrons (covalent bond) or transferring electrons (ionic bond).

charge: a property of atoms based on the numbers of protons and electrons; more protons than electrons would make the atom positive, more electrons than protons would make the atom negative, and identical numbers of protons and electrons would make the atom neutral.

electron: negatively charged particles that have a charge of –1.

element: an atom that has a particular number of protons. Elements make up all matter.

ion: an atom that has an overall positive or negative charge.

mass: the measure of how much matter is in something.

molecule: a collection of atoms bonded together.

neutron: particles with no charge.

pH scale: a measurement of how acidic or basic a substance is.

proton: positively charged particles that have a charge of +1.

reaction: a change that occurs when two or more substances interact.

valence electrons: electrons on the outermost level of the electron cloud.

CHAPTER 10 ANSWER KEY

PAGE 349

There must be something in shells that isn't in rocks that reacts with vinegar.

PAGE 350

ITEM	VINEGAR	WATER
Baking soda	Reaction	No reaction
Table salt	No reaction	No reaction
Flour	No reaction	No reaction
Sugar	No reaction	No reaction
Milk	No reaction	No reaction
Bath bomb	Reaction	Reaction
Dirty penny	Reaction	No reaction
Dark chocolate	No reaction	No reaction
Banana	No reaction	No reaction
Coffee	No reaction	No reaction
Limestone rock	Reaction	Reaction
Granite rock	No reaction	No reaction
Soap	Reaction	No reaction

PAGE 353

ITEM	ACID	BASE	NEUTRAL
Baking soda		X	
Table salt			X
Flour			X
Sugar			X
Milk	X		
Bath bomb		X	
Dirty penny			X
Dark chocolate	X		
Banana	X		
Coffee	X		
Limestone rock			X
Granite rock			X
Soap		X	

PAGES 354–355

VINEGAR	
REACTION	**NO REACTION**
Baking soda	Table salt
Bath bomb	Flour
Dirty penny	Sugar
Limestone rock	Milk
Soap	Dark chocolate
	Banana
	Granite rock

WATER	
REACTION	**NO REACTION**
Bath bomb	Baking soda
Limestone rock	Table salt
	Flour
	Sugar
	Milk
	Dirty penny
	Dark chocolate
	Banana
	Coffee
	Granite rock
	Soap

PAGE 355

1. The items that reacted to the vinegar are *more/ less /neither* acidic than the vinegar. The items that did not react to the vinegar are *more/less/ neither* acidic than the vinegar.

2. The acidity of the items that reacted with the water *increased/ decreased/ remained the same.* The acidity of the items that did not react with the water *increased/decreased/ remained the same.*

Some substances react with each other when one is an acid and one is a base. But sometimes, there is no reaction and the pH of the combined substance becomes close to neutral. So, there must be something more going on than just some substances being an acid or a base.

PAGE 359

		NUMBER OF PARTICLES	CHARGE OF EACH PARTICLE	TOTAL CHARGE OF PARTICLES
⊖	ELECTRON	2	-1	-2
⊕	PROTON	2	+1	+2
⬤	NEUTRON	2	0	0
			Total charge of the atom:	0

PAGE 360

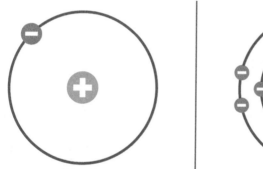
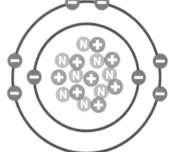

	NUMBER OF PARTICLES	TOTAL CHARGE		NUMBER OF PARTICLES	TOTAL CHARGE
⊖ ELECTRON	1	-1	⊖ ELECTRON	8	-8
⊕ PROTON	1	+1	⊕ PROTON	8	+8
Ⓝ NEUTRON	0	0	Ⓝ NEUTRON	8	0

PAGE 361

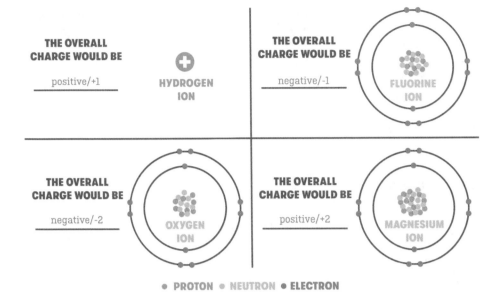

THE OVERALL CHARGE WOULD BE

positive/+1

HYDROGEN ION

THE OVERALL CHARGE WOULD BE

negative/-1

FLUORINE ION

THE OVERALL CHARGE WOULD BE

negative/-2

OXYGEN ION

THE OVERALL CHARGE WOULD BE

positive/+2

MAGNESIUM ION

● PROTON ● NEUTRON ● ELECTRON

PAGE 362

The answer is **choice D**, losing an electron.

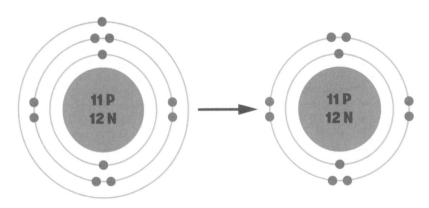

PAGE 363

In addition to a substance potentially being an acid or base, some substances are made up of ions. Some ions can even react with neutral water, such as potassium. Therefore, sometimes the pH of a substance can determine if it will react, and sometimes the substance is made of ions that can determine if it will react.

PAGES 364–365

Mendeleev predicted properties of undiscovered elements by determining the periodic patterns of known elements and using those patterns to determine the properties such as the mass and group of unknown elements.

PAGE 372

GROUP	PROPERTY
Alkali metals	The misfit group of atoms
Alkaline earth metals	Contains the most reactive known element
Post-transition metals	Metals that can violently react with water
Metalloids	Super chill and peaceful elements
Reactive nonmetals	The atoms tend to have a charge of +2
Noble gases	Crumbly, metal-looking elements

There are probably more ways than you thought to determine if a substance will react or not. Different groups of elements on the periodic table react with other elements or even with water. If you look more closely at the groups, there are probably some more patterns within the table that we haven't figured out yet that can tell us if an element will react or not.

PAGE 374

Bromine, Calcium, Radium, Hydrogen, Sodium, Chlorine,

Oxygen, Helium, Beryllium, Cesium, Argon, Iodine

PAGE 375

F Sulfur is more likely to give up two valence electrons and become positively charged.

T Sodium and chlorine come together to share sodium's single valence electron so that each has a full set of valence electrons.

T Carbon has four valence electrons.

F Barium is likely to come together with rubidium to complete the set of valence electrons.

The most reactive elements on the periodic table seem to be the elements that contain one valence electron or need one more valence electron. Therefore, having close to a full set of eight valence electrons makes the elements of an atom more reactive. Atoms with full sets of valence electrons almost never react.

PAGE 378

Chocolate and caffeine are made up of the same elements, carbon, hydrogen, nitrogen, and oxygen, but in different configurations, giving them different properties. Sugar and acetic acid (vinegar) are both made of carbon, oxygen, and hydrogen with different configurations, giving them different sets of properties.

PAGE 379

There are many reasons why the combination of some substances causes a reaction, such as the pH of a substance and the number of valence electrons in the atoms. For example, when acids and bases combine, there tends to be a reaction. The more acidic and/or more basic the substance is can determine how large a reaction could be. Atoms that have either one extra electron or need one more to make a full valence set also tend to be very reactive, even with water, which is neutral.

NOTES

11 MOTION AND STABILITY: FORCES AND INTERACTIONS

You are ziplining between two tree houses. You hook yourself into the zipline attached to the first tree house, jump, and start zooming toward the other tree house. But, you start slowing down and then stop about halfway there. Yikes, you're stuck! The physics concepts of velocity, acceleration, and force can help you. Ready to learn how?

CHAPTER CONTENTS

How do you get all the way from one tree house to another without getting stuck along a zipline?

SPEED, VELOCITY, AND ACCELERATION

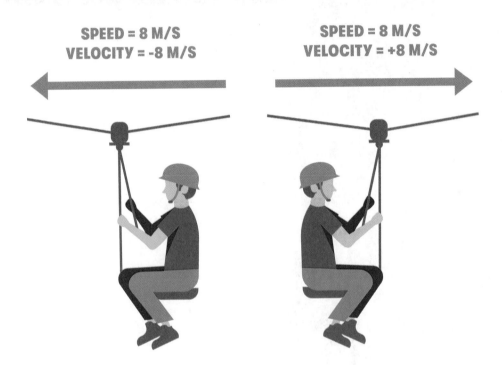

SPEED = 8 M/S
VELOCITY = -8 M/S

SPEED = 8 M/S
VELOCITY = +8 M/S

As you move, you have speed. You have speed climbing up the ladder to get to the tree house. You have speed when you let go and zipline across to the other tree house. You have speed when you drop to the ground. But you also have direction. You climb *up* the ladder. You zipline *across*. You drop *down*. The word velocity describes both the speed and direction that you are traveling.

SCALARS AND VECTORS

SCALAR	VECTOR
Distance	Displacement
Speed	Velocity
Mass	Force
Temperature	Acceleration

Velocity is described as a vector because it describes both speed and direction. Values that have only a size are called scalar. Velocity without a direction is called speed. So walking at a set pace is a scalar value. Walking at a set pace in a specific direction is a vector. The distance you walked along that path, such as 3 miles, is a scalar because it is just a size. When you add the direction to that distance, such as 3 miles toward the west, it becomes displacement. Displacement is a distance with a specific direction.

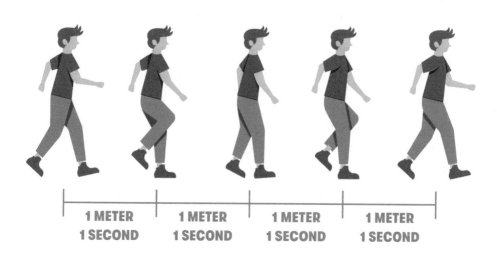

| 1 METER | 1 METER | 1 METER | 1 METER |
| 1 SECOND | 1 SECOND | 1 SECOND | 1 SECOND |

Velocity is measured as distance over time. Examples of velocity are meters per second or miles per hour. A constant velocity means that you cover the same distance during each time period. The person in the image is walking at a constant velocity of 1 meter per second.

VISUALIZING VELOCITY

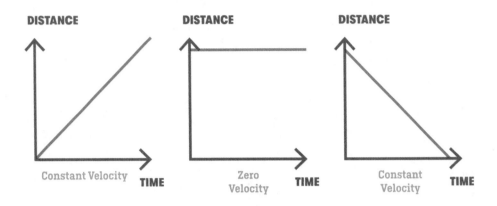

You can graph your velocity by plotting how your displacement (remember, displacement is the vector form of distance) changes over time. Graphs can give you a lot of information. For example, when you graph your displacement over time and you get a straight line with a positive slope, you have a constant velocity. And the steeper the slope (remember slope from math class?), the faster you are going. Therefore, the shallower the slope, the slower you are going.

And when you get to a flat, horizontal line when graphing your displacement over time, you aren't even moving. Maybe you had to stop and wait for the stoplight to turn green.

Now let's say that instead of crossing the street, you turned around and went back home. The slope of the line when you graph your displacement over time would have a negative slope. And that negative slope just means that you are traveling in the opposite direction because displacement and velocity are vectors.

GRAPHING A RUN

Let's say you went for a run and used a GPS to track yourself. Afterward, you hooked up the GPS to a computer and it displayed the following graph:

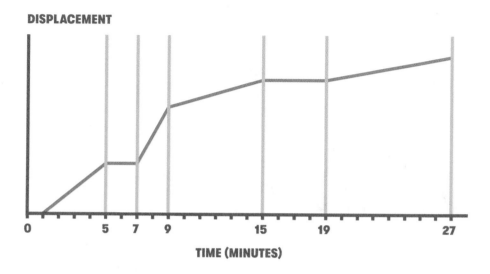

DISPLACEMENT

TIME (MINUTES)

The slope of each line segment tells you a lot. Let's take a closer look at them. What do you think you were doing during each of the time periods?

Well, between 0 and 5 minutes, the slope of the line is positive, so you're not stopped. There are line segments that are both steeper and shallower than the line segment between 0 and 5 minutes, so you weren't walking or sprinting. Therefore, between 0 and 5 minutes, you were *jogging*.

 Circle the word that best completes the statement.

Between 5 and 7 minutes, I was: stopped   walking   jogging   sprinting

Between 7 and 9 minutes, I was: stopped   walking   jogging   sprinting

Between 9 and 15 minutes, I was: stopped   walking   jogging   sprinting

Between 15 and 19 minutes, I was: stopped   walking   jogging   sprinting

Between 19 and 27 minutes, I was: stopped   walking   jogging   sprinting

GETTING UP (OR DOWN) TO SPEED

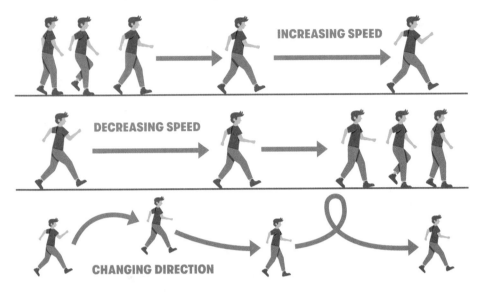

Now let's say that you started out at a walking pace and then began to increase your speed until you were sprinting. When you change your speed, you are accelerating. Speeding up is called accelerating and slowing down is called decelerating. **Acceleration** is the change of speed over time. For example, you accelerate when you go from stopped to sprinting in a race.

 Determine if each of the following phrases is an example of velocity or acceleration. Then, organize each phrase into the corresponding category.

- Walking along a straight path
- Speeding up as you bike down a hill
- Climbing up the ladder of the tree house
- Jumping off a zipline

VELOCITY	ACCELERATION

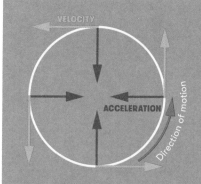

Because acceleration is a vector, meaning that it has both a size and a direction, you are also accelerating if you change direction while running at the same speed. So if you are running around a circular trail at a constant pace of 2 meters per second, you are also constantly accelerating because you are constantly changing direction. So if either your speed OR direction changes, you are accelerating!

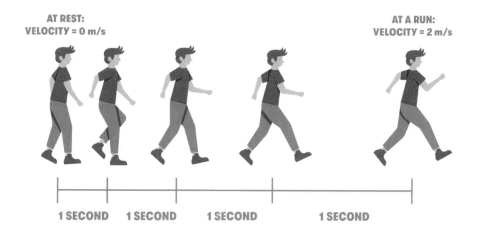

AT REST:
VELOCITY = 0 m/s

AT A RUN:
VELOCITY = 2 m/s

1 SECOND 1 SECOND 1 SECOND 1 SECOND

You decide to use your GPS on another run to graph how your velocity changes. Your speed, according to your GPS, as you accelerate from 0 meters per second to 2 meters per second at the start of your run looks like this on the graph:

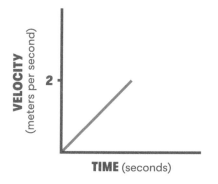

And then let's say that you kept your pace of 2 meters per second, along a straight path, for the next 10 minutes. What do you think the graph would look like? If you were running at the same speed and in the same direction, you weren't accelerating, so the slope of the graph would be zero.

SLOPE AND ACCELERATION

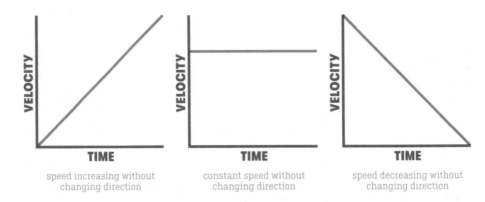

speed increasing without changing direction

constant speed without changing direction

speed decreasing without changing direction

Now, let's pause for a moment here and reflect on the slopes. The positive slope of a line on a velocity over time graph shows that you are constantly accelerating. The steeper the slope, the faster you are accelerating; the shallower the slope, the slower you are accelerating. When the slope of a line is zero, meaning that it is a flat, horizontal line, there is no acceleration. BUT there IS velocity. Because the acceleration is zero, the velocity is constant. So you are still moving; you are just moving at a constant velocity. And when the slope of a line is negative, that means that your velocity is decreasing. In other words, you are slowing down. The steeper the negative slope, the faster you are slowing down.

Now let's finish applying these concepts to your GPS-tracked run. So far, you have accelerated from 0 to 2 meters per second. The graph for that portion of your run looked like this:

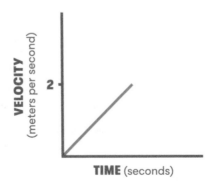

Next, remember that you ran at a constant pace, 2 meters per second, for 10 minutes. Because you weren't accelerating, the slope of that line segment would be zero. Therefore, your graph would look like this:

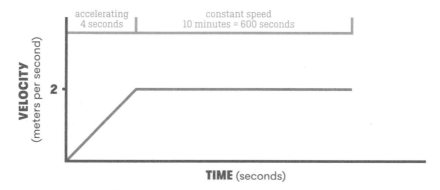

And then, you approached your tree house and slowed back down. It took you 2 seconds to come to a complete stop from your constant pace of 2 meters per second. Therefore, the slope of that line segment on your graph, as you slowed back down, would be negative. It would look something like this:

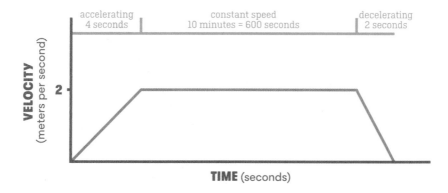

If you calculated the slope of each line segment of a velocity vs. time graph, you would have your acceleration.

 Let's revisit our question from the beginning of the chapter. Can you explain what happens as you jump off and begin to zipline between the tree houses, in terms of velocity and acceleration?

_____

_____

GRAVITY

Gravity is a *force* (more on that word soon) that causes you to accelerate as you drop. When you are stuck on the zipline, you aren't moving, meaning you have no velocity. Then, when you let go, you accelerate (increase your speed) until you hit the ground. This is probably something you should avoid doing!

 On Earth, the acceleration due to gravity is about 10 meters per second per second (or meters per second squared, m/s^2) or 32 feet per second per second (or feet per second squared, ft/s^2).

If you drop a ball (safely!) from the edge of a cliff, its velocity would continue increasing as it falls. After 1 second, the ball will go from 0 to 10 meters per second. After 2 seconds, the ball's speed will increase to 20 meters per second.

How fast will the ball be going at the following times?

3 seconds: _____ meters per second

4 seconds: _____ meters per second

5 seconds: _____ meters per second

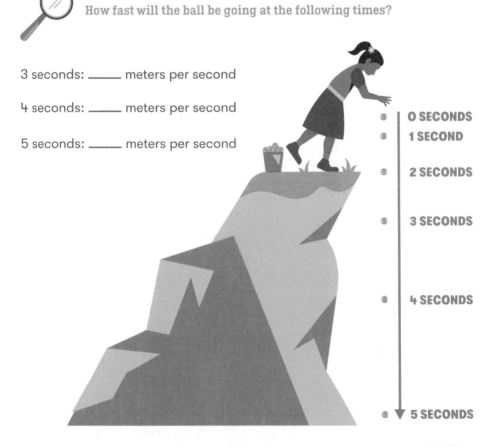

0 SECONDS
1 SECOND
2 SECONDS
3 SECONDS
4 SECONDS
5 SECONDS

Good thing your zipline is much closer to the ground! It only takes you about half a second to drop from the zipline to the ground.

 Based on this information, how fast were you going the instant before you hit the ground?

_____

_____

_____

_____

FACTORS THAT AFFECT GRAVITY

 If Earth's gravity were to suddenly turn off, we would all go flying off into space. Anything that isn't bolted down to Earth's surface would drift away. Even the Moon would travel away. But don't worry, Earth's gravity isn't going anywhere anytime soon! Why? Because Earth has mass. And everything that has mass has gravity. Yes, even you!

THERE IS GRAVITY IN SPACE!

Gravity can act over a large distance, such as between the Earth and the Moon. So why is it common to say that astronauts float in space because there is no gravity? In fact, the acceleration due to gravity on the International Space Station is only very slightly less than what you feel on the surface of Earth! Traveling further into outer space? The gravitational influence from the Sun is estimated to extend over two light years! Although the acceleration due to gravity decreases the farther you go, it is still there. And past that point? Another star's gravitational influence takes over.

So why do astronauts float on the International Space Station? Gravity keeps the International Space Station, and all other objects, in orbit around Earth. Gravity causes an acceleration as it changes the path of the space station. Have you ever been on a free-fall ride at an amusement park? This is the same idea—essentially, the space station, and everything and everyone inside, is in a constant free-fall toward Earth. This free-fall causes everything inside to "fall" at the same rate, which allows the astronauts to float around in the space station.

If you put this book down on the table in front of you and you sit back, there would be a very slight gravitational attraction between you and the book. Although, you'd have to sit there a very long time to actually see anything happen. That is because both you and the book are so tiny compared to the Earth. Earth has much, much more mass than either you or the book, so it has a much greater influence on both you and the book. The more mass an object has, the greater its gravitational influence.

In the table below, use the mass of each object to determine which has the most gravitational influence and put a 1 in the Gravitational Influence column. Put a 2 in the Gravitational Influence column for the object that has the next highest amount of gravitational influence, and so on.

ITEM	MASS (KILOGRAMS)	GRAVITATIONAL INFLUENCE (1–5)
Book	1 kg	
Earth	5.97×10^{24} kg	
Moon	7.35×10^{22} kg	
Person	70 kg	
Sun	1.99×10^{30} kg	

WEIGHT VERSUS MASS

If it weren't for gravity, you would weigh 0 pounds! What?! That's right. Because of gravity, all objects on Earth have weight. But be careful. Weight is not the same thing as mass. Mass is the amount of matter that makes up an object. Weight is how gravity influences the mass of an object.

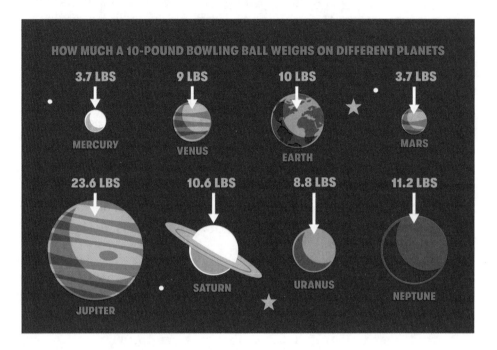

HOW MUCH A 10-POUND BOWLING BALL WEIGHS ON DIFFERENT PLANETS

3.7 LBS	9 LBS	10 LBS	3.7 LBS
MERCURY	VENUS	EARTH	MARS

23.6 LBS	10.6 LBS	8.8 LBS	11.2 LBS
JUPITER	SATURN	URANUS	NEPTUNE

If you take an object that weighs 10 pounds on Earth and send it around the solar system, it will display different weights on each planet because each planet has a different mass. Therefore, each planet has a different gravitational influence. The mass, however, stays exactly the same as you take the object from planet to planet. The more mass a planet has, the more the object will appear to weigh on that planet.

Now let's think back to the question at the beginning of the chapter. How can you use your amazing new knowledge to describe what happens when you get stuck on the zipline halfway between the two tree houses?

_____

_____

_____

FORCE

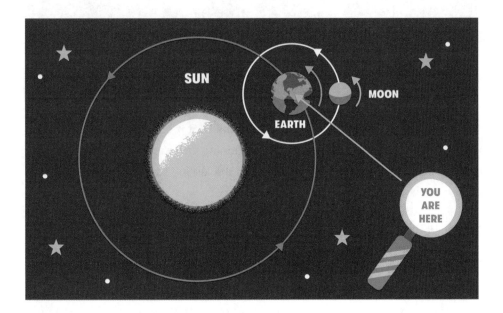

Recall from the beginning of the previous section that gravity is a force. What is a force? Basically, a force is a push or a pull. Earth's gravity pulls you down and keeps you on its surface. You push on a door to close it behind you after walking into your room. You apply a force to pull a drawer open and then to push the drawer closed.

Gravity is a noncontact force. This means that it can influence the motion of objects without physically touching them, such as an apple falling from a tree or you dropping from the zipline to the ground.

Contact forces are forces that influence the motion of objects with a physical push or pull, such as a baseball player hitting a curve ball with his bat. When you pick up this book off the table or push your dinner plate away from you after eating, you are applying a contact force on the book and the plate. But sometimes, when a force is applied to an object, the object doesn't move. Have you ever tried to push a large tree? Did you get it to move? Most likely, the tree didn't budge. So why can you push the dinner plate away but not a tree?

BALANCED AND UNBALANCED SYSTEMS

Take a look at this image. What do you see? The two people are perfectly balanced on the seesaw. This means that gravity is pulling down on each person in exactly the same way. But if a third person came over and joined the person on the right of the seesaw, the seesaw would tip so that the two people on the right dropped to the ground. The seesaw would no longer be balanced.

Forces can either be balanced or unbalanced. Balanced forces result in an object not accelerating. For example, let's say two people are pushing exactly the same amount on opposite sides of a box. Will it move? Nope! The forces are balanced because they are equal forces in opposite directions.

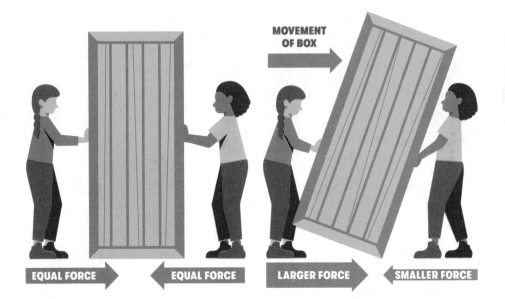

EQUAL FORCE ➤ ◄ EQUAL FORCE   LARGER FORCE ➤ ◄ SMALLER FORCE

Now let's say that one person begins to push much harder than the other. What will happen? The box will begin accelerating in the same direction as the larger force. The forces are not balanced because one force is larger than the other.

Let's think back to the question at the beginning of this chapter. How can you include forces in your explanation for describing your motion as you get stuck ziplining from one tree house to the other?

_____

_____

_____

FRICTION

Now you start thinking about cool things to build, and you also decide to build a skateboard ramp. But what material should you make the ramp out of to give you the smoothest ride?

You begin to test different materials: a large piece of plywood, a sheet of plastic, and a sheet of metal.

You set up each piece of material against a tree stump and put your skateboard at the top of each ramp. (Don't try riding the ramp until a grown up helps you make sure it's secure.) Predict which material will create the fastest ramp, the slowest ramp, and the one in between.

MATERIALS	RANK FOR SPEED
Plywood	
Plastic	
Metal	

As you may have predicted, some materials may be better suited for a ramp than others. But why is that?

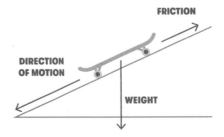

FRICTION

DIRECTION
OF MOTION

WEIGHT

You time how long it takes the skateboard to travel down each of the ramps, and here's what you find.

MATERIALS	TIME IN SECONDS
Plywood	2 seconds
Plastic	1 second
Metal	0.5 seconds

Some materials that are rough cause a lot of friction, which can slow down or stop an object. Other materials are smoother and cause less friction, but even less friction can still slow an object down. Friction is a force that is applied in the opposite direction to which an object is traveling, or in other words, it exerts resistance on an object in motion.

Which material (wood, plastic, or metal) has the highest amount of friction? Which has the least? Why do you think so?

_____

_____

_____

After your experiment, you decide to build your skateboard ramp out of metal, because it had the least amount of friction, which means that it will give you the smoothest ride.

Let's think back to the question at the beginning of the chapter. How can you use friction to explain what happens when you get stuck on the zipline halfway between the two tree houses?

_____

_____

PULLEYS

Let's go back to that tree house at the beginning of the chapter. Now you want to hang out there for a while, but it's hard to carry supplies in your hands as you go up and down the ladder. You decide to build a system that allows you to put your snacks, books, and stuff in a bucket, climb up the ladder, and then pull a rope that goes through a pulley to lift the bucket. The pulley system makes bringing supplies up to the tree house so much easier!

 Use what you have learned about forces to describe what is happening at each of the numbered locations on the image. Match each phrase to the correct numbered location.

The rope is applying a force to the bucket.

Gravity is pulling the bucket down.

You are applying a force to the rope.

1. _____

_____

2. _____

_____

3. _____

_____

LAWS OF MOTION

 Let's say you put your backpack down on the table in your tree house. What is it going to do? It's going to sit there until you pick it up again or accidentally knock it off, right?

This is half of Newton's first law of motion. Isaac Newton first shared his laws of motion in 1687 when he published *Mathematical Principles of Natural Philosophy*, oftentimes just called *Principia*, the book's Latin name. There are three laws that are used to describe the many types of motion and why motion occurs. They are very cleverly named the first law of motion, the second law of motion, and the third law of motion.

NEWTON'S LAWS OF MOTION IN PLAIN ENGLISH

	NEWTON'S FIRST LAW	NEWTON'S SECOND LAW	NEWTON'S THIRD LAW
WHAT NEWTON SAID	Every object persists in its state of rest or uniform motion in a straight line unless it is compelled to change that state by forces impressed on it.	For a constant mass, force equals mass times acceleration.	For every action, there is an equal and opposite reaction.
TRANSLATION	Things will stay in motion or at rest unless something messes with them.	Force, mass, and velocity all affect one another.	This one pretty much speaks for itself. When you head a soccer ball, the ball is also beaning you with equal force!

THE FIRST LAW

Newton's first law is that an object at rest tends to stay at rest, or an object in motion tends to continue along its path unless some external force is exerted on the object. What exactly does that mean?

Part 1: If you put your backpack on the table, it will stay there unless you apply a force.

Part 2: A soccer ball traveling in a straight path across the soccer field will continue unless you apply a force to change its direction or stop it.

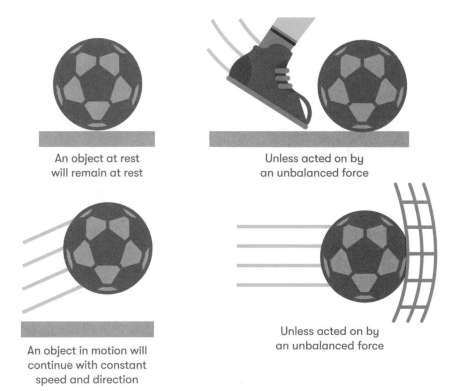

An object at rest
will remain at rest

Unless acted on by
an unbalanced force

An object in motion will
continue with constant
speed and direction

Unless acted on by
an unbalanced force

An external force is a force (contact or noncontact) applied to an object by another object. The backpack is an object. You apply an additional force as you push on your backpack. The soccer ball is an object. The net of the goal applies an additional force by stopping the soccer ball.

Another important word to know when talking about motion is inertia. Inertia is the resistance of an object to a change in its movement. Objects with higher amounts of inertia, like a car, are less likely to move than objects with lower amounts of inertia, like a ball, if you apply the same force.

Let's think back to the question from the beginning of the chapter. How can you incorporate Newton's first law to describe how to get all the way from one tree house to the other without getting stuck along the zipline?

_____

_____

_____

THE SECOND LAW

Newton's second law of motion: a force applied to an object causes an acceleration. Now let's break this one down. A force is applied to an object, such as a push on the backpack or a kick of the soccer ball. The object, the backpack or soccer ball, has mass. That mass begins to accelerate after the force is applied.

Remember, acceleration is a vector. This means that the acceleration can either be a change in velocity, a change in direction, or both. Newton's second law shows how force, mass, and acceleration are related. It is summarized as the equation $F = ma$ (force equals mass times acceleration).

Let's think back to the question from the beginning of the chapter. How can you incorporate Newton's second law to describe how to get all the way from one tree house to the other without getting stuck along the zipline?

_____

_____

THE THIRD LAW

Newton's third law: every action force has an equal and opposite reaction force. If you push your backpack to one side of a table, your backpack pushes right back onto you. When you use your head to change the direction of the soccer ball, the soccer ball applies a force right back at your head!

You will most likely feel the ball pushing back on your head, but why don't you feel the backpack pushing back on you? The forces may be equal and opposite, but you have much more mass than the backpack does. This means that the acceleration of the larger object is smaller, and the acceleration of the smaller object is bigger. Let's see how that works. Remember Newton's second law: $F = ma$. Let's assume that the backpack has a mass of 25 kilograms and the overall force is 100 N:

$$100 \text{ N} = (25 \text{ kg})a$$
$$a = 4 \text{ m/s}^2$$

Now, let's assume that you have a mass of 100 kg and the overall force remains 100 N:

$$100 \text{ N} = (100 \text{ kg})a$$
$$a = 1 \text{ m/s}^2$$

For example, have you ever watched two figure skaters push apart from each other? If you watch really closely, you'll see that the smaller skater moves away a bit faster than the larger skater. But why is that?

The force is equal and opposite, right? Yes! This is where we combine Newton's second and third laws: when they push away from each other (equal and opposite force), the skater with the larger mass accelerates less than the skater with the smaller mass: big mass × small acceleration = small mass × big acceleration.

Let's think back to the question from the beginning of the chapter. How can you incorporate Newton's third law to describe how to get all the way from one tree house to the other without getting stuck along the zipline?

_____

_____

_____

CHAPTER 11 VOCABULARY

acceleration: the change in speed over time.

contact force: a force applied with a physical push or pull.

displacement: the vector change in position and/or direction of an object.

external force: a force applied by one object to another.

force: a push or a pull that can influence the motion of an object.

friction: the force caused by the resistance of one object moving against another.

gravity: a noncontact force that pulls masses together. Gravity is also the force that causes you to accelerate as you drop from a height back to the ground.

inertia: the resistance of an object to change its movement.

mass: the amount of matter that makes up an object.

noncontact force: a force applied to an object without a physical touch.

scalar: measurements that only have a size.

speed: how fast an object is traveling. Distance traveled per unit of time.

vector: measurements that have both a size and direction.

velocity: the speed and direction an object is traveling.

weight: how gravity influences the mass of an object.

CHAPTER 11 ANSWER KEY

PAGE 395

Between 5 and 7 minutes, I was stopped/walking/jogging/sprinting.

Between 7 and 9 minutes, I was stopped/walking/jogging/sprinting.

Between 9 and 15 minutes, I was stopped/walking/jogging/sprinting.

Between 15 and 19 minutes, I was stopped/walking/jogging/sprinting.

Between 19 and 27 minutes, I was stopped/walking/jogging/sprinting.

PAGE 396

VELOCITY	ACCELERATION
Walking along a straight path	Speeding up as you bike down a hill
Climbing up the ladder of the tree house	Jumping off the zipline

PAGE 399

You are initially at rest. You begin to accelerate along the zipline when you jump off, which increases your velocity. Your velocity slows down as you decelerate and reach the middle of the zipline. You have no velocity when you get stuck halfway across the zipline and are just hanging on the bar. When you let go, your velocity increases as you drop to the ground because gravity causes an acceleration.

PAGE 400

3 seconds: 30 meters per second

4 seconds: 40 meters per second

5 seconds: 50 meters per second

PAGE 401

Gravity caused you to accelerate from zero to 5 meters per second after you let go of the zipline.

PAGE 403

ITEM	MASS (KILOGRAMS)	GRAVITATIONAL INFLUENCE (1–5)
Book	1 kg	5
Earth	5.97×10^{24} kg	2
Moon	7.35×10^{22} kg	3
Person	70 kg	4
Sun	1.99×10^{30} kg	1

PAGE 405

Gravity causes a downward acceleration on all masses, including you. When you jump off the tree house and begin to zipline, gravity is pulling you down. Gravity also pulls you down when you get stuck on the zipline and have to jump off.

PAGE 408

You apply a force when you jump off the tree house. Gravity is a force that pulls you down as you zipline. Gravity is a bigger force than the force you applied, so the forces are unbalanced, causing you to get stuck halfway across the zipline.

PAGE 409

Metal will create the fastest ramp, followed by plastic, and then plywood.

PAGE 410

The wood has the highest amount of friction because the skateboard takes the longest amount of time to travel down the wood ramp. The metal has the lowest amount of friction because the skateboard takes the shortest amount of time to travel down the metal ramp.

All objects have friction; therefore, the friction between the rope and zipline apparatus causes you to slow down and stop halfway across zipline.

PAGE 411

1. You are applying a force to the rope.
2. The rope is applying a force to the bucket.
3. Gravity is pulling the bucket down.

PAGE 414

Top: You are at rest, and then apply a force by jumping off the tree house to begin moving along the zipline. Friction and gravity are forces that cause your motion to stop along the zipline.

Bottom: You apply a force to yourself, who has mass, as you jump off the tree house. You then accelerate across the zipline. Gravity and friction apply forces to your mass, which cause you to decelerate along the zipline.

PAGE 416

When you push on the tree house as you jump, the tree house applies a push back at you, which causes you to accelerate across the zipline. In order to make it all the way across the zipline, you must have to apply a larger force when you jump off. And if you don't make it across, you jump down and land on the ground, which pushes back up on you.

NOTES

12 ENERGY

You're riding your bike along a trail. As you ride, you notice something new. Wow! Look at those wind turbines! Those weren't there before. That's good—the city must be using more renewable energy. But how do wind turbines work? You're about to learn about energy, and how it works.

CHAPTER CONTENTS

How can you get electricity from wind?

WHAT IS ENERGY?

So what is this thing that we call energy? Well, energy is actually the result of forces applied over distances.

Recall Newton's second law of motion: a force that is applied to an object will cause it to accelerate. Now let's take that law one step further. Let's say you apply a force to a box. The box begins to accelerate. You push the box across the floor some specific distance. The force you applied to the object over that distance is energy.

The force you apply to the box is 100 newtons (isn't it so cool that the unit for force is named after Isaac Newton?). You push the box 5 meters. To calculate the energy, you multiply the force times the distance you pushed the box. The unit of energy is called a joule.

energy = force × distance

energy = 100 newtons × 5 meters = 500 joules

WORK SMART, NOT HARD!

You may have heard or read about the term "work" when learning about energy. This isn't the same work you do at school or adults do at their jobs. Work, in science-language, means that a force is applied over a distance, which is basically the definition of energy. Energy and work are very closely related. Think about work as a type of energy. In fact, the science-y definition of energy is the ability to do work.

POTENTIAL AND KINETIC ENERGY

 The force on the object can also come in all different forms. Remember, forces can be both a direct contact force of one object on another, such as a physical push or pull, or an indirect noncontact force on another object, such as gravity. It even takes energy to power our bodies. You eat food, which your body breaks up, and then you have energy to get up and run!

There are lots of different types of energy. But don't worry, we'll go through each one in detail! So let's just cover the basics for now.

It takes energy to drive a car, power a home, and even melt ice cream. But even though there are lots of different types of energy, they can pretty much all be classified as either potential or kinetic.

POTENTIAL ENERGY

POTENTIAL ENERGY

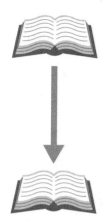

Potential energy is the amount of energy that is stored, ready, and waiting to do something. For example, what would happen if you held this book above your head, and then let go? Obviously, it would fall to the ground. Therefore, when you hold the book over your head, it has the potential to fall if you release it.

Circle the word that correctly completes the sentence.

The potential energy of the book when it is on the floor is the *same/not the same* as when the book is above your head.

The book dropping is an example of gravitational potential energy. Gravitational potential energy is the work done on an object as it falls to the surface or to a lower position on Earth's surface due to the force of gravity. At the top of the hill, the rock is still on the surface of the Earth, but gravity wants the rock to roll down the hill. This will give the rock a lower position on the surface, or a lower elevation. The rock has a lot of potential energy at the top of the hill and little to no potential energy at the bottom of the hill. This is because when the rock reaches the lowest elevation possible, the rock has nowhere else that it can go on its own.

DO THE MATH: POTENTIAL ENERGY

You can calculate the amount of gravitational potential energy an object has by understanding how the mass of an object, the influence of gravity, and its height above the ground are related. The equation for finding the amount of gravitational potential energy an object has is **PE = mgh.** PE is short for potential energy, of course. The m is the mass of the object, the g is the acceleration due to gravity, which we will round to 10 m/s^2, and h is the height of the object above the ground.

You hold the book 1.5 meters above the ground. The book has a mass of 0.5 kilograms. So the potential energy of the book is

$$PE = mgh$$

$$PE = 0.5 \text{ kg} \times 10 \text{ m/s}^2 \times 1.5 \text{ m}$$

$$PE = 7.5 \text{ joules}$$

So potential energy is pretty much entirely dependent upon height. Look at this image:

ENERGY COASTER

Rank the locations on the roller coaster from highest to lowest potential energy.

HIGHEST					**LOWEST**

TYPES OF POTENTIAL ENERGY

Gravitational energy is just one type of potential energy. Other types include chemical energy, nuclear energy, and stored mechanical energy.

CHEMICAL ENERGY	The energy stored in the bonds of atoms
GRAVITATIONAL ENERGY	The energy stored in the position of an object
NUCLEAR ENERGY	The energy stored in the nucleus of an atom
STORED MECHANICAL (OR MOTION) ENERGY	The energy stored in an object before it is released by an applied force

WIND TURBINES IN ACTION

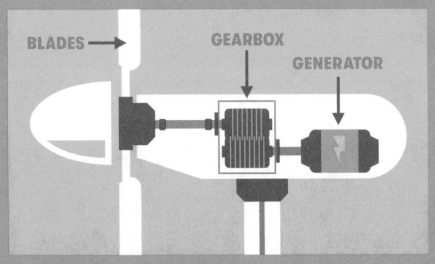

While many people use the terms wind turbine and windmill interchangeably, they are actually slightly different. Wind turbines primarily generate electrical energy, while windmills primarily generate mechanical kinetic energy. There are many parts to a wind turbine that allow it to use wind to make electricity to power your home! Let's take a look at the key parts.

- Blades: the long arms of a wind turbine

- Gearbox: connects the blades and generator, and it increases the rotational speed of the blades before reaching the generator

- Generator: receives energy from the high-speed gears in the gearbox, and it sends out electrical energy

 So let's get back to the wind turbine that you saw on your bike ride. You notice that it isn't moving right now. What is the energy of the wind turbine?

KINETIC ENERGY

Kinetic energy is the energy of motion. After you let go of that book above your head, for example, the book has kinetic energy as it falls to the floor. But it stops moving when it hits the ground. And because it stops moving, it no longer has kinetic energy. Kinetic energy is the energy of motion, like the book moving from above your head to the floor.

DO THE MATH: KINETIC ENERGY

You can calculate the amount of motion or mechanical kinetic energy an object has by understanding the relationship between the mass of an object and how fast it is going. The equation for finding the amount of motion kinetic energy an object has is $KE = \frac{1}{2} mv^2$. KE is short for, you guessed it, kinetic energy. The m is the mass of the object, and the v is the velocity of the object.

Let's assume that just before the book hits the ground, it is traveling at 5 meters per second. Thus, the kinetic energy of the 0.5-kilogram book is

$$KE = \frac{1}{2} mv^2$$

$$KE = \frac{1}{2} \times 0.5 \text{ kg} \times (5 \text{ m/s})^2$$

$$KE = 6.25 \text{ joules}$$

So the amount of kinetic energy something has depends on how fast it is going. Take a look at this image again:

ENERGY COASTER: ROUND 2

 Rank the locations on the roller coaster from highest to lowest kinetic energy.

HIGHEST   **LOWEST**

TYPES OF KINETIC ENERGY

Mechanical energy, which describes the motion of the book falling to the floor, is one type of kinetic energy. There are several other forms of kinetic energy, such as electrical, electromagnetic, sound, and thermal.

ELECTRICAL ENERGY	The movement of electrons
MECHANICAL ENERGY	The movement of objects from one place to another
ELECTROMAGNETIC ENERGY	The movement of electromagnetic (light) waves
SOUND ENERGY	The movement of energy through colliding particles
THERMAL ENERGY	The movement of heat

So let's get back to the wind turbine that you saw on your bike ride. As you watch, the blades begin to slowly spin. What is the energy of the wind turbine?

_____

_____

_____

_____

_____

CONSERVATION OF ENERGY

ALL POTENTIAL ENERGY

POTENTIAL ENERGY DECREASING

KINETIC ENERGY INCREASING

ALL KINETIC ENERGY

At the top of a water slide, you have potential energy. This is because you have the ability to begin sliding down to the lake, thanks to gravity. Since you aren't moving yet, you have zero kinetic energy. Let's say you give yourself just enough of a push to begin moving and you begin to slide down.

The amount of kinetic energy you have actually increases as you move faster and faster down the slide. At the same time, the amount of potential energy you have decreases as you get closer to the bottom of the slide. So, as the kinetic energy increases, the potential energy decreases by the same amount. This is because energy is always conserved and can never be lost.

The law of conservation of energy means that energy cannot be created or destroyed. This is because all energy has the ability to transfer. Think about the slide example. The energy was not lost. That is because the potential energy *transferred* into kinetic energy as your speed increased down the slide. That is one of the most important rules of energy.

Let's look at how energy is transferred in the slide example. Take a look at the image on the previous page.

- At number 1, you are sitting at the top of the slide and haven't begun to move yet. You have all gravitational potential energy and no mechanical kinetic energy.

- At number 2, you are moving down the slide. The amount of potential energy is decreasing as the amount of kinetic energy is increasing. The potential energy is transferred into kinetic energy.

- At number 3, the instant before you land in the water, you have all kinetic energy and no potential energy. The amount of potential energy has entirely transferred into kinetic energy.

- At number 4, you land in the water. You have no more potential energy and no more kinetic energy.

So if energy isn't created or destroyed, what happens to the kinetic energy as you land in the water? Write your prediction below.

_____

_____

When you landed in the lake, water shot up into the air during the splash, which means that some of your kinetic energy transferred to the kinetic energy of the water. You also probably heard a loud splash, which means that some of your kinetic energy transformed into sound energy.

TRANSFERRING AND TRANSFORMING ENERGY

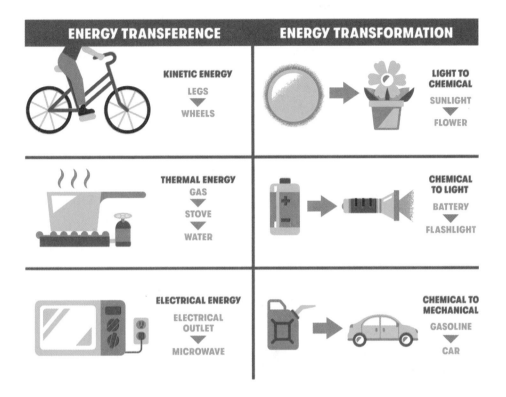

ENERGY TRANSFERENCE	ENERGY TRANSFORMATION
KINETIC ENERGY LEGS ▼ WHEELS	**LIGHT TO CHEMICAL** SUNLIGHT ▼ FLOWER
THERMAL ENERGY GAS ▼ STOVE ▼ WATER	**CHEMICAL TO LIGHT** BATTERY ▼ FLASHLIGHT
ELECTRICAL ENERGY ELECTRICAL OUTLET ▼ MICROWAVE	**CHEMICAL TO MECHANICAL** GASOLINE ▼ CAR

Transformed? How is that different from transferred? Energy is transferred from object to object, such as from you to the water, causing the splash. Energy is transferred between similar types. The potential energy you have at the top of the slide and the kinetic energy you have moving down the slide both have to do with your motion. This means that they are similar. And therefore, potential energy can transfer into kinetic energy.

When energy changes from one type to another, like kinetic energy to sound energy, it is transformed because the types of energy are not similar. Let's say you ate an apple as a snack. The chemical energy from the apple is transformed into mechanical kinetic energy that allows you to climb up the ladder of the slide.

Let's repeat that primary rule of energy again: energy is neither created nor destroyed. Energy can be transferred or transformed.

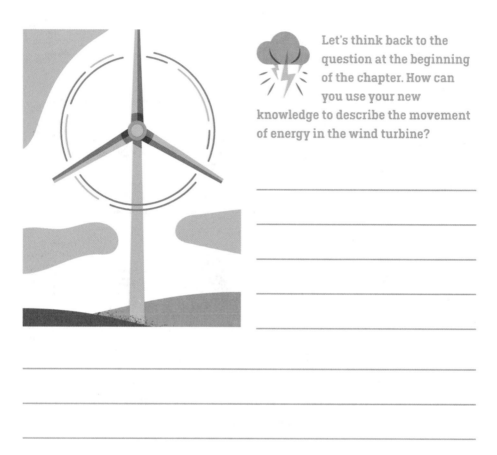

Let's think back to the question at the beginning of the chapter. How can you use your new knowledge to describe the movement of energy in the wind turbine?

_____

_____

_____

_____

_____

_____

_____

_____

ENERGY ALL AROUND US

TYPES OF ENERGY

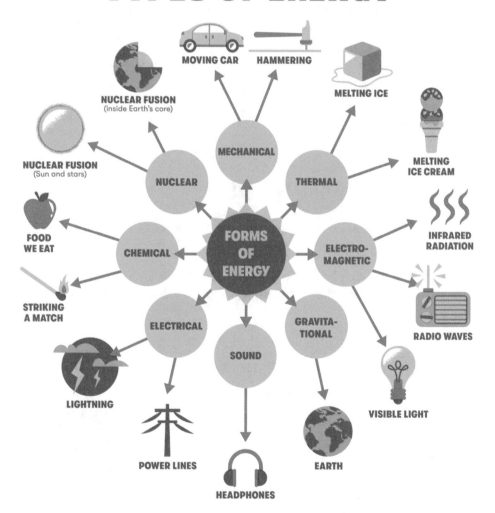

Energy is all around us, and it takes on so many different forms. Humans use different types of energy with every single thing they do. Even the atoms that make up your body are constantly transferring and transforming energy!

We have already covered bits from potential energy and kinetic energy and how energy moves, so let's recap:

- Potential energy is the energy that is stored, ready, and waiting to do something.

- Kinetic energy is the energy of motion.

- Energy can be transferred or transformed, but never created or destroyed.

Different types of energy are transferred or transformed as wind causes the wind turbine to turn. The primary goal of using a wind turbine is to generate electrical energy. But what is electrical energy?

ELECTRICAL ENERGY

Electrical energy is what happens when you flip the switch to turn on the light. It allows you to press a button on a microwave to heat up your food. It allows you to charge your smartphone and also allows you to use your smartphone when it isn't even plugged in. But what exactly is electrical energy?

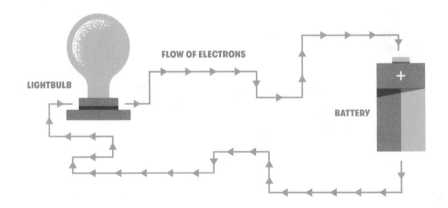

Electrical energy is a form of kinetic energy. And kinetic energy is the energy of motion. The movement of teeny tiny electrons causes electrical energy. Remember what electrons are? Those are the negatively charged particles that zip around the nucleus in an atom.

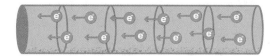

So the electrons that cause electrical energy are not attached to any atom; they are free and traveling around by themselves. When these free electrons travel through a wire, such as the wires through our homes or smartphones, it is called current.

The more current that flows through a wire, the more electrical energy it has. Generally, the heavier the *gauge*, or thickness of a wire, the stronger the electrical current that can flow through it.

THERMAL ENERGY

You unplug your smartphone from the charger and notice that the wire connecting the phone to the outlet is warm. Electrical energy allows the phone to charge, and electric charge is just the flow of electrons. So what else might be going on that causes the wire to warm up?

 Recall what you learned about friction—it is the force caused by objects rubbing against each other as they move. Friction goes in the opposite direction an object is moving in, and it can cause the object's movement to slow down or stop. In the wire, there is friction between the wire itself and the movement of electrons. That friction causes some of the mechanical kinetic energy to leave the electrons and transform into thermal energy. Thermal energy is the heat that you feel.

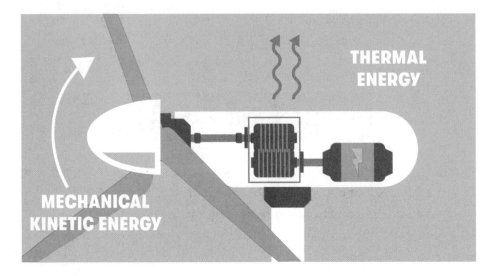

The wind has kinetic energy that causes the wind turbine blades to turn—the mechanical kinetic energy of the wind is transferred to the mechanical kinetic energy of the blades. The mechanical kinetic energy of the blades then transforms into electrical energy, which is sent through the wires and to our homes. BUT, because of friction, some of that energy is released as thermal energy—heat.

ELECTROMAGNETIC ENERGY

Electromagnetic energy can be thought of as light energy, like sunshine. The energy from the Sun is transmitted through space and eventually reaches Earth.

Solar panels, like wind turbines, offer alternative energy. Solar panels collect electromagnetic energy from the Sun. Solar panels have converters that take that collected electromagnetic energy and transform it into electrical energy. So electromagnetic energy is just sunlight? Well, let's dive in and surf the electromagnetic spectrum.

Remember that energy cannot be created or destroyed. But for right now, let's call sunlight the beginning of the chain of energy transference and transformation.

NUCLEAR ENERGY INSIDE THE SUN

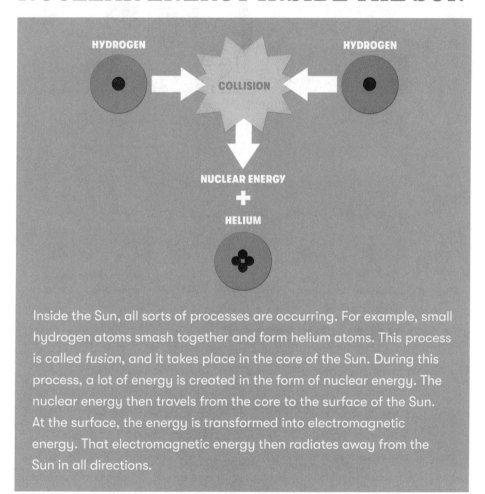

Inside the Sun, all sorts of processes are occurring. For example, small hydrogen atoms smash together and form helium atoms. This process is called *fusion*, and it takes place in the core of the Sun. During this process, a lot of energy is created in the form of nuclear energy. The nuclear energy then travels from the core to the surface of the Sun. At the surface, the energy is transformed into electromagnetic energy. That electromagnetic energy then radiates away from the Sun in all directions.

ELECTROMAGNETIC SPECTRUM

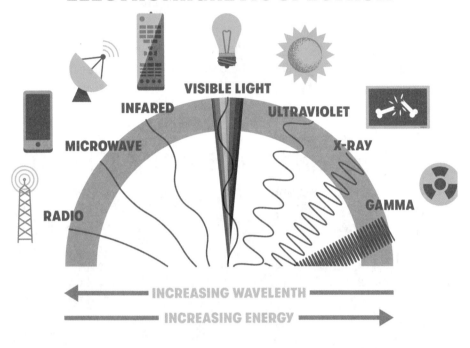

INCREASING WAVELENTH

INCREASING ENERGY

RELATIVE SIZE OF WAVES

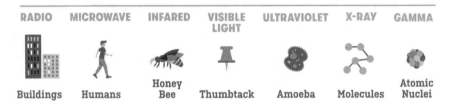

RADIO	MICROWAVE	INFARED	VISIBLE LIGHT	ULTRAVIOLET	X-RAY	GAMMA
Buildings	Humans	Honey Bee	Thumbtack	Amoeba	Molecules	Atomic Nuclei

ELECTROMAGNETIC ENERGY

The electromagnetic energy from the Sun is sent out in all directions, including toward Earth. Electromagnetic energy (more on this in the next chapter) is made up of a wide range of energies, from low energy radio to high energy gamma rays. In the middle of the range is a tiny section known as the visible spectrum. This is the narrow band of light that we can see with our eyes. Most of the electromagnetic energy coming from the Sun lands in the middle of that visible range. This is why the Sun looks yellow.

Solar panels can collect a range of electromagnetic energies to transform into electrical energy. The transformation takes place in a piece of equipment called an inverter.

HOW ENERGY MOVES

Energy needs something to travel through. That something is called a *medium*. Mediums can be solid, liquid, or even gas. For example, electrical energy typically travels through wires or pieces of metal. This is why you never stick a metal fork into an electrical socket. Thermal energy can travel through many different solids, liquids, and gases. That's why you can feel heat coming off of a pot of boiling water if you put your hand near it. Kinetic energy is based on the speed of the object itself, and it can transfer when the objects collide. Think of this like a large group of air particles moving together to make wind. The wind has kinetic energy, and some of that kinetic energy is transferred when it hits the wind turbine.

 Let's think back to the question from the beginning of the chapter. How can you incorporate all the awesome knowledge you just learned to explain how you get electrical energy from wind?

_____

_____

_____

_____

CHAPTER 12 VOCABULARY

conservation of energy: energy can either be transferred or transformed, but it can never be created nor destroyed.

current: the flow of electrons carrying electrical energy.

electrical energy: a form of kinetic energy in which electrons move.

electromagnetic energy: the movement of light waves.

energy: the measurement of forces applied over a distance or the ability to do work. Energy can be transferred or transformed, but never created or destroyed.

gravitational potential energy: the work done on an object as it falls to a lower position due to Earth's gravity.

kinetic energy: the energy of motion.

newton: the standard unit of force.

potential energy: the energy that is stored, ready, and waiting to do something.

thermal energy: the movement of heat.

transferred: the movement of energy from one location to another.

transformed: the change of energy from one form to another.

work: a force is applied over a distance.

CHAPTER 12 ANSWER KEY

PAGE 427

The potential energy of the book when it is on the floor is *the same/not the same* as when the book is above your head.

PAGE 429

Note that 2 and 5 are at the same height, so they have the same potential energy.

HIGHEST				LOWEST
1	3	2 or 5	2 or 5	4

PAGE 430

The wind turbine has potential energy because it has the potential to begin moving when the wind blows on it.

PAGE 432

HIGHEST				LOWEST
2	4	5	3	1

PAGE 433

The wind turbine has kinetic energy because the blades are moving.

PAGE 436

Some of the kinetic energy you have as you land in the water transfers to the water, causing the water to move upward and creating the splash. Some of the kinetic energy gets transformed into sound energy, which you can hear in the splash.

PAGE 438

The wind has kinetic energy, which gets transferred to the wind turbine when it hits it. The kinetic energy gets transformed into electrical energy inside the wind turbine, which gets sent to your home and everywhere else in the city to power it.

PAGE 445

The wind has kinetic energy. Some of the kinetic energy gets transferred to the wind turbine when the wind hits it. The blades move slowly, so they have low kinetic energy. The gearbox increases the kinetic energy through a series of gears. The high kinetic energy powers a generator. The generator transforms the kinetic energy into electrical energy. The electrical energy gets sent along wires to power the town or city. Friction in the wind turbine creates thermal energy, which is released as heat.

NOTES

13 WAVES, ENERGY, AND INFORMATION

You're minding your own business when suddenly, your cell phone buzzes. You smile at the grumpy cat meme that someone texted you. You begin to wonder how someone was able to take a picture of the cat, which was then shared by millions of people around the world, appearing exactly the same each time. How does that happen? Keep reading to find out.

CHAPTER CONTENTS

How is information sent wirelessly from one communications device to another?

THE WAVES OF SIGHTS AND SOUNDS

All of the sights you see and all of the sounds you hear have something in common—the information arrived to you on waves. Not quite like the waves in the ocean. Sight and sound are two types of information that we receive to understand the world around us. That type of information travels as energy.

Do you remember learning about energy in the previous chapter? We are going to build on that information to learn how energy moves from one place to another.

The energy that carries what you see and hear is carried on mechanical waves.

You dip your finger in a puddle and watch as the ripples travel away. We are going to use those ripples as our analogy. When you dip your finger into the water, you are transferring energy from your finger to the water.

Remember the water slide from the previous chapter?

When you landed in the water, you created ripples that traveled away from the water slide, just like the ripples you made in the puddle with your finger. The energy that is transferred to the water then travels through the water on a mechanical wave. Let's dive in deeper.

MECHANICAL WAVES

Let's review what energy is: energy is the ability to apply a force over a distance. Remember, a force can be either a physical push or pull (contact force) or a distant push or pull (noncontact force). For example, you pushing on a door is a contact force. Gravity is a noncontact force that pulls you to the ground.

The energy that is transferred between either contact or noncontact forces is sent over waves. These waves are known as mechanical waves. There are two primary types of mechanical waves: longitudinal and transverse waves.

LONGITUDINAL WAVES

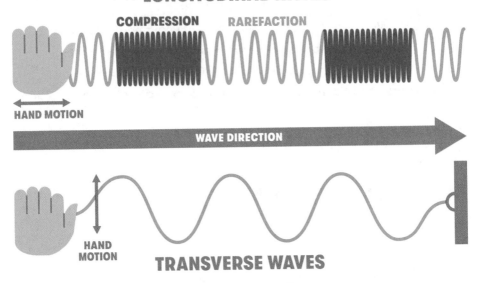

COMPRESSION   RAREFACTION

HAND MOTION

WAVE DIRECTION

HAND MOTION

TRANSVERSE WAVES

EXAMPLES OF LONGITUDINAL WAVES	EXAMPLES OF TRANSVERSE WAVES
Sound	Light
Springs, like in a pogo stick	Ocean waves
Seismic P-waves	Ripples in a lake or puddle

LONGITUDINAL WAVES

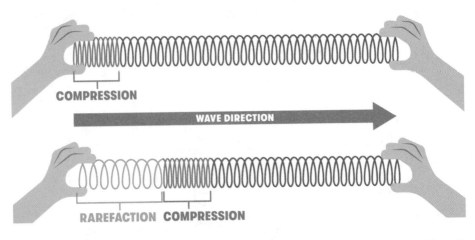

COMPRESSION

WAVE DIRECTION

RAREFACTION   COMPRESSION

Longitudinal waves send energy through vibration. The energy travels in the same direction as the vibration. Is there a bed with a mattress nearby? If so, go sit or lie down on it. If not, think about what happens when you sit or lie down on a mattress.

When you lie down on the mattress, you compress the springs underneath you as you sink in. In other words, you are applying a downward force on the springs. Energy transfers from the top of the springs to the bottom.

PADDING

COILS

Now let's say that you decide to try a different mattress. You lie down and realize you don't sink in as much as the first mattress. Why is that?

Take a look at the following two mattresses. Circle which one you think is the first mattress you tried.

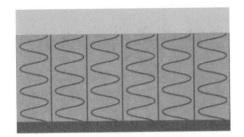 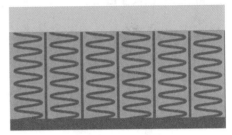

What's the difference between these two mattresses? One has coils that are thin with wide gaps. The other has coils that are thick with thin gaps. If you circled the mattress with the thin coils, you are correct! Thin coils compress more than thick coils.

Circle the word that correctly completes the sentence.

On the mattress with thin coils, there is *more/less energy* transferred from the top of the spring to the bottom.

On the mattress with thick coils, there is *more/less energy* transferred from the top of the spring to the bottom.

So energy transfer has to do with how thick the springs are. A spring is an example of a longitude wave. And, as you will see very soon, energy transfer also has to do with what material the wave travels through. But let's take a closer look at the parts of a longitudinal wave first.

PERIOD:
how long it takes for one wavelength to travel from its beginning to end.

WAVELENGTH:
the distance between each compression or rarefaction.

FREQUENCY:
how many wavelengths pass through per second.

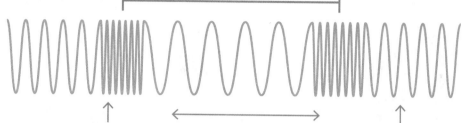

COMPRESSION:
when the medium is squished together.

VIBRATION DIRECTION:
the medium vibrates or moves forward and backward along the direction of motion.

RAREFACTION:
when the medium stretches out.

 A surfer riding a wave, a person talking, or a person looking up directions on her phone. Which one do you think is an example of energy traveling along a longitudinal wave?

_____

_____

_____

BUMPER CAR VIBRATIONS

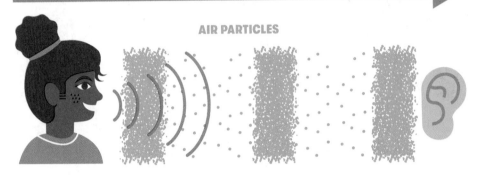

SOUND DIRECTION

AIR PARTICLES

Think of air particles as bumper cars. Now think of what happens when you drive a bumper car purposefully into another bumper car. The bumper car you hit gets pushed forward into another bumper car. And then that bumper car gets pushed forward into another bumper car, and so on. That's pretty much what happens when we talk.

When we talk, our windpipe creates vibrations. Think of those vibrations like that first bumper car coming out of your mouth. That bumper car hits another air particle disguised as a bumper car, and so on until that last bumper car hits an ear. Those bumper car air particles travel on a longitudinal wave.

 Use the diagram below to label the compression, rarefaction, wavelength, and direction of motion on your bumper car wave.

BUMPER CAR EFFECT

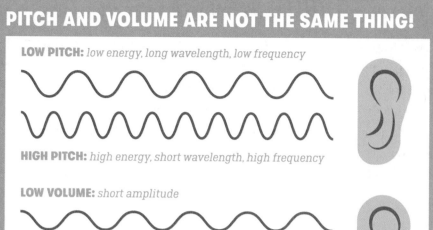

PITCH AND VOLUME ARE NOT THE SAME THING!

LOW PITCH: *low energy, long wavelength, low frequency*

HIGH PITCH: *high energy, short wavelength, high frequency*

LOW VOLUME: *short amplitude*

HIGH VOLUME: *tall amplitude*

When you are listening to music, sometimes you hear the bass and sometimes you hear soprano. This refers to the pitch. The pitch depends on the frequency of the sound. The higher the frequency, the higher the pitch.

Volume, on the other hand, how loud you want your music, depends on the amplitude, or height, of the wave (more on amplitude below). You increase the amplitude when you turn the dial on your stereo or hit the up button on your smartphone. The higher the amplitude, the louder the music.

Have you ever heard the phrase, "no one can hear you scream in space"? Sound waves, and all longitudinal waves, need something to travel through. What waves travel through—air, water, or other liquid or solid material—is called a medium (plural, *media*). Because there is no air or water in space, there are no little bumper car particles, so the sound wave has nothing to travel through. Therefore, it is true that a scream can't be heard in space, by human ears, anyway. But if you are lucky, someone will see you and rescue you because light travels on a different kind of wave.

TRANSVERSE WAVES

So what's the difference between longitudinal and transverse waves? When you throw a stone in a lake (or stick your toe in a puddle), the ripples move outward, but they also wiggle up and down as they move. That is how a transverse wave moves. Instead of bumper cars, transverse waves do a wiggle dance. They send energy through up-and-down vibrations perpendicular to the direction of motion. Let's investigate transverse waves further.

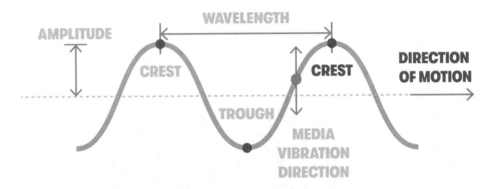

crest: the tip top of the wave.

trough: the bottommost bottom of the wave.

wavelength: the distance from crest to crest or trough to trough.

amplitude: how tall each crest or trough is.

media vibration direction: perpendicular to the direction of motion.

period: how long it takes for one wavelength to travel from beginning to end.

frequency: how many wavelengths pass through per second.

Let's look at another example of transverse waves. Have you ever used a pogo stick?

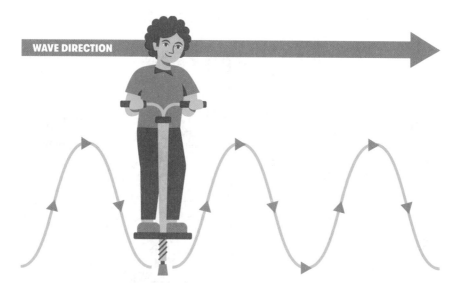

Let's say you are a glob of energy. And you decide to use a pogo stick to bounce down the sidewalk. You are bouncing up and down, yet you are moving forward at the same time.

 Let's test your knowledge of transverse waves. Look at the image below and then fill in the blanks using the terms provided on the previous page.

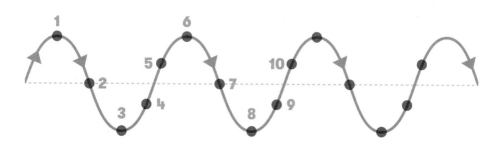

As you follow the energy glob from point 1 to point 6, you are tracing out a(n) _____. The _____ can be measured as the height difference between points 2 and 3. Point 8 is the _____, and point 1 is the _____.

We have said a couple of times now that light is a transverse wave, so let's enlighten ourselves about light.

ELECTROMAGNETIC SPECTRUM

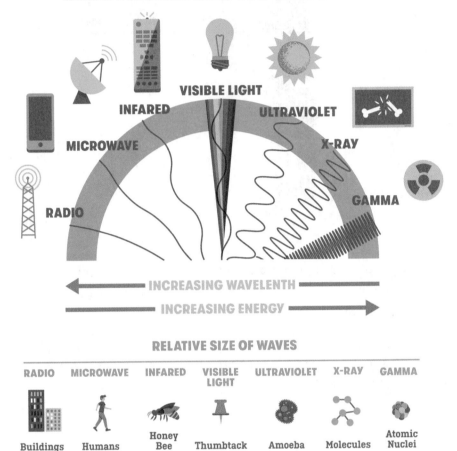

VISIBLE LIGHT

INFARED

ULTRAVIOLET

MICROWAVE

X-RAY

RADIO

GAMMA

← INCREASING WAVELENTH →

INCREASING ENERGY →

RELATIVE SIZE OF WAVES

RADIO	MICROWAVE	INFARED	VISIBLE LIGHT	ULTRAVIOLET	X-RAY	GAMMA
Buildings	Humans	Honey Bee	Thumbtack	Amoeba	Molecules	Atomic Nuclei

Light is part of the electromagnetic spectrum. Do you remember learning about electromagnetic energy in the previous chapter? Light is a part of that spectrum. All of the different types of light on the electromagnetic spectrum travel along transverse waves. The largest wavelengths are so big that they are the size of skyscrapers.

Those really big waves are called radio waves.

RADIO WAVES

Now let's say you turn on the radio and your favorite song is playing. That song is being played in one location, wherever that radio station is located. The people at the radio station take the song, convert it into an electronic signal, and send it out on those really big radio waves. The radio waves travel from the radio station to your radio, which converts the radio waves back into sound waves, so you can listen to your favorite song.

MICROWAVES

Some people use microwaves to heat up their leftovers. You put your cold leftovers in, press a few buttons, and a few minutes later you have hot food. Microwaves are named after the type of electromagnetic energy they use. Heat energy travels along microwaves, which are about the size of ants, to your food to warm it up.

INFRARED LIGHT

Between visible light and microwaves on the electromagnetic spectrum, you'll find infrared light. Infrared wavelengths range from the size of the head of a pin down to microscopic. We experience longer infrared waves ("far infrared") as heat—think the warmth of a radiator or a fire. Infrared lamps are often used in restaurants to heat food. Shorter infrared waves ("near infrared") are used in many remote controls, like those for a TV.

VISIBLE LIGHT

Visible light falls between infrared and ultraviolet on the electromagnetic spectrum. Coincidence? No. Take a look at the color prism on the opposite page. At one end of the visible spectrum is red—and infrared is just beyond that (*infra* means "below" in Latin). At the other end of the visible spectrum is violet. Ultraviolet is just beyond that (*ultra* means "beyond" in Latin). Luckily for us, the visible light spectrum happens to correspond with the wavelengths that are visible to receptors in our eyes.

ULTRAVIOLET LIGHT

At its longer wavelengths (UV-A), ultraviolet light is familiar to us as "black light," which makes ordinary colors appear to glow. The shorter ultraviolet wavelengths (UV-B) are the rays that can give us sunburn, while the smallest (UV-C) are extremely harmful to humans even in small doses, but are used by humans to disinfect food and to kill harmful microorganisms.

X-RAYS

X-ray machines direct X-rays, which are about the size of an atom, toward your broken bone. This type of energy can travel through your skin, but not your bones. This is why your bones look white in the image. Doctors can use X-rays to see exactly where your bone is broken so they can best treat it.

GAMMA RAYS

The smallest wavelengths on the electromagnetic spectrum belong to gamma rays. They also have the most energy of any wave on the spectrum, emanating as they do from neutron stars, pulsars, supernova explosions, and regions around black holes. On Earth, gamma waves are generated by nuclear explosions, lightning, and radioactive decay.

All of these examples move energy from one place to another along transverse waves.

LONGITUDINAL WAVES, TRANSVERSE WAVES, AND EARTHQUAKES

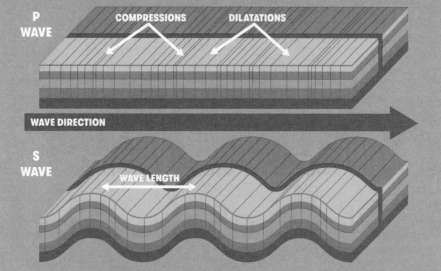

P WAVE — COMPRESSIONS — DILATATIONS

WAVE DIRECTION

S WAVE — WAVE LENGTH

Have you ever experienced an earthquake? During an earthquake, two types of waves travel through the planet—longitudinal and transverse waves. Longitudinal waves are called P-waves because they travel fast and are usually the first or primary waves to be detected. Transverse waves are called S-waves because they travel more slowly, and are generally the second waves to be detected.

Let's take a quick moment to reflect. How do you think mechanical waves can help you begin to understand how information is sent from one device to another?

_____

_____

_____

_____

_____

MOVEMENT OF MECHANICAL WAVES

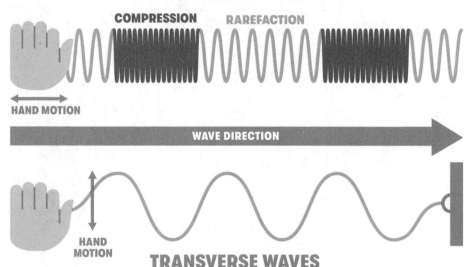

LONGITUDINAL WAVES

COMPRESSION RAREFACTION

HAND MOTION

WAVE DIRECTION

HAND MOTION

TRANSVERSE WAVES

So we have mechanical waves—both longitudinal and transverse. Both types of waves move energy from one place to another in different ways. So far, we have just looked at how these waves travel in a single direction—a straight line. But can they turn? And what happens when they hit something?

WAVE BEHAVIOR

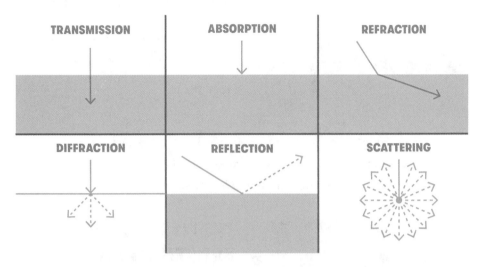

Waves can pass straight through an object as if it weren't even there, which is called transmission. Waves happily continue on their direct path, or they can hit something and be totally stopped in their path. When that happens, they are sometimes absorbed into whatever they run into. Have you ever felt a dark-colored sidewalk or street on a hot day? Energy carried on waves was absorbed into that pavement and caused it to heat up.

Remember the law of conservation of energy: energy can be transfered or transformed but never created nor destroyed.

Let's take a closer look at what else can happen. Waves can bend as they travel, which is called refraction. Diffraction is a special type of refraction in which waves are bent in more than one direction. Waves can also bounce right back off of the object they run into. That is called reflection. Scattering is a special kind of reflection in which waves are reflected in more than one direction. Let's take a more detailed look at refraction and reflection.

REFRACTION

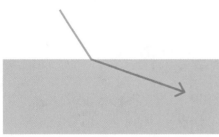

REFRACTION OF MECHANICAL WAVES

Have you ever noticed that when you try to walk in water, you can't go as fast as you can when you walk on the ground? The same thing happens to waves! Let's say a wave is traveling through the air and then hits the water. It moves more slowly through the water, which causes the wave to bend. That phenomenon is called refraction. Let's look at an example called the broken straw.

THE MYSTERIOUS BROKEN STRAW

When you put a straw into a clear glass filled with water and look at it from the side, the straw looks like it broke apart. It looks that way because of the bending of light.

The light going through the air headed toward the water is called the incident wave. The "normal" is the angle perpendicular to the surface of the water, or perpendicular to wherever the change of medium occurs. The angle of incidence is what angle the light hit the water at.

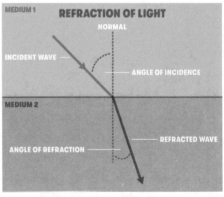

The angle of refraction is, you guessed it, the amount the light that was refracted or bent. The refracted wave is the new direction the light takes. That's why when you look at the straw from the side, the straw looks like its broken where the air hits the water.

Refraction can also be observed by taking a prism and holding it up to the light. Do you have a prism handy? Or even a disc such as a CD, DVD, or Blu-ray (ask someone over 30 if you're not sure what these are). If you do, go ahead and hold it up to the light. If you are using a disc, hold the shiny side up to the light and move it around. What do you see? Wow, look at all those beautiful rainbows—that's refraction!

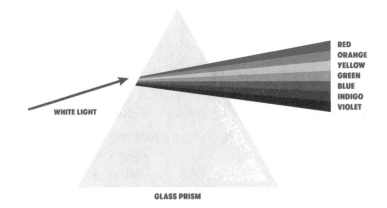

WHITE LIGHT

RED
ORANGE
YELLOW
GREEN
BLUE
INDIGO
VIOLET

GLASS PRISM

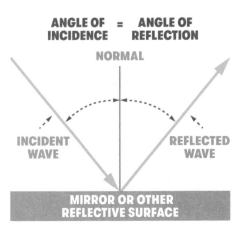

Think back to the electromagnetic spectrum. Each color of that rainbow has its own unique wavelength of light. When the light hits the prism, each one of those wavelengths bends a slightly different amount. This breaks the light up into the colors that make up the rainbow. The same thing happens when you see a rainbow in the sky after it rains. In that case, the prisms are water droplets in the air.

REFLECTION OF MECHANICAL WAVES

ANGLE OF INCIDENCE = ANGLE OF REFLECTION

NORMAL

INCIDENT WAVE

REFLECTED WAVE

MIRROR OR OTHER REFLECTIVE SURFACE

Let's bounce on over to see what happens when waves are reflected. Waves travel in a straight path and then smack into something solid, like a mirror. The wave hits it and bounces right back off, like a basketball bouncing off a polished court floor.

You might notice that some of these terms are almost the same as the terms describing what happens when waves are refracted. The light headed toward the mirror is called the incident wave. The angle of incidence is the angle at which the light wave hits the mirror. The angle of reflection is equal to the angle of incidence, and it is the angle at which the light wave bounces back off the mirror. And the reflected wave is, of course, the light wave that is reflected back off of the mirror.

A THOUGHT EXPERIMENT

Let's do another experiment, but let's make this one a thought experiment. Lasers travel in a straight line and change direction when they reflect off of a mirror.

 On the image below, draw the path the laser will take as it travels from start to finish, ending at the target. Remember, lasers have to follow the rules of physics. Use the diagram on the prior page if you get stuck. Note that not all mirrors may be included in the path.

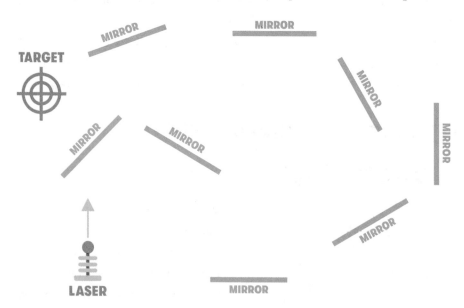

Did you make it through the laser maze? How many mirrors did you need to make the laser reach the target?

Let's take a look at another example of how waves can be reflected.

ECHOLOCATION

Some animals, such as dolphins and bats, use echolocation to find their next meal.

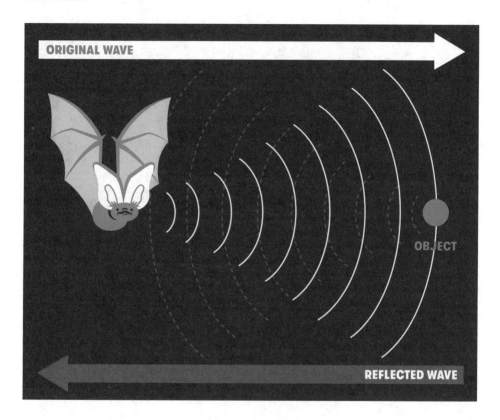

 This is very similar to how sonar works on submarines. Sound waves get sent out and then travel in a straight line until they hit an obstacle or object. The sound waves get reflected back toward the animals or submarine. Submarines typically change direction when they detect obstacles. But bats and dolphins can tell that some of those reflected waves bounced off of their next meal, so they head straight for them.

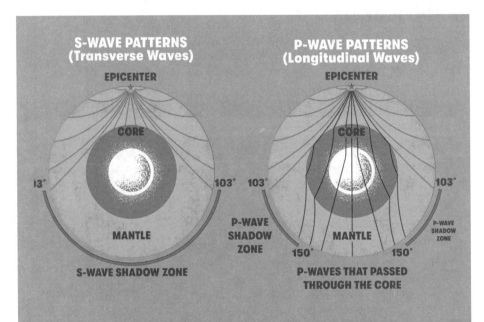

S-WAVE PATTERNS
(Transverse Waves)

EPICENTER

CORE

13°

103°

MANTLE

S-WAVE SHADOW ZONE

P-WAVE PATTERNS
(Longitudinal Waves)

EPICENTER

CORE

103°   103°

P-WAVE
SHADOW
ZONE

P-WAVE
SHADOW
ZONE

MANTLE

150°   150°

P-WAVES THAT PASSED
THROUGH THE CORE

Here's another interesting fact for you about P- and S-waves: they were used to help scientists determine what the layers inside Earth are made out of. Scientists knew that different types of materials expand and contract in differing amounts (P-waves) and that different types of materials refract and reflect waves in differing amounts (S-waves). By modeling the detection of the different types of waves for many, many earthquakes, scientists were able to find out what the layers inside Earth are made of and how thick they are.

How can you take the movement of mechanical waves to further develop your understanding of the question from the beginning of this chapter? How is information sent from one device to another?

_____

_____

_____

_____

SIGNALS

ANALOG AND DIGITAL INFORMATION SIGNALS

The energy that travels by either longitudinal or transverse waves also carries a good amount of information with it. But how can the information be sent from one specific place to another? Like the grumpy cat picture you received from a friend as a text message?

That is called the exchange of information signals. There are two main types of signals: analog and digital.

Take a look at these clocks. Write their similarities and differences in the Venn diagram below, but remember to leave some room. You may want to add some new details as you read on.

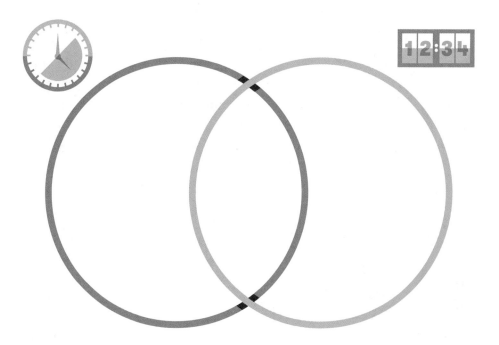

Let's start with the types of signals that are all around us: analog signals.

ANALOG SIGNALS

When you speak or sing, you are sending out an analog signal. Cats meowing, dogs barking, and even the sound of traffic on a busy street—basically, everything in nature is analog.

Until the advancement of computers during the 20th century, signals were read in analog. Because analog signals are continuous, with an infinite number of possible values, they are usually read on a meter or dial with an indicator needle that can register the highest value, the lowest value, and everything in between. Think about a second hand moving around a clock and you'll get the idea.

Let's look at an example. You might hear an adult say, "this doesn't sound nearly as good as it did on my old vinyl records!" Well, there is some truth to that. The sound from a vinyl record is continuous sound. The songs you hear through your mp3 player are not. Let's investigate the sound from records first.

When you are listening to analog signals, such as music from a vinyl record, the signals cover all of the sound. This means that you don't miss anything when you listen to the music shared over analog waves.

So how does that compare to the sound you hear from the music on your mp3 player? The signals you hear from vinyl records differ from signals generated by a computerized device, which are digital signals. Take a look at the signals from a vinyl record and a smartphone or portable mp3 player:

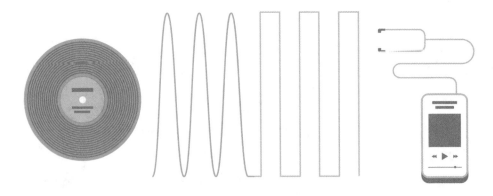

Add your observations to the Venn diagram on page 473 if you still have room. If you don't, use the space below.

_____

_____

_____

Most of the music that you listen to today has been converted from an analog signal to a digital signal. The example on the previous page shows that the signals are different. Keep reading to find out exactly how analog and digital signals are different.

DIGITAL SIGNALS

To understand digital signals, which are signals that are used to represent analog signals, you need to understand binary signals.

BINARY SIGNAL

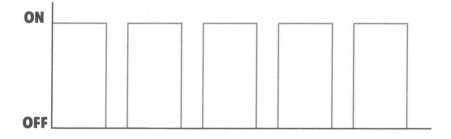

Binary signals are signals that have two modes—off and on. Computers are an example of binary in action: they run on binary code. All of the software on your computer, all of the apps on your smartphone, and even the video games that you play on consoles are built on binary code. All the information your computer processes gets translated into long strings of 0s and 1s. The 0s represent "off" and the 1s represent "on." Each of the 0s and 1s is called a _bit_.

THE ALPHABET IN TWO KINDS OF BINARY CODE

Even each letter typed into this book can be rewritten as a sequence of 0s and 1s.

LETTER	BINARY EQUIVALENT	MORSE CODE	LETTER	BINARY EQUIVALENT	MORSE CODE
A	01000001	.-	N	01101110	-.
B	01000010	-...	O	01101111	- - -
C	01100011	-.-.	P	01110000	.- -.
D	01100100	-..	Q	01110001	- -.-
E	01100101	.	R	01110010	.-.
F	01100110	..-.	S	01110011	...
G	01100111	- -.	T	01110100	-
H	01101000	....	U	01110101	..-
I	01101001	..	V	01110110	...-
J	01101010	. - - -	W	01110111	.- -
K	01101011	-.-	X	01111000	-..-
L	01101100	.-..	Y	01111001	-.- -
M	01101101	- -	Z	01111010	- -..

First, write your name using the regular alphabet.

Now, try converting your name into binary code. There's an extra line because binary letters take up a lot of space!

MORSE CODE

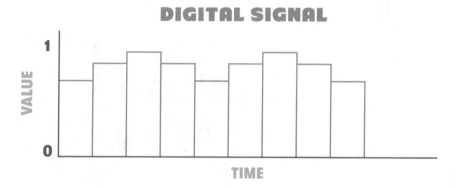

Can you read the line of code above? Morse code is an example of binary code made up of dots (.) and dashes (–). It is typed out using a single lever that completes a circuit and sends electrical energy along a wire to a receiver.

COMPUTERS

DIGITAL SIGNAL

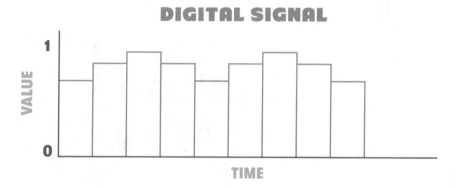

Computers use digital signals that are built upon binary signals to run. Digital signals are similar to binary signals in that each segment is given a specific value. This value is often called the discrete value.

Let's compare digital and analog signals to get a better idea of digital signals. What do you notice? Add your observations to your Venn diagram if you have room or use the space below.

_____

_____

_____

And now, let's take the analog signal and convert it into a digital signal. Picture yourself walking down a hill.

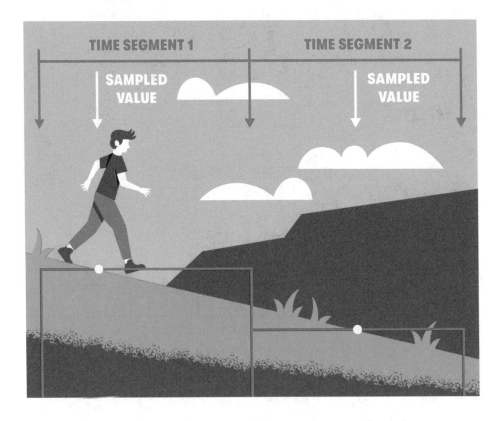

Think of the hill as the original, analog signal. It gets sampled once per time segment. This means that any point within the time segment is fair game to be picked to be the sample. So you pick your point and turn it into a series of bits. This is why digital signals look very similar to binary code signals. Digital signals are called square waves. Can you guess why?

ANALOG VS. DIGITAL SIGNALS: SIMILARITIES AND DIFFERENCES

Analog waves are great for sound and video because they allow for the recording of every note of an instrument and every flicker of movement. Whereas with digital signals, you only hear sampled bits. Let's think back to our vinyl record versus portable mp3 player. A lot of people have trouble telling the difference between what they hear on their mp3 player or computer and what they hear on a vinyl record. If you have access to both, try it out for yourself. If not, you can at least see why.

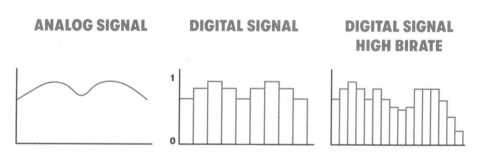

During the process of converting an analog signal to a digital signal, the analog signal gets sampled at each specific time segment. This is called the "bitrate" or "sample rate." The higher the bitrate, the closer the digital signal matches the analog signal.

 It's your turn! Use the following analog signal to draw what its corresponding digital signal would look like.

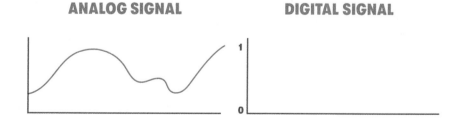

THE PROS AND CONS OF ANALOG AND DIGITAL SIGNALS

Both analog signals and digital signals have their positive and negative qualities. Let's summarize a few of them.

ANALOG SIGNALS	
PROS	**CONS**
They are ideal for sound, visual, and motion pictures.	Making copies of analog signals causes the signals to degrade.
They require less bandwidth than digital signals.	They are not as accurate as digital signals.

DIGITAL SIGNALS	
PROS	**CONS**
They can be shared and copied over and over without losing any quality.	They require more bandwidth than analog signals.
They are universal.	They can't give perfect reproductions of sound.
They are easy for computers to read, edit, and send.	Sampling leads to rounding errors.
They can be compressed.	
They can be encoded.	

 Think back to that text message of a cat that you received on your smartphone. How can you use the knowledge you gained to develop your understanding about how information transfers between devices? How is information sent from one device to another?

_____

_____

_____

CHAPTER 13
VOCABULARY

absorb: to take in or soak up energy.

amplitude: the height of a wave.

analog signal: a continuous signal that can be found everywhere in nature.

angle of incidence: the angle of light as it hits a surface.

angle of refraction: the angle of light that is refracted or bent after it hits a surface.

binary signal: a signal made up of only two values.

compression: the compacting (squishing together) of a wave traveling through a medium. The opposite is **rarefaction**.

crest: the highest point on a wave.

diffraction: a type of refraction in which waves are bent in more than one direction.

discrete value: a specific value within a digital signal.

digital signal: signals used to represent data.

echolocation: the process of "seeing" things by measuring sound waves reflected off an object.

frequency: the number of wavelengths that pass through a point per second.

incident wave: the direction a wave travels before it hits an obstacle.

infrared light: electromagnetic radiation that has wavelengths between microwaves and visible light. Far-infrared light is emitted as heat, and near-infrared radiation is used to send signals.

longitudinal waves: waves that send energy through vibration in the same direction as they travel.

mechanical waves: waves that carry energy.

medium: the stuff (air, liquid, or solid) that waves travel through.

microwaves: electromagnetic radiation that has wavelengths between radio waves and infrared radiation. Microwaves are commonly used to heat food and are used in communications and radar.

period: the time it takes one wavelength to travel from its beginning to its end.

pitch: the frequency of sound. The higher the frequency, the higher the pitch.

P-waves: longitudinal waves that travel through Earth's interior and originate from an earthquake.

radio waves: electromagnetic radiation with the longest wavelengths and lowest energy. These wavelengths can be the size of skyscrapers!

rarefaction: the stretching out of a wave traveling through a medium. The opposite is **compression**.

reflection: the process of waves bouncing off an object.

refraction: the process of waves being bent as they travel.

scattering: a type of reflection in which waves are reflected in more than one direction.

S-waves: transverse waves that travel through Earth's interior that originate from an earthquake.

transmission: the process of a wave passing through an object as if the object wasn't there.

transverse waves: waves that send energy through vibrations perpendicular to the direction of travel.

trough: the lowest point on a wave.

ultraviolet light: electromagnetic radiation that has wavelengths between visible light and X-ray radiation. Long ultraviolet radiation (UV-A) is often used in black lights. Shorter ultraviolet radiation (UV-B) can cause a sunburn if you forget your sunscreen. Even shorter ultraviolet radiation (UV-C) can be harmful and cause cancer in humans. UV-C is also used to kill harmful microorganisms.

vibration direction: the direction in which the wave traveling through a medium vibrates—up and down, perpendicular to the direction of motion for transverse waves and forward and backward along the direction of motion for longitudinal wave.

visible light: electromagnetic radiation that has wavelengths between infrared radiation and ultraviolet radiation. These are the wavelengths that humans can see.

volume: how loud a sound is; determined by the amplitude of a wave.

wavelength: the distance from peak to peak or compression to compression in a mechanical wave.

X-ray radiation: electromagnetic radiation that has wavelengths between ultraviolet and gamma ray radiation. X-rays are often used by doctors to diagnose broken bones.

CHAPTER 13
ANSWER KEY

PAGE 456

On the mattress with thin coils, there is (more)/less energy transferred from the top of the spring to the bottom.

On the mattress with thick coils, there is more/(less) energy transferred from the top of the spring to the bottom.

PAGE 457

The surfer riding a wave is an example of a longitudinal wave.

PAGE 458

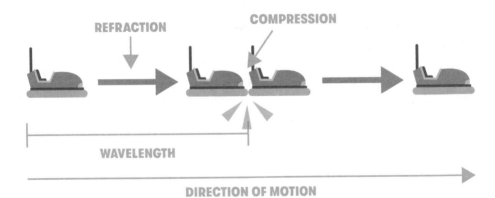

PAGE 461

As you follow the energy glob from point 1 to point 6, you are tracing out a(n) **wavelength**. The **amplitude** can be measured as the height difference between points 2 and 3. Point 8 is the **trough** and point 1 is the **crest**.

PAGE 465

Information and energy travel along longitudinal and transverse waves. Waves can carry information from one place to another.

PAGE 470

Remember, for light reflecting off a mirror, the angle of incidence equals the angle of reflection.

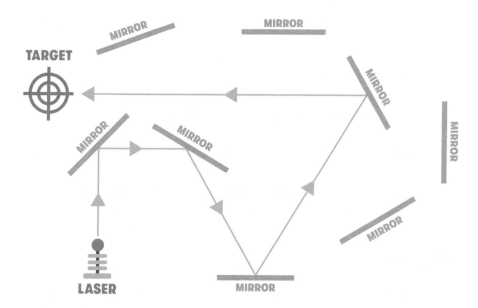

PAGE 472

Information that is carried on the mechanical waves can be reflected, refracted, or transmitted to make sure it gets to its target destination.

PAGE 473

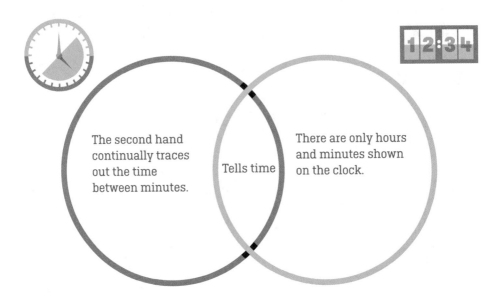

The second hand continually traces out the time between minutes.

Tells time

There are only hours and minutes shown on the clock.

PAGE 475

You could add in the left had circle that analog is continuous sound; in the right hand circle, you could add that digital is not continuous.

PAGES 476–477

Because this is based on your personal name, there are lots of correct answers.

PAGE 478

Analog: smooth, curvy signal

Digital: boxy, not continuous signal

PAGE 479

DIGITAL SIGNAL

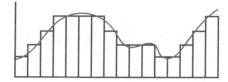

PAGE 480

Information is a type of energy that is carried on mechanical waves, either longitudinal or transverse. Waves can be reflected and refracted to make sure they reach their target destination. If you take a picture of a cat, you are taking an analog signal and converting it to a digital image. That digital image is then converted into a signal that can be sent from one device to another.

14

HOW TO THINK LIKE A SCIENTIST

Look around you. What do you see? Maybe some trees, rocks, and animals if you are outside. Maybe some walls and a roof if you are inside. What do each and every single one of these things have in common? They all suddenly become a lot more interesting when you look at them through the eyes of a scientist!

CHAPTER CONTENTS

SCIENCE AS A WAY OF UNDERSTANDING THE WORLD

 Let's pretend you are sitting in the middle of a forest. You look around and see countless trees in all directions around you. All of those trees are connected to each other. Fungi help to create underground networks called **mycorrhizal networks**, which allow the trees to communicate and share nutrients.

This network works very similarly to the **neural network** within our own bodies. When you fall and skin your knee, for example, a pain message is sent from your knee to your brain through your body's information highway. That highway is made up of nerve cells that generate electrical signals that are sent from one part of your body to another, typically ending up at your brain.

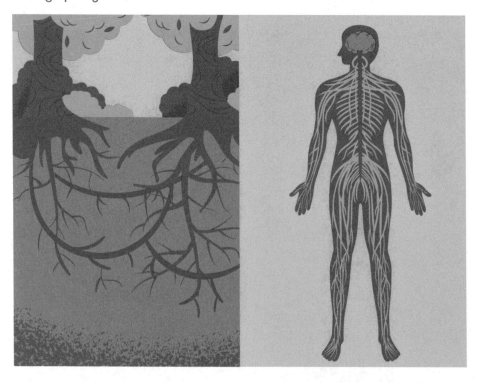

If that skinned knee of yours was actually an invasive species beginning to grow in the opposite side of the forest, chemical signals would be sent across the entire forest to warn all of the trees of the danger. The trees could then utilize their defense systems to inhibit the growth of that invasive species.

Science not only connects much more of the world than we can see with our eyes, but it often follows similar patterns. Before we get into that, let's dive into what science really is.

WHAT IS SCIENCE?

So what is science anyway? Science gives us a way of understanding the world, from the tiniest atoms to the entire universe. Science gives us a way to organize the chaos and fill in the gaps. Most of all, science gives us the tools and knowledge to improve the world, like a vaccine to prevent a deadly virus. That sounds great and all, but that doesn't really narrow it down. Let's start with the more technical definition of science: science is the process of studying, testing, questioning, organizing, and building upon current knowledge about the natural world through observation and experimentation. This is all done through the use of the scientific method.

 Think back to the introduction of this book when we first mentioned the scientific method.

THE SCIENTIFIC METHOD

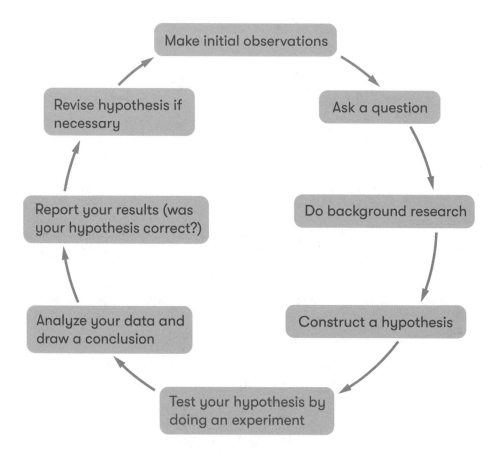

Usually, the scientific method is taught as though it happens in a straight line. But, in reality, science rarely follows a specific path or pattern, as you can see in the flowchart above. Science is a form of exploration—it's incredibly dynamic with lots of twists and turns, many of which are not predicted. Scientists typically don't work alone, either—different groups of scientists, sometimes in different fields of science, can tackle different parts of the scientific method either at the same time or with long gaps in between. The best scientists are those who are creative, open minded, and resourceful.

EXPLORING

Exploration is essential to starting a path following the scientific method. You may explore the forest, for example, by walking through it and looking at all the plants and animals that live there. You may explore a new neighborhood by walking around and introducing yourself to the people who live there. Let's look at what "exploring" means to a scientist.

HOW SCIENTISTS EXPLORE

OBSERVING	Make observations of the natural world around you. Observations include using your five senses (seeing, feeling, listening, smelling, and tasting) as well as using scientific tools such as telescopes, microscopes, radar, satellites, sensors, and other forms of technology.
QUESTIONING	Ask questions based on the natural world around you, from the tiniest atoms to the entire universe.
SHARING	Share your ideas, background knowledge, and data with others. Discuss your findings with those in that field or other fields to make sense of the information you gathered and to spark new ideas.
FINDING	Look for inspiration around you, in discussions with others, in exploring background knowledge, and in trying something new.
LEARNING	Use various resources to learn all you can about the type of science surrounding your question, such as library books, scientific publications, and discussions with experts in the field. Use what you find to guide other aspects of exploration.

If you had to make a flow chart of those five actions, how would you order it? Go ahead and draw it here:

If you think about it, there's more than one way that these five words can be connected. In fact, if you think about it closely, each of these actions is connected directly to the other. Something like this:

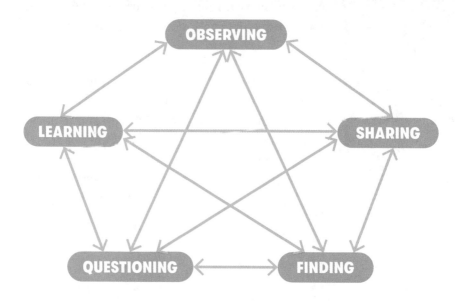

EXPLORATION

OBSERVING

LEARNING

SHARING

QUESTIONING

FINDING

Exploration is only one part of the scientific method. And as you go through the other areas, you will notice that there is overlap. Remember that science doesn't follow a specific recipe and can have a countless number of approaches. In general, you will first have an idea or question and then figure out how to go about testing it. Exploring your idea or question comes from observing the natural world around you and sharing what you have observed or learned. Often, that idea comes from exploring!

MAKING OBSERVATIONS

Let's start with the first step in the scientific method—making an initial observation. One of the earliest known instances of science was when early *Homo sapiens* (humans) looked up toward the sky. What do you think they noticed?

 If you need a hint, think back to Chapter 1.

Those early humans saw the shape of the Moon change each night and noticed that the patterns of stars drifted over the course of the year. They noticed that the length of the day varied throughout the year and that the Sun's path across the sky changed with it. They also noticed that specific star patterns were visible during different seasons. These were just a few of their observations, and those observations lead to questions.

QUESTIONS, LOTS OF QUESTIONS

Have you ever heard the saying, *there is no such thing as a silly question*? Questions are what drive science forward, sideways, and sometimes branching off into other new disciplines. Any question is fair game when it comes to science.

Each chapter of this book focused on a specific question to guide you—the phenomenon. The phenomenon question at the beginning of each chapter guided you as you explored a big scientific question. These questions were simple and straightforward. The subjects may have been familiar—but they were still in need of explanation. Some scientific questions do not require several years in graduate school and a PhD to answer. Questions can be as simple as "what kind of rock is that?" or "why do trees have rings?" Science questions are also not set in stone—they can be tweaked along the way as you dive deeper into your research.

Those questions, along with your initial observations, are part of the exploration aspect of the scientific method.

TESTING

Scientists are often pictured with test tubes and funny looking contraptions when it comes to thinking about testing their ideas and their evidence. While some scientists do use test tubes in their research, such as biochemists trying to find a new drug to fight a virus, most scientists use a variety of other methods in their testing phase. Scientific testing is made up of two parts: gathering data and interpreting the data.

 For the biochemists, gathering the data could be testing the new drug with a variety of solutions (remember, in chemistry, a solution is a mixture such as salt water), whereas interpreting the data could mean seeing how the drug reacts with the different solutions. Let's take a closer look.

HOW DO SCIENTISTS TEST?

	GATHERING		INTERPRETING
Hypothesis	Propose an explanation for your initial idea or question that can be used as the base of your tests.	**Support**	The data you gather can be used to support your initial hypothesis.
Expected	Think about what type of data and results you would expect to gather during the testing phase.	**Oppose**	The data you gather can oppose or rule out your initial hypothesis.
Actual	Determine what type of actual data and results came out of your experiments.	**Inspire**	The data you gather can inspire you to alter your initial hypothesis or to come up with an entirely new idea.

After you have your initial idea and question, it's time to develop a hypothesis and then test it. Testing your hypothesis involves collecting data. You then take the data you collect in your experiment and compare it to your hypothesis. Let's take a look first at how these ideas can be connected.

TESTING

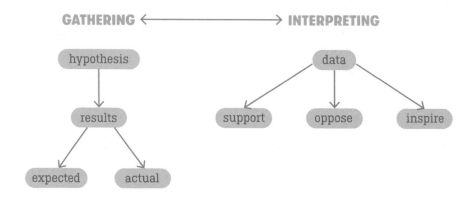

GATHERING ←——————————→ INTERPRETING

hypothesis → results → expected / actual

data → support / oppose / inspire

Now let's get into some of the nitty-gritty details. Usually, before you start an experiment, you have some notion of what results you may get.

 Think back to Chapter 10 where you predicted what would happen when some substances were added to others, the expected results. Were all of your predictions what actually happened? Maybe, but most likely not. The actual results of experiments are often different, sometimes even the complete opposite, of your expected results.

All experiments involve collecting data of some sort. That data can then be used to support your hypothesis (agrees with your hypothesis) or determine if your hypothesis needs to be tweaked or completely rewritten. Maybe the

data will lead you to an entirely new idea to pursue.

So what are experiments and data? In the case of Chapter 10, the experiment was combining substances, such as baking soda and vinegar, and the data was noting if a reaction occurred or not. But not all experiments involve mixing substances together.

 Think back to Chapter 4 and the experiment where you looked at how the water level in a bowl changed over the course of a week. The data you collected was the height of the water each day. The interpretation of the data was the explanation of the changing water levels.

Think back to Chapter 5 as well.

Several sets of data of Earth's average global temperature and the amount of carbon dioxide in the atmosphere were gathered by scientists. The data were interpreted and found to be connected, which allowed scientists to explain why global temperatures change.

 Finally, think back to Chapter 1. Astronomers will often gather large amounts of data over long periods of time using telescopes and sensitive cameras. For example, the Kepler Space Telescope spent about nine years looking at the same patch of sky. Astronomers looked for the tiniest blips in the data that could potentially be extrasolar planets, planets that orbit outside our solar system. From there, astronomers were able to further their understanding of how planetary systems formed, what types of stars planets are typically found orbiting, and even further define conditions for life to exist on those extrasolar planets.

Once you have your data, there are many ways to analyze it to determine if it fits with your hypothesis and initial idea.

ANALYSIS

Analyzing data is a very important step to understanding it. For example, a biochemist testing a new drug collects data on how the drug performs in a variety of situations. Analyzing the data about the drug involves answering questions, such as why it is showing to be effective against the disease, or if it is ready for human trials. Analysis also takes into account sharing and discussing the findings with other scientists—based on the data, the scientists could collectively discuss if they think the drug could be effective against the disease or if they have additional ideas for testing.

Analysis can also be broken up into two linked loops: connecting and building.

Have a look at the table on the next page for an overview of the different ways scientists analyze data.

HOW SCIENTISTS ANALYZE DATA

CONNECTING		BUILDING	
Feedback	Share your data and conclusions with experts in that field and incorporate the feedback in your analysis in a process called peer-review.	**Questioning**	Your results could lead to further questions and ideas, starting a new cycle of the scientific method.
Discussion	Share your ideas, data, and conclusions with colleagues and bounce ideas off of each other to gain new insights and creative approaches.	**Theorizing**	Your results could support a known theory or provide evidence to alter a theory or even disprove a theory.
Replication	This is a very important part of the experiment process— can your experiment be repeated by others? This ensures that your results are accurate.		
Publication	Publishing your data and results helps drive science forward.		

Just like with testing, analysis is broken up into two linked flowcharts, something like this:

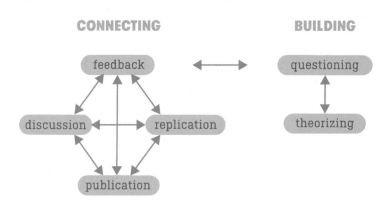

ANALYSIS

Data can be analyzed in many ways, depending on the type of data you collect. The data you collected in Chapter 10 was "yes" or "no," depending on whether or not a reaction occurred. In a further analysis, you could retest the same substances to see if you get the same results. Then you could group the yeses together and then find out what they have in common.

Scientists will share their findings with other experts and colleagues to see if there are any other insights that could be brought to their research, and to review their procedures and data in preparation for publication.

However, the process does not stop with publication. Published results can lead to further ideas, theories, and questions that you or others can tackle, starting the process over again. The discovery of penicillin in 1928 by Alexander Fleming (1881–1955), for example, changed the entire field of studying antibiotics and other disease-treating drugs. Penicillin was the first widely produced and distributed antibiotic, and it is credited with saving countless lives. Before antibiotics, the smallest cut could turn lethal. Today, there are hundreds of different types of antibiotics to treat many different types of bacterial infections, from tiny cuts to diseases such as cholera and tuberculosis.

Galileo Galilei (1564–1642), as another example, used his telescope in the early 1600s to build upon **Nicholas Copernicus**'s (1473–1543) theory of the motion of objects in our solar system around the Sun. Even though Galileo was put under house arrest for the rest of his life thanks to his publication, he was ultimately able to use his data to confirm that Earth and the other planets orbited around the Sun, instead of everything orbiting around Earth.

As you can see, there really is no start or end to the scientific method. But each particular hypothesis is typically wrapped up in some sort of conclusion, whether the data supports your hypothesis or not.

CONCLUSIONS

You have your hypothesis, data, and analysis—now what? Like the end of a good book, the scientific method has a conclusion. But at the same time, that ending may be a cliff hanger, prompting you to get the next book. Or, in terms of the scientific method, it may be the cliff hanger leading the scientist, or yourself, to the next problem to be solved or discovery to be made. Let's take a closer look.

HOW SCIENTISTS DRAW CONCLUSIONS

DEVELOPING	Data, analysis, and conclusions can lead to improved or brand new technologies, including those used in everyday life, medicine, engineering, and even lead to new ways of doing scientific research.
ADDRESSING	Research can lead to addressing problems or issues in science, technology, and even society.
INFORMING	Findings can lead to informing the public and even prompt policy changes.
SOLVING	Questions and experiments can be used to solve problems such as food and housing shortages, illness, climate change, and everything in between.
BUILDING	No matter what is accomplished, even if the experiment and data opposed the initial hypothesis, knowledge and curiosity are constantly being built upon.

Developing, addressing, informing, solving, and building are all connected to each other, something like this:

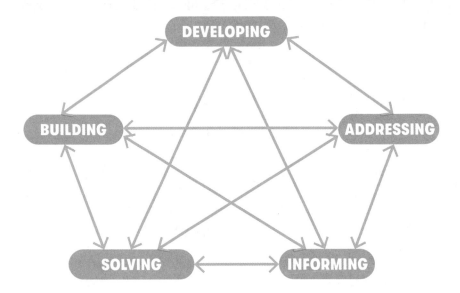

CONCLUSIONS

DEVELOPING

BUILDING

ADDRESSING

SOLVING

INFORMING

Even if your data did not support your hypothesis, the data could identify a new piece of technology or idea in science that no one has explored yet, or it can help answer a question in a different scientific field.

BRINGING THE SCIENTIFIC METHOD TOGETHER

Let's bring exploration, testing, analysis, and conclusions together. By now, you probably have a pretty good idea of what that is going to look like. Is this what you were thinking?

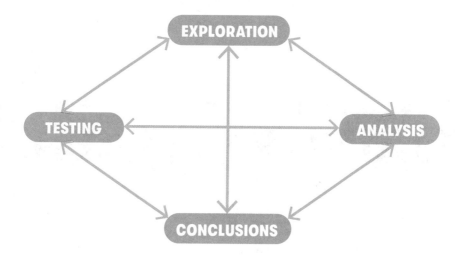

As you have seen, the scientific method is as far from linear as you can get. There are many twists and turns you can take from your very first idea.

HAVE A PLAN, BUT BE FLEXIBLE

Early humans looking up at the sky thousands of years ago set some questions in motion that astronomers are still trying to answer today. And each question answered can raise several more questions in a continuous, never-ending cycle. Some scientists spend their entire careers looking to answer one single question.

Remember, science doesn't necessarily follow the original plan or procedure. Several parts of the scientific method remain the same—such as making observations, formulating a hypothesis, gathering and analyzing data, and drawing conclusions. But the path between them may not be exactly what you have planned. However, it is important to begin the process with a plan that includes the what, why, and how of what will be explored. Just remember that if something doesn't go exactly to your plan, it is perfectly okay! Take that feedback and adapt as you go.

As a scientist, it is important to learn how to go with the flow and look for new opportunities and ideas. Ideas can come naturally from others' research and discoveries, or they can come from the most unlikely places.

WHAT KIND OF SCIENTIST ARE YOU?

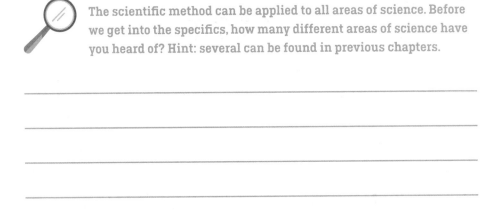

The scientific method can be applied to all areas of science. Before we get into the specifics, how many different areas of science have you heard of? Hint: several can be found in previous chapters.

_____

_____

_____

_____

So far, in this book, we have discussed many topics in science in the areas of Earth and space, life, and physical sciences. Some of the specific specialties within those broad categories that you have already learned about include astronomy, geology, paleontology, meteorology, climate science, biology, ecology, physics, and chemistry.

But did you know that there are many, many others? And that they all can be further broken down into subspecialties? And some of those subspecialties can be separated even further? Don't worry, we won't get into that right now!

Let's just take a look at some of the specialties in the physical sciences:

PHYSICAL SCIENCES	
PHYSICS	**ASTRONOMY**
• **Mechanics**: the study of motion of objects in force fields, electric fields, and magnetic fields.	• **Astrophysics**: the study of applying the laws of physics and chemistry to the universe.
• **Nuclear physics**: the study of the interactions of and forces within atomic nuclei.	• **Celestial mechanics**: the study of the motion of objects under the influence of gravity.
• **Particle physics**: the study of the building blocks of matter and their interactions.	• **Cosmology**: the study of the evolution of the universe.
• **Thermodynamics**: the study of the flow of energy within a system.	• **Galactic astronomy**: the study of galactic evolution and motion.
• **Quantum physics**: the study of the tiniest stuff known in the universe.	• **Planetary science**: the study of the formation and evolution of different types of planets.
• **Electromagnetism**: the study of the interactions between electric and magnetic fields.	• **Solar physics**: the study of the Sun.
• **Optics**: the study of the interactions between light and matter.	• **Exoplanets**: the study of planets in other solar systems.
• **Biophysics**: the study of the physical aspects of biology, such as atoms and molecules.	• **Relativistic astrophysics**: the study of the extremes in the universe, such as black holes.

PHYSICAL SCIENCES	
CHEMISTRY	**EARTH SCIENCE***
• **Materials chemistry**: the study of the materials that make up the world	• **Atmospheric science**: the study of the structure, properties, and movements of Earth's atmosphere
• **Nuclear chemistry**: the study of the properties and changes to atomic nuclei	• **Climatology**: the study of the atmosphere and weather patterns over long periods of time
• **Physical chemistry**: the study of how matter behaves on the atomic scale	• **Geology**: the study of the structure of Earth, its processes, and materials
• **Inorganic chemistry**: the study of the properties and reactions of inorganic compounds	• **Geochemistry**: the study of applying the laws of chemistry to aspects of geology
• **Analytical chemistry**: the study of processing and communicating information about matter	• **Mineralogy**: the study of the naturally occurring minerals that make up Earth and other planets
• **Geochemistry**: the study of the chemistry of geologic activity	• **Paleontology**: the study of prehistoric plants and animals
• **Biophysical chemistry**: the study of the physical and chemical aspects of biological systems	• **Oceanography**: the study of the physical, chemical, and biological aspects of Earth's oceans
• **Spectroscopy**: the study of how light interacts with matter	• **Planetary science**: the study of the planets and their systems

Earth science is sometimes considered part of the physical sciences.

Don't worry if you don't understand a lot of those words right now. These are topics that you might learn more about later in your schooling.

Even within the subspecialties, you may notice some overlap. For example, *astrophysics* combines aspects of astronomy and physics and involves the study of the physics of the entire universe. Another example is *astrobiology*.

Similarly, life sciences can also be broken down into various sections and subsections: biology, anatomy, genetics, botany, ecology, neuroscience, pathology, paleontology, and many, many more.

Physical and life sciences together make up natural science. Natural science is the study of natural phenomena, from tiny atoms to the entire universe. There are also formal sciences and social sciences. Formal science includes mathematics and computer science, which are used in all areas of natural science. Social science includes the study of human behavior; it includes subspecialties such as anthropology, archeology, linguistics, psychology, political science, and history.

So what about engineering? Engineering is *not* science, but it is closely related. Science focuses on exploring the known and unknown within the natural universe. Engineering focuses on finding solutions for real-world problems. Think about a computer—physics allows you to understand why and how electricity flows and how information can be sent; engineering allows you to take those physics principles to build circuit boards, CPU, RAM, and the other parts of a computer; and computer science allows you to program those physical parts to run simulations and experiments for every other field of science.

Now think about a bridge that connects two pieces of land on either side of a river. An engineer builds the bridge based on the composition of the soil on either side from geologists, how the bridge will impact the ecosystem from ecologists, what the bridge should be made out of from materials scientists, if the bridge could stand up to earthquakes from seismologists, and even how the wind will affect the structure of the bridge from atmospheric scientists and physicists. Building a bridge involves so many steps and so many different experts.

COLLABORATION AMONG DISCIPLINES

Many different fields work together to help answer some of the big questions. Let's take Earth's climate as an example. If you look back at the table, you will see climatology under Earth science. Because climatology specifically deals with Earth's climate, it makes sense that it is filed under Earth science. But climatology is actually made up of different parts from each branch of science. Let's take a closer look.

 Climatology includes the entire planet—this means everything within the atmosphere, biosphere, geosphere, and hydrosphere. Let's start with changes in the atmosphere and weather, such as rain. Rain and other forms of precipitation can greatly affect all life forms and even change entire ecosystems. Ocean currents also affect the overall climate of an area. Greenhouse gases in the atmosphere have been on the rise, primarily by human actions, and those gases not only trap more heat within the atmosphere and affect weather patterns, but they can react with other substances, sometimes negatively. Everything works in a feedback loop, and one change can affect everything else.

Thus, climatology involves the work of many experts in all branches and many specific subsets of each branch, such as meteorologists, atmospheric scientists, botanists, zoologists, ecologists, oceanographers, biochemists, and several others. Science relies on the collaboration between many different specialties to answer questions such as *why is our climate changing?*

Many branches of science affect everyone, not just scientists. Let's take a closer look at how science can affect society and how society can affect science.

SCIENCE AND SOCIETY: THE NEVER-ENDING LOOP

When you think of how science and society are connected, what is the first thing that pops into your head? You don't have to write it down; just keep it in your mind. There are many examples that are more obvious and others that are pretty subtle. Let's start with one of the big ones—medicine.

Almost everyone has had to take medication at some point, from something over the counter to fight a fever, to strong drugs that fight cancer, to a vaccine that prevents a disease such as polio. All medications go through many loops around the scientific method before they are ready to be available for the public. This process takes several years and includes many rounds of testing different compounds, several trials of each (often on human volunteers), peer review to make sure the science and process are accurate and replicable, publication in medical journals, and sometimes even back to the beginning if a slight change to the medication is needed.

Sometimes, the needs of society drive science forward at a much faster rate. Let's look at vaccines, for example. Vaccines are used to protect against deadly diseases such as polio, measles, pertussis, and even the flu. The typical path of a single vaccine takes 5–10 years or even more, and it has to follow very strict procedures to become available to the public.

Very rare occurrences, such as the COVID-19 pandemic that began in 2020, can drive the process forward at an accelerated rate to meet the needs of society. A vaccine for COVID-19 started becoming available to certain populations within months. So did they bypass the typical procedure? Nope! Other coronaviruses, one of which causes

COVID-19, have actually been studied for more than 50 years by experts, including immunologists (scientists who study the immune system) and microbiologists (scientists who study tiny organisms such as bacteria and viruses).

Most people have been exposed to some of the many hundred coronaviruses in their lives, some of which cause mild illnesses including the common cold. Scientists around the world collaborated to build upon all the previous research on coronaviruses to determine what made the strand that caused COVID-19 different. They applied that combined research, as well as the latest technologies, to develop, test, publish their results, and then make the vaccine available to the public, saving many thousands or even millions of lives.

Let's look at another example of science driving science forward—climate change. Climate change affects every single living thing on Earth.

 As you read in Chapter 5, humans are the primary cause of climate change, and the effects can already be seen in every corner of the world. Severe droughts in some locations and increased storm strength in others have already caused widespread damage and loss of life. Scientists across all disciplines and many young activists are coming together to figure out if climate change can be slowed, stopped, or even reversed. Ideas are being researched, tested, shared, and published to not only involve all citizens of Earth to do their part in reducing actions that led to climate change but to help promote policy change at the highest levels of government.

Throughout many of the chapters in this book, you followed along with different scenarios that took place in a forest. Forests are thought to be one of the keys to combating climate change—one of the more important reasons is that they take in and store a large amount of carbon dioxide. Deforestation not only destroys the habitats of the many species that call their forest home, but it releases a great deal of carbon dioxide back into the atmosphere, increases soil erosion, and can pollute the water supply. Helping forests regrow and remain healthy is vital in at least slowing climate change, and as a member of society, you can help—no science degree required!

WHAT'S NEXT?

Science is about answering the questions of the natural world around us. The only prerequisite you need to become a scientist is curiosity, creativity, and a passion to learn. That's it. Yes, you will need to take a variety of math and science courses in school to build your foundation, but those are subjects that can be learned. Passion cannot be learned; it is within you. Your passion may steer you toward studying the universe as an astronomer, figuring out how to fight infectious diseases, or helping to reverse climate change. Science has no limit to how far it, or you, can go.

But even if you choose not to become a scientist, you can take the principles of science with you. Here's a handy checklist that you can take with you, wherever you decide to go:

☐ Never stop being curious.

☐ Continue to notice the natural world around you.

☐ Always keep an open mind.

☐ Never stop learning.

☐ Never stop exploring.

CHAPTER 14 VOCABULARY

actual results: the results or data that come from an experiment.

engineering: the study and practice of finding solutions for real-world problems.

expected results: the type of results or data that are expected before completing an experiment.

extrasolar: an object or objects that exist outside of our solar system.

formal science: the study of formal language such as mathematics and computer languages.

Homo sapiens: the primate species that includes humans.

immunologist: scientists who studies the immune system.

microbiologist: scientists who studies very tiny organisms such as bacteria and viruses.

mycorrhizal networks: underground networks of fungi that connect to tree roots and allow trees to communicate and share nutrients with each other.

natural science: the study of naturally occurring phenomena, from the tiniest pieces of atoms to the entire universe.

neural network: the network of nerve cells in the body that send signals from any location within the body to the brain.

science: the process of studying, testing, questioning, organizing, and building upon knowledge about the natural world.

social science: the study of human behavior in society and culture.

TEXT CREDITS

Page 165, Human Population Growth by Century: Max Roser, Hannah Ritchie and Esteban Ortiz-Ospina (2013) - "World Population Growth." Published online at OurWorldInData.org. Retrieved from: 'https://ourworldindata.org/world-population-growth'. Original data sourced from History database of the Global Environment (HYDE), PBL Netherlands Environmental Assessment Agency, and from the United Nations.

Page 166, Global Fresh Water Usage Since 1900: Data published by Global International Geosphere-Biosphere Programme (IGB). Original data sourced from Flörke, M., Kynast, E., Bärlund, I., Eisner, S., Wimmer, F., Alcamo, J. 2013. Domestic and industrial water uses of the past 60 years as a mirror of socio-economic development: A global simulation study. Global Environmental Change 23: 144-156.

Page 170, Average Temperature on Earth: NOAA National Centers for Environmental information, Climate at a Glance: Global Time Series, published July 2021, retrieved from https://www.ncdc.noaa.gov/cag/

Page 177, Release of Greenhouse Gases Since 1850: NOAA Global Monitoring Laboratory, Annual Greenhouse Gas Index (AGGI), published spring 2021, retrieved from https://gml.noaa.gov/aggi/aggi.html

Page 180, Sources of Greenhouse Gases, Worldwide: Data published by United States Environmental Protection Agency, "Global Greenhouse Gas Emissions Data." Original data sourced from: IPCC (2014). Climate Change 2014: Mitigation of Climate Change. Contribution of Working Group III to the Fifth Assessment Report of the Intergovernmental Panel on Climate Change [Edenhofer, O., R. Pichs-Madruga, Y. Sokona, E. Farahani, S. Kadner, K. Seyboth, A. Adler, I. Baum, S. Brunner, P. Eickemeier, B. Kriemann, J. Savolainen, S. Schlömer, C. von Stechow, T. Zwickel and J.C. Minx (eds.)]. Cambridge University Press, Cambridge, United Kingdom and New York, NY, USA.

Page 184, Global Carbon Emissions and Global Average Temperature Change: Wuebbles, D.J., D.R. Easterling, K. Hayhoe, T. Knutson, R.E. Kopp, J.P. Kossin, K.E. Kunkel, A.N. LeGrande, C. Mears, W.V. Sweet, P.C. Taylor, R.S. Vose, and M.F. Wehner, 2017: Our globally changing climate. In: Climate Science Special Report: Fourth National Climate Assessment, Volume I [Wuebbles, D.J., D.W. Fahey, K.A. Hibbard, D.J. Dokken, B.C. Stewart, and T.K. Maycock (eds.)]. U.S. Global Change Research Program, Washington, DC, USA, pp. 35-72, doi: 10.7930/J08S4N35.

ABOUT THE CREATORS OF HOW TO SURVIVE MIDDLE SCHOOL: SCIENCE

Rachel Ross is a science writer and educator who lives in Northern California. She holds a Master's degree in astronomy from James Cook University in Australia. Rachel served as a specialist in education and outreach at Las Cumbres Observatory in Southern California, where she also worked as a researcher and an operator of the telescope network.

Maria Ter-Mikaelian is a freelance science writer with a PhD. in Neuroscience from New York University with eight years of college teaching experience. She has written educational video scripts for the PBS channel *It's Okay to be Smart* and articles for the children's science magazine *Smore*. She lives in Brooklyn with her husband, son, and dog.

Sideshow Media is a print and digital book developer specializing in illustrated publications with compelling content and visual flair. Sideshow excels at making complicated subjects accessible and interesting to young readers and adults alike. The company is led by its founding partner, Dan Tucker. www.sideshowbooks.com

Carpenter Collective is a graphic design and branding studio led by partners Jessica and Tad Carpenter. They focus on bringing powerful messages to life through branding, packaging, illustration, and design. They have worked with clients ranging from Target, Coca-Cola, and Macy's, to Warby Parker, Adobe, and MTV, among many others. They've earned a national reputation for creating powerful brand experiences and unique visual storytelling with a whimsical wink. See more of their work at carpentercollective.com